STALEMATES

NEW LIGHT ON *WHAT* DRIVES
PEOPLE TO ADULTERY

STALEMATES

The Truth About Extramarital Affairs

Marcella Bakur Weiner, Ed.D.
and
Bernard D. Starr, Ph.D.

NEW HORIZON PRESS
Far Hills, New Jersey

Library of Congress Catalog Card Number 89-43163

Marcella Bakur Weiner
Bernard D. Starr
Stalemates

ISBN 0-88282-036-2
New Horizon Press

Acknowledgements

We are greatly indebted to Corrine Streich whose creative thinking contributed to an early structuring of this book as well as the title.

We also want to acknowledge a number of people who gratiously read and critically evaluated various parts of the manuscript. Our appreciation to Dr. Marjorie Taggart White for her sensitive reading and insightful comments. Dr. Jerry Bass and Jason Starr reviewed and commented on much of the manuscript. Many of their suggestions were incorporated into revisions. Dr. Leon Lewindowski's medical expertise was invaluable in sharpening some of the language in the discussion of AIDS.

Our thanks to William Weiner for his encouragement, patience and continuous availability as informal consultant.

Dr. Jeanne Teresi's statistical analysis of the AIDS survey data yielded some of the surprises which appear in the book. We thank her. Our sincere thanks to Avi Ashman, Lorraine Bersin, Jeanette Hainer, Sallie Moore, Aniko Nemeth, Dr. Lala Straussner, Dr. Lynn Tepper, and "Richnik's Singles" for their assistance in data collection for chapter seven. We also thank Dr. Arline Rubin for her assistance in gathering data on sexual attitudes and practices.

The distinguished therapists, Dr. Seymour E. Coopersmith, Dr. Albert Ellis, Dr. Gerald Epstein, Dr. Barry Lubetkin, Dr. Marjorie Taggart White and Dr. Shirley Zussman, who shared their thoughts and experiences in chapter eight ("Therapists

View Affairs'') gave their valuable time unstintingly. They contributed greatly to this book.

We are deeply appreciative of the contributions of Dr. Robert E. Gould and Dr. Harold W. Jaffe to "Sexual Practices in the Age of AIDS." Their forthright statements, as different as they may be, will undoubtedly guide many readers on this troubling issue which touches everyone.

This book could not have come about without the support, perseverance and confidence of our literary agent, Margaret Russell.

Our typist, Liz Fenelius, is to be applauded for her understanding of both computers and authors.

Harry L. Wagner, our editor, researcher and outstanding Jack-of-all writing-trades deserves very special mention. His wonderful writing skill and ability to suggest solutions to thorny problems while always maintaining good humor despite deadlines made our task much lighter. We are grateful.

DEDICATIONS

To my Aunt Rebecca whose many years of living have translated theories into a form of living art for me.

Marcella Bakur Weiner

To the entire gang in Romont. Let's keep the spirits up!

Bernard D. Starr

DISCLAIMER

This book accurately conveys the themes central to extramarital affairs and is based upon our professional experience.
However, the individuals mentioned in this book are not specific
individuals but composites, and all names are fictitious.

CONTENTS

PREFACE

It might be stretching the point a bit to claim that this book is a labor of love, but it is certainly a labor *about* love. The authors hope that this work will help readers examine their own situations and needs and determine how best to meet them.

We have based our findings on our clinical cases as psychologists and therapists, on research with other individuals, and on interviews with prominent therapists, which yielded an additional pool of thousands of cases for our information base. Still, this is not a statistical treatment of the subject. The authors are not particularly interested in what percentage of people have had this or that type of extramarital affair (if in fact such information can ever be really reliable). We feel that when it comes down to understanding *your* position and *your* affair, raw statistical data are not especially useful or personally comforting. Our experience has been that each extramarital affair is unique and requires sole concentration on the specifics of that particular relationship.

Still, we feel that the experience of others can be useful to you in making judgements about your own situation. To this end, we have concentrated on the wide spectrum of possible affairs and on the variety of experiences and outcomes we have encountered in studying those involved in them. Some proved self-enhancing while others proved self-destructive, but all involved real people in real relationships. Naturally, some of the purely descriptive facts and some information of a strictly personal nature have been altered to protect the individuals involved—and to protect the confidentiality of the client/therapist relationship.

As you will see, one sensibility that permeates this whole work is heightened neutrality. As therapists and social scientists we do not deplore or condone affairs. We do recognize that they exist and represent a powerful force in the lives of many people. They have been around for a long time, and they are likely to continue—even the menace of AIDS does not seem to have materially dampened their occurrence. Given this fact of life, our approach is to stress information and reflection. Is an affair right for you? Given who you are, what might you expect in the way of pleasure or pain from an affair? If you are having an affair now, how much has it added to your life? Detracted from it? Only you can answer these questions, and we believed that what you will learn in these pages will help you answer them in a way that is most self-fulfilling for you.

In earlier societies, extramarital affairs were generally limited to one class and were socially tolerated only when the man was the one who strayed. Now the classic "rules of the game" seem to have changed radically. Throughout much of our society, affairs no longer bring down public denunciation and private ruin on those involved in them. But, if the rules are not now as clearly defined, there are, in the words of the poet Robert Frost, "roughly speaking, zones." Some things are dangerous, some things are thoughtless and cruel, and some may prove quite destructive to self or loved ones. The authors' intent here is to give you a sense of some of those "zones," with an eye toward helping you see how they apply in your case. An unreflected life may or may not be worth living, but an affair unreflected is a loose cannon on deck. This book is designed to help you get it back under control.

Chapter One

LES LIAISONS DANGEREUSES

"Oh yes," you say, "I've seen the movie and read the book. And why on earth anyone would want to learn about extramarital affairs now is simply beyond me. The 'Go-Go' days are over—where have you been since the Sixties, on a desert island off the coast of Albania?"

Well, Why a Book on Affairs Now?

The authors understand perfectly that sexual relationships of any kind are occasions for some anxiety. Nevertheless, or perhaps because of this, we feel strongly that today more than ever is the time to talk rationally and sensibly about our sexual and emotional lives. Despite all the discussion in the media about a pullback from involvement, a nation practicing "passionate celibacy" just isn't in the cards. People will continue having sexual relationships—and, yes, even extramarital ones.

To get on with our lives as sensibly as possible in this time of stress, we need more, not less, information. We need to know more, not less, about sexual behavior, different options, probable consequences, and various strategies. We must think more, not less, about our own needs and desires and how in a dangerous and uncertain world we can best fulfill them. We need to consider more, not less, how we relate to others and they to us, what our mutual responsibilities are, and what our mutual satisfactions can be. Most of us can't be lured into real depravity, and few of us will be frightened into near sainthood. Human relations, including sexual ones, will, as before, be played out on some middle ground, and, as before, they will involve choices. Choices require discernment—and discernment implies knowledge. Ignorance is no basis for choice.

Even if you have no intention of having an affair, it is more than likely that you have fantasized about the lover you would like to have—if the world were different. Have you never had a dream of making love to a stranger or to a known friend? Can you identify with Justine, described by her friends as a "happily married woman," who was in therapy ostensibly for a problem involving her aging mother and who told her therapist the following in an offhand manner?

> When we're out to dinner with friends, I sit down with my wonderful husband of 15 years and look around the table at the men my friends have married—and I think about which ones I'd like to be in bed with and what it would be like. All this while casually eating my salad. Then I catch myself and am properly horrified.
>
> I never think of affairs at other times and would die before I'd actually try one. I was beginning to think there was something about salads and affairs that went together.
>
> What that's all about I really don't know and you're the only person I've ever told this to. I feel plain weird. Do other women ever feel this way, too?

Whatever decision *you* come to about extramarital affairs, we have designed this book for you. We do not presume to be exhaustive; we doubt that's possible. But we do present a number of different ways of thinking about affairs and those involved in them. Further, we believe that within this wide range of considerations, a few, at least, will address your special situation. This is a book for you and, in a way, about you. It deals with the experiences of many people and covers a variety of situations. Some will be quite familiar to you; others will be totally incomprehensible. Nevertheless, there is something to be learned from each one.

From Flirtation to Infidelity. Why do people go into affairs? There are as many answers to that as there are affairs. Society provides a number of ways for sexes to flirt with each other and develop non-sexual relationships: dancing, parties, picnics, club meetings, dinners, and on and on. At a dance, a married woman accepts a man who is not her husband into her arms, and when the music ends, she lets him go. No harm done. Society accepts that even if people are married, they are not blind. They need the stimulation of being with others; of interacting with others; of having their social, intellectual, and sexual selves validated by others. Wise societies know this and make provisions for such encounters to take place in settings where they can be contained and managed.

There come times, however, when these socially approved methods of socialization are not enough. Certain individuals feel compelled to go beyond what is acceptable. Sometimes it happens in a flash; sometimes over many months. In any case, what was a non-sexual relationship becomes a sexual one, and an "affair" is begun. This book concerns that time when you may have moved, or contemplated moving, from socially approved forms of flirtation to the more ambiguous, far more stimulating, world of affairs. We will look at some of the considerations that may have led you to such a move, and we will examine some of the consequences. The step from flirtation to infidelity can be a very small one indeed, but it can have giant consequences for everyone involved.

Just what are you apt to find in an affair? Pretty nearly anything you can imagine. Affairs are so complex, have so many dimensions, and reach into so many areas of life that you can find in them many focuses. There is passion, immortality, lust and selfishness certainly, but there is also tenderness and caring. Rejection, hurt, and betrayal play their part, but so do exhilaration, comfort, and loyalty. There is no one answer to the powerful attraction of affairs or one overriding motive for them. The most general statement is that they have occurred, are occurring now, and, in all likelihood, will continue to occur. This very fact says something important about sex and its power to speak to the self.

Make no mistake, sex can be empowering and self-affirming. Perhaps no aspect of an affair has such a hold on participants as this sense of self-affirmation. Suddenly, energies that seemed to have been drained out of one miraculously reappear. A life that seemed routine and dull takes on new vitality and intensity. People tap into a core of energy in themselves that they'd forgotten—or never realized they had. The step into an affair is a step of discovery. What one then discovers constitutes the story of the affair, and, as you will see in the rest of this book, there are many stories with many different ends. Discovery is a dicy business, and one of its least pleasant aspects is that there is no gain without pain.

What Do We Know about Affairs Today? There is no end of anecdotal evidence on extramarital affairs. Literature has investigated the topic from Greek tragedy through Roman comedy to French farce and Hollywood romances. It would not be accurate, though, to label this "hard data," as informative and entertaining though some of it might well be. Still, we will have to make do with what is available. In the 1940s Dr. Kinsey found in his groundbreaking report that 50% of the married men interviewed had had affairs as against 25% of the married women. In 1982, a magazine survey (inconclusive, to be sure) came up with statistics of 48% for the men and 38% for the women. Sociology professor Pepper Schwartz of the University of Washington, was quoted in the *New York Times* (June 1, 1987) on women and infidelity by writer Trish Hall as saying, "If you look at people under 25, there are equal amounts of extramarital sex: 25% of both men and women. They're starting earlier, and equally."

In the 40-year period from the Kinsey Report to today, men seem to have changed their extramarital behavior little, while women appear to have changed theirs radically. Again, the figures may be in dispute (Shere Hite's *Women and Love,* 1987, reported over 70% of women married over five years as having sex outside their marriages), but the data seem to bear out a trend that most of us will recognize. Women today, including married women, do not think and act the way their mothers and grandmothers did. They generally have fewer children, more interests outside the home and family, and, consequently, more chances to experiment sexually as well as socially and professionally.

An interesting finding appeared in a study by Annette Lawson in her recent book, *Adultery.* She links premarital sexual behavior to affairs in marriage, with those who had engaged in premarital sex being more likely to have extramarital affairs than those who did not. She states that the more lovers one had before marriage, the more likely one was to continue the pattern after marriage. This behavior pattern, however, while strong in men, was not as clearly defined in women. Especially among older people, the roles are likely to be fixed, with older men generally having more premarital and extramarital sex than the women of their age group. The younger men and women, though, in keeping with the observation in the *Times,* show evidence of being equally active before and after marriage. Are we moving towards a "unisex" sexual behavior?

Another factor to consider is the increase in longevity for us all. Despite myths to the contrary, older people are sexually active and sophisticated. They may also be involved in affairs. This was revealed to the authors when we were collecting data from interviews with older persons (60–92) which was used in our book, *The Starr-Weiner Report on Sex and Sexuality in the Mature Years.* In constructing our questionnaire, we asked about sexual attitudes and behaviors. We erred, however, on the side of conservatism and, not wishing to alienate any of our would-be-respondents, we included no questions about extramarital affairs. When the data was in and we had encouraged the respondents to make their own suggestions and comments, we were taxed with omitting any data or questions on affairs.

Whether the older people taking us to task for the omission were themselves involved in affairs or knew of people who were, they made it clear that this was a subject they wished to know more about. An older population does not necessarily mean a more conservative one.

Incidentally there's another statistic of longevity and marriage that may prove interesting here. Mr. Lawrence Stone, reviewing the book *Putting Asunder: A History of Divorce in Western Society* in the *New York Review of Books,* makes the following fascinating observation:

> Over a decade ago, I suggested that the rise in divorce in the late nineteenth century could be interpreted as a functional substitute for death . . . A graph of American marriages dissolved both by divorce and by death between 1860 and 1980 shows that although the dissolution rate by death of a proportion of marriages was falling steadily after 1960, the slack was taken up by the rise of divorces. As a result, the rate of dissolutions a year per 1000 marriages remained almost exactly the same from 1860 to 1960. It was only after 1960 that the situation changed abruptly, as the number of divorced soared to wholly new heights, quite unrelated to any continued decline in the adult mortality rate, which in fact has been flattening out.

This is an intriguing statistic. Marriage is " 'til death do us part." For the last 100 years, however, death has been arriving later and later, considerably stretching out the time that a young couple would stay married to well beyond what was the norm in earlier times. The availability of divorce averaged out the disparity, but the suggestion is there that as your population grows older, the incidence of single, life-long marriages becomes more and more problematical. In fact, as the review points out, divorce is now running at unprecedented proportions. Perhaps there is a "fatigue factor" in marital relationships that tends to put a time limit on even very successful ones. The 50- or 60-year marriage, so wistfully looked back on now, was always a rarity; it never really was the norm.

More importantly, perhaps, these surveys seem to indicate a major change in attitude, certainly among women and more recently in men, too. Along with the "sexual revolution" of the free-booting 1960s there seems to have come a more lasting revolution of "rising expectations."

For instance, we've already mentioned the critical role that sex plays in an affair. This would seem only logical as we define an affair as having sex with a partner who is not a spouse, and it would seem only natural to take as crucial that aspect of an affair which defines it. This may have been the case earlier, but now it would seem that the emphasis is changing. Lynn Atwater, a sociology professor at Seton Hall University, questioned 250 women on what they considered the most important aspect of their affairs. She fully expected the answer to be sex or sexual fulfillment. What they said, however, was "communication." The switch in emphasis seems to be true of men also, as both men and women now seek partners in their liaisons who can serve as confidant and trusted friend as well as paramour. This change in men's thinking has been dramatically referred to by Lawson as a "feminization of love."

Now, "communication" is a big word, and, like charity, it can cover a multitude of sins. In certain cases, it might be used to mask sexual desire on the basis that it sounds more refined. On the other hand, it seems likely that the desire—the demand— for "communication" is evidence on the part of both sexes of a change in their view of marriage. They want marriage to be an equal partnership, and they want their needs—for appreciation, for career, for self-fulfillment, for recognition as a co-partner— to be met in marriage. When this doesn't happen, women—and more recently men—are no longer willing to put up with it or make do. More and more, they will seek satisfaction for these needs outside of marriage. And if that includes sex, well, so be it. With so many increased demands from within and so many blandishments from without, is it any wonder that marriage has been taking a beating for the past two decades?

Clouding the picture still further is the ominous presence of AIDS. If affairs are by their nature risky business, sex itself

now appears to be fraught with more peril than delight. Today
more than ever one feels the mordancy of Max Beerbohm's quip
on sex: "The pleasure is fleeting, the price enormous, and the
position ridiculous."

Nevertheless, people still do get married, and some of them
will eventually have extramarital affairs. But on what basis and
to what ends? That is the subject of this book.

Achieving the "Cohesive Self"

It would seem evident, but it's worth stating again that people
generally embark on an affair because, in one way or another, it
makes them *feel good*. We have never in our many years of
practice heard anyone say: "I went into this affair to feel bad."
Initially, at least, the affair appeared as a plus to the partners,
something that promised to make their lives more exciting, more
rewarding, more fulfilling.

It may be well now to explain that for purposes of this
book, we will consider an "affair" as a sexual relationship
between two adults, at least one of whom is married. We will
concentrate only on affairs that involve consenting adults, leaving out those situations that involve coercion of any kind or the
participation of partners other than adults—children or the
mentally incompetent, for instance. Nor do the discussions here
touch on affairs that result from extreme pathological behavior
such as nymphomania, satyriasis, drug or other substance
abuse, etc. Extramarital affairs involving problems of this nature
require specialized help and are not amenable to the rational
discourse practiced here.

Our concern is rather with those whom society considers
"normal," the person the French call *l'homme moyen sensuel,*
the sensual-man-(woman)-in-the-street. Our purpose is not to
advocate or denigrate affairs per se, but to provide you with
information and insights which you can use to examine your
own situation and needs.

Our goal in all such examinations is for each individual to
achieve what psychologists call the "cohesive self"—a person-

ality that is integrated, whole, "together," and functioning on a high level. The cohesive self is a self that allows an individual to use their talents and sensibilities to the fullest extent possible.

In general, people struggle toward this goal, albeit more often than not subconsciously. They do things that make them feel good or that promise to do so, as a reflection of their search for their own unique cohesive self. Marriage is one way, a very common way, that people use to find themselves or complete themselves and tap into their potential. When a marriage becomes an impediment rather than an aid to such self-realization—a situation we call "stalemated"—the dissatisfied partner is liable to look elsewhere. The "elsewhere" need not necessarily mean an affair. A new job, a new set of interests, new friends are all part of the search, and they may fill the bill without ever bringing an affair into the picture. Nevertheless, when one senses, even subconsciously, that one is in a "stalemated" situation, one becomes susceptible to an affair. If opportunities for affairs had presented themselves earlier, the individual may not have recognized them or may not have been interested in pursuing them. All of a sudden, now, he or she is—and a relationship starts. To the participants it may seem like a bolt out of the blue. Many people are simply amazed at finding themselves in an affair, at a complete loss to explain how it happened. The dynamics of inner change, though, have been working all along, and they can come to the surface at the slightest provocation, a smile, a touch of the hand, a chance meeting, anything. As Hamlet said, "The readiness is all."

This does not mean that an affair always spells the end of a marriage or that the inclination indicates that an individual is bent on getting out of a marriage. Even an ex-President, Jimmy Carter, admitted that he "lusted in his heart" after a woman, but he did not leave his marriage or become unfaithful. Inclination and fantasy are universal, but action is local and specific. Moreover, as you will see later (Chapters 5 and 8), having an affair may be a strategy to actually continue a marriage. The married partner in an affair may find that *both* relationships are required for him or her to achieve a cohesive self.

Should we even consider that an affair is always the correct response to a stalemated situation? Just because one is ready for an affair doesn't mean that this is the longed-for solution. Many of the case studies in this book reflect instances where affairs resulted in a great deal more damage than self-realization. Extramarital affairs, whether frivolous one-night stands or long-term romantic relationships, constitute an exceedingly dangerous strategy. Because they involve the self and others—mates, children, co-workers, etc.—they have many uncontrollable factors. There may be times when an affair is seen to represent a beneficial move, but affairs, under any circumstance, always bear the label, "EXPLOSIVE; HANDLE WITH CARE."

Given these drives and concomitant dangers, what can we say about the future of affairs? We expect it will sound a little like Jimmy Durante's old song, "Did You Ever Have the Feeling That You Wanted to Go But You Wanted to Stay?"

The Cloudy Crystal Ball

As we head into the end of the 20th century, there's a strong push-me/pull-you aspect to our emotional lives. On the one hand, people want it all and want it now. Men and women are impatient of restraint. The soaring divorce rate seems to indicate that married couples "go for the divorce papers at the first fight," as a young woman described it to us. With both partners working in the typical married family, there's not much time or energy left to make needed repairs when the relationship gets into rough water.

Today our high-pressure, work-oriented society makes it hard on lovers trying to keep an affair progressing. A middle-aged man told us wryly that he had complained to his paramour about the fact that their excessive work commitments were interfering with their finding time enough to enjoy their wonderful sex together. She, a highly organized executive, quipped back at him, "Put it on the list. It'll get taken care of." Though affairs are more numerous now, there's a real desire to find and keep family values. Marriage is still popular, and for most men

and women definitely the relationship of choice. Moreover, there
is growing awareness of the often devastating effect divorce has
on children, as evidenced in the book *Second Chances* by Judith
Wallerstein and Sandra Blakeslee. Their study, conducted over
a 15-year period, did not advocate staying in a bad marriage for
the sake of the children. It did make a strong finding, however,
that divorce neither soothes nor repairs but for the most part
intensifies the negatives of life, with serious consequences for
the parents and children alike. There's no evidence yet, but we
may see more of a disposition in the future to put divorce off, at
least until the kids are grown. In this case, affairs may stage
some sort of social comeback. A partner who finds a marriage
stultifying but is unwilling to leave, might turn to a well-managed
affair (see chapter 5) as just the thing to keep family—and self—
from breaking up. In earlier times when divorce was virtually
impossible, affairs, at least for the man, were publicly deplored
but privately condoned. Strict monogamy was always the ideal—
but it remained largely an ideal. Thus a future with a lower
divorce rate and a higher affair rate is a distinct possibility. This
time around, though, there's little chance that women can be so
rigorously excluded.

Also, as we mentioned before, the graying of the family
may have an inflationary effect on the incidence of affairs. Noted
sociologist Dr. Ruth Bennett points out that people are marrying
later and living longer. With many of them still sexually active
in their 50s, 60s, and even beyond, we may expect that some
will feel a drive for one last fling before time runs out. Thus
demographics and long-term economic interests may set the
scene for a high level of continued interest in, and pursuit of,
extramarital affairs. (Personal Communication, Dr. Ruth Bennett, March 21, 1987.)

Conversely, an affair may open a dissatisfied spouse's eyes
to the real value of the marriage. For instance, instead of proving
to be an exciting fantasy world, an affair may turn into a
nightmare, leading to a reassessment of the quality of the marriage, and a "I-didn't-know-how-great-it-was-to-be-healthy-un-
til-I-got-sick" kind of thing. An affair may provide a frame of

reference by which to judge the marriage—and the marriage doesn't always have to be the loser.

There's no sure way to say just what role affairs will play in the near future, other than that they will occur. Our premise here is that affairs are neither "healthy" nor "neurotic." They are, rather, unique to each individual. How an individual can judge whether an affair can be or can never be considered a viable option is the pressing business of the rest of this book.

Exercising Understanding and Judgment

It may seem hopelessly naive of us to talk about understanding and judgment where people are engaged in extramarital affairs. Affairs are not noted for fostering rational decision-making. Usually, they're a "Damn-the-torpedoes. Full-speed-ahead" type of situation, with the consequences to be faced later. It is our contention, nevertheless, that self-awareness and self-knowledge are the main recourses against self-destructive behavior.

As we discover more about ourselves and how we got to be the way we are, we have a better chance to exercise control over what we do. Also, it's more likely that we can derive the maximum benefit from those activities we choose—note the emphasis on choice—to pursue if we know what we're about. Moving blindly from one relationship to another through life is not an effective way to achieve the cohesive self, or to deal with stalemated situations. The basic tenet of therapy, and, incidentally, of this book, is an essentially optimistic one. *You* have alternatives, and *you* can choose among them. To help you appreciate this and use it in your interpersonal relations, we have arranged the rest of this book to proceed logically from the general to the particular as we go on to examine affairs from a variety of viewpoints and possible outcomes.

First, we deal with two basic psychological needs—mirroring and idealization—that form the underlying dynamic in interpersonal relationships. Numerous case studies amplify the many ways these two needs manifest themselves in affairs.

Then we go on to investigate the affair itself with a treatment of the inherently risky nature of affairs and how different types of people react to the risk-taking. Also discussed is the option of continuing marriage and affair(s) in a situation of parallel play. The idea here is to keep both while losing neither, a neat but not impossible trick—but not for the faint-hearted. The book then goes into the question of what happens when the affair goes beyond parallel play and either ends or escalates into a new commitment.

We also consider affairs in other social contexts. We examine how AIDS has changed our attitudes towards sex in general and affairs in particular. The discussion is detailed, and in some ways controversial, but the authors feel that this is a topic that must be grappled with if we are to make sense of our emotional lives today. Next we explore the views of six different therapists on the value (if any) of extramarital affairs. There is no single "line" on affairs in therapy; opinions on their value and on ways of handling them vary widely among different schools of therapy and among individual therapists. You will find this information especially useful if you are looking or thinking of looking for a therapist to counsel you in your particular situation. Then we take up the problem of the "Rejected Partner" and what those hurt by a married partner's affair can do to cope.

Lastly, we offer you a set of approaches you can use to assess your responses to affairs and to judge their applicability to your special situation. We can't go so far as to say that the unconsidered affair is not worth having, but we do believe that the kind of thinking urged here will prove invaluable to you, regardless of what decision you come to.

As adults, few of us are ignorant of the existence of extramarital affairs. We may not know that one began the Trojan War or that another one brought about the end of a Tolstoy novel. We *do* know that affairs are the stuff of TV soap operas (on and off the screen), racy newspaper headlines, and, not infrequently, our own personal lives. Affairs are amusing for some, titilating for others, and a way of life for others. For all of us, the extramarital affair is a universal social artifact.

At the same time, affairs incite almost universal condemnation. Thus a book about affairs, such as this one, is faced with distinctly unpleasant choices. If it is not to offend, it must dissemble. If it is to inform in a relatively impartial manner, it runs the risk of seeming by that very impartiality to condone what decent people everywhere deplore. The authors urge on the reader a willingness to defer questions on the morality of affairs until we have discussed some of the dynamics that underlie them. You, the reader, can tap into your own sensitivities to extramarital affairs—whether you are considering an affair, are already involved in one, or are, like most of us, simply curious about yourself.

Chapter Two

MIRRORING

Mirror, mirror on the wall
Who is the fairest of them all?

The wicked queen in "Snow White and the Seven Dwarfs" asks her magic mirror this question, and bets her life on the answer. She's safe only so long as the mirror reassures her by telling her she is the fairest. Of course, in the way of mirrors, the dread answer finally does come. No, the Queen is no longer the most fair—Snow White is. The gamble is lost. To recoup, the Queen enters into a series of actions, each more desperate than the last. It is a self-destructive path, and she self-destructs.

The Brothers Grimm first wrote the fairy tale "Snow White" in the 1880s, and it has been a favorite ever since. The story of a young girl, struggling for independence, and her hateful stepmother (read also good versus evil) is a timeless one. The wicked stepmother, dominant, arrogant, and envious of her beautiful stepdaughter, appears also as a metaphor in Betsy Cohen's provocative 1986 book *The Snow White Syndrome: All About Envy*. Cohen focuses on envy *per se* as the Queen's primary motivating force, evidenced by her asking the mirror repeatedly for affirmation of her youth and beauty. The mirror is always truthful, however, as these things happen in fairy tales, and dutifully reports back to her the inevitable sad truth: she is no longer the fairest of all, Snow White has taken that honor.

If only this fairy tale mirror had been aware of new psychological theory, or self-psychology. Then it would have been attuned to the Queen's lack of self-feeling, and it would have continued to provide for the Queen's need for appreciation and affirmation. In this case, the "Bad Queen" would have become the "Good Queen," for that is the basis of self-esteem. When we feel good about ourselves, we are able to act good towards ourselves—and towards others. Truth is not always the most desirable quality in a mirror.

A World of Mirrors

The need of the Queen for approval and reassurance is a need shared universally by all people. We all have a need for *mirroring*. Mirroring simply being the term used to describe our individual needs for affirmation and acceptance by others. The need for mirroring begins at birth and continues throughout our lives. We need to see our own sense of self-worth mirrored in the eyes of those we love and trust. When an infant takes its first faltering steps to the applause and encouragement of its parents, more than motor skills are at stake. A secure sense of self is being molded, too. An absence of positive mirroring in early life can have serious long-term effects on an individual's relations with others. This is especially true of one's love affairs as mirroring is often the vehicle through which two lovers intensify their celebration of each other. After all, the lover is the one who, unlike the Queen's mirror, tells his or her partner, "*You* are the fairest of them all." But will it last? Will it be enough? Many relationships—marriages and extramarital affairs as well—are determined by the mirroring needs of the partners. Where they are well-matched, a rich relationship can result. Where one or both partners have obsessive needs—like those of the Queen—the results are apt to be frustration and pain.

Perhaps the two most important skills you need to master to have successful adult emotional relationships are: the ability to find a good mirror for yourself and the ability to be a good mirror to your partner. For lovers, mirrors come in twos.

Reflections in a Lover's Eye

Because our needs for mirroring are real and lifelong, the only question is whether to cope with them in a positive rather than in a destructive manner. Many an extramarital affair begins as a response to unmet mirroring needs. In this case, it is not so much a question of "stalemates" as of flawed mirrors. We cannot see in our partner what we so much want to see. And then, across a crowded room, waiting for a bus, chatting with a coworker, the glass brightens and an image is struck. It's tricky, though, picking our way through this mirror maze.

Mirror Images. Sam was Denise's lover. Her former "lover" had been her husband, Vic. Vic proved to be a bad mirror, reflecting his own negative feelings about life and himself. He criticized everything and everyone. With him, Denise had become convinced that she *was,* not merely *had,* "fat legs." Like the distorting mirrors in a funhouse, she felt all of her to be ". . . just my big fat legs, out of proportion with all the rest of me, out of sync with the world. I thought people would look at me and just immediately stare at my legs. He had so convinced me of this un-beauty that I was always wearing pants and refused to put on a bathing suit. I would sit there, on the beach, looking like a big scarecrow, all covered up, clothes flapping in the breeze, hot and sweaty, but afraid to peel any of them off. My fat legs became an obsession. I read every book on diets, thinning, slimming, cellulite, exercise, massage, or surgery. My mirror, like Vic, saw nothing but legs. I was miserable. Then I met Sam, and everything turned itself around."

She looked flushed with excitement, radiant and glowing. "Beauty may be in the eyes of the beholder, but let me tell you, it gets translated into the eyes of the 'holder,' too. I now feel like a perfect Venus. The 'ugly duckling' has bloomed."

Like all of us, Denise needed to feel "fairest of them all." Although she is aware that her thighs were "less than Hollywood perfect," her husband was only able to point out her flaws. On the other hand, her lover, Sam was able to provide the nourishment that good mirroring gives. The husband focused on the negative, the lover on the positive. What Denise found was what the "good affair" provides—the mirroring lacking in early life. Vic, Denise said, felt he was "being honest." He felt he was "telling it to her straight" when he was critical of her. Yet, this very criticism is only the replaying of an old scene. It opens up old wounds. Every person who says, "Tell it to me straight," is apprehensive, for, at bottom, is the desire for "straight" to be "great, beautiful." A good mirror will always temper honesty with feeling and compassion.

Denise waited 30 years to meet her good mirror. She had not known this type of reflector in her early years. The child of actor parents, Denise could not compete with their careers for their attention. Her father left home with a much younger actress when Denise was small. Her mother drank for a while as a way of soothing herself, but she soon turned back to her career and consequently spent little time with Denise. When she did, she was highly critical of the child, always finding some minor flaw that needed to be pointed out. "Walk with your shoulders straight back," or, "Learn to cross your legs at the ankles when you sit," and other similar comments, were always being tossed at her.

Denise was sent to dancing school at age seven to "make her more graceful." After a short time, and even though Denise enjoyed the lessons, she was told by her mother, "Unfortunately, since you are naturally clumsy, there's no point in our wasting money on this." Obviously, this was not the supportive mirroring that a young child craves. Denise felt herself hopelessly un-beautiful, and acted that way, because the way we are made to think about ourselves early on becomes a part of us.

As is often the case, her marriage at age 24 to Vic simply repeated the pattern. This is often what happens with faulty early mirroring. Unused to supportive mirroring, the person does not know how to find it, does not even know if it exists at all. There was nothing new in the way Vic viewed Denise. It was all too familiar to her. His "honest responses" only focused on failings, as he perceived them. He rarely complimented her.

Denise was thoroughly accustomed to this, but even so, she came to feel that she was living in an arid desert, where life would eventually wither away.

Through treatment, Denise finally divorced Vic, the mirror with the "crack" that she had been unable to see when she chose him. In finding Sam, her married lover, she finally got some of the positive mirroring that had been denied in her life. She lapped it up like a puppy deprived of food. She could now be "ugly, smelly, bad, angry, dirty, jealous" and still feel accepted. With Sam, she did not have to worry about how her legs looked, or any other part of her. His love, translated into his appreciation and admiration of her total being, was unqualified. She became the image of her fantasy, the one who is loved completely. She felt—and acted—beautiful—a rose, not a weed.

The Mirror Junkie. How much mirroring does it take to make up for early deprivation and damage? There's no set answer, and some people become "mirror junkies," wandering through life forever seeking, forever hungry. They crave reassurance, and they demand reassurance—constantly. In a marriage, this can put an intolerable strain on the supplying partner—the overburdened mirror.

It was exactly this situation that moved Ed away from his wife Brenda and into an affair. Their marriage was the second for both of them. Brenda's marriage had ended with the early death of her husband, still in his 30s, and Ed's had terminated in divorce when his wife, in a career change, had suddenly announced that she was moving to another state and wanted to be "free." Surprised and hurt, Ed comforted himself as best he could with ideas of, "We each make choices, and I can't stop her from doing what is good for her." Nevertheless, his needs for closeness were still there, and when he met Brenda a short time later at a popular travel resort, she seemed right for him.

Brenda was sweetly pretty, with small, even features, and, more importantly, she seemed to be looking for closeness as much as he was. They did everything together, skiing, skating, reading to each other, watching TV, traveling, and dining out.

Ed often suggested that they have more friends and include others in their dining out, but Brenda was reluctant. She wanted—just Ed. She relied greatly on his approval.

At first, he was lavish with appreciation and attention, because it seemed to bind them closer. Sometime later, however, he began to feel enslaved. He said: "I now feel as if I'm strangling. Whatever she does, wherever she is, she seems to need my continuous appreciation. It's as though if I don't give my stamp of approval, nothing counts. She won't buy underwear unless I'm there with her. I feel sucked into a bottomless pit. How many times each day can I tell her I love her, that she's beautiful, that the new underwear was made just for her, that I care? It becomes a drag."

Brenda needed her mirror to be there continuously. As in the myth of Narcissus gazing at his reflection in a pool, Brenda needed Ed to be her constant pool. And Ed felt himself running dry.

Ed wanted to stay in the marriage. He was ready to give it all he could, and he was unwilling to face another "failure." Still, as he said, he had, "run out of vitamins." He continued, "I feel like someone must who has a close relative in a wheel-chair, always taking care of him and offering him hope. She's so needy so much of the time. I can't keep it up."

Thus, when he met Theresa, his sister's new roommate, it seemed natural that they begin an affair. Terry was independent and full of energy, as he was. More to the point, she did not have Brenda's excessive need for reassurance. Of course, she was happy for his attentions, his telling her how he felt about her, his remarking on her clothes and achievements, his admiration for the way she handled herself. But Ed knew that Terry, unlike Brenda, could have managed without them. No longer a literal "care-giver," Ed felt that he could now attend to his own needs. He could listen to his own inner voice and reflect on his own inner experiences. In a very real way, Terry gave Ed back to himself.

Giulietta, the courtesan in Offenbach's opera *Tales of Hoffmann,* beguiles Hoffmann into yielding up his reflection in the mirror to her as payment for her favors. It is a symbol of Hoffmann's loss of self in the relationship. So it is with mirror junkies like Brenda. Through their incessant demands for attention and reassurance, they metaphorically soak up their partner's image, giving nothing in return. The mate of a mirror junkie has no recourse. In order to regain an image of self, he or she must find a truer mirror: a reflector, not an absorber. Ed found his with Terry.

Through a Glass Darkly. People cope with unmet mirroring needs in many different ways. Some, like Brenda, become mirror junkies. Others take an opposite tack, a mirror-image approach so to speak. Instead of trying to control others through seductive persuasion, through clinging and demanding, as Brenda did, they seek to fulfill their mirroring needs by allowing others to exploit them. Masochistic in their style, these people choose partners who are violent, unpredictable, liable to fly into "narcissistic rages" at the slightest "violation" of their fragile selves. For the masochistically inclined, abuse is at least better than indifference.

Gloria was a case in point. She was a "rage-ee," the victim of a "rage-er." Not only was this true of her marriage but of her present love affair as well.

"I had seen Joey drinking when we first got married—five years ago. I was young. I knew that he got a little sloppy, a little out of control after a few strong martinis, but I didn't think it mattered all that much. Once or twice, even before we got married, he became a little abusive towards me, but he said it was all in fun. He's a big guy and he likes to wrestle, so he would wrestle with me. He'd have my hands twisted around my back in what he thought was fun. I didn't think it was, and I'd ask him to stop it. It was hurting me. I'd show him the red marks around my wrists, but he'd laugh and say not to be such a baby. He'd say women today were tough and didn't have to be treated like out of some Victorian novel. I believed him. I'd feel ashamed of myself for rubbing my wrists and holding back tears. Then things got worse. His drinking got rougher—and so did his so-called 'horseplay.' I thought of leaving him, but he said he'd kill me if I did. So, instead, I found someone else—Rick." Gloria then went on to explain how things had developed in her new affair with Rick.

"At first, it seemed a lot better than with Joey. He never wanted to roughhouse the way Joey did. And he drank the way I do—a couple here and there but nothing much to speak of. Then somehow it started happening again. I began feeling like I had with Joe. Somehow, I was always at fault, always feeling either shame or criticism—or something. I just wasn't feeling good, and I don't know how it happened."

Gloria stopped, as though trying to sort out this puzzle in her head, looking for the missing pieces, for the parts that would put it all together and give her some understanding and, hopefully, some peace. Finally she was able to go on:

"He was married. I was married. So it was tough getting together. I was really scared of being found out because Joey was so violent. So I had to be real careful. When I'd make a suggestion to Rick about how we could meet and not be found out—or when I'd just question a plan of his, like the time he said we should use his house because his wife would be gone for the afternoon—he wouldn't answer. He'd just go into a fury. I got all scared inside and didn't know what to do. After all, all I did was ask a question. At first he'd give me a look that made me feel like a disgusting little kid, then he'd scream something like: 'I just told you what we're going to do. What is it with you, are you stupid or something? I know my wife, and I know when she'll be back.' He didn't seem to understand where I was coming from, what I was feeling. I thought to myself—what's the good of this affair if it's not much better than the marriage?"

In going from Joe to Rick, all Gloria had done was change her men—not her mind. Lots of people do this. Freud called this behavior the "repetition compulsion." It involves the reliving, again and again, of the same pattern of failure. The scenario is always the same, and the old feelings are constantly reactivated. Take Gloria, for instance: her mother had died shortly after she was born, and her father abandoned her when she was little

more than two. She was raised by her aunt—her father's sister—
who resentfully agreed to take the young child in.

Still young and beautiful, Gloria's aunt led an active life
that included relationships with many men. Little Gloria was
often left alone with less-than-competent baby-sitters. She remembered crying herself to sleep many nights with no one there
who seemed to care or, by the age of eight, with no one actually
around. Her aunt kept telling Gloria that she would be back
"sometime later." When Gloria pleaded for the aunt to stay
home, she was reminded, in no uncertain terms, that she should
be grateful she had a house to live in and that she should not be
such a baby—words later repeated in a different setting by her
husband.

In Gloria's case, the unmet early mirroring needs of her
childhood badly hampered the adult. Gloria made a mistake with
Joey, and was not able to compensate for it in her affair with
Rick. Instead, she merely repeated it. With little sense of self-
worth, Gloria did not yet possess the skill of recognizing what
or who would be a good mirror for her. What she needed was a
partner who could transform some of her masochism into a
sense of self-caring. What she had chosen were partners who
exploited her feelings of weakness and played on her sense of
inadequacy. Because they were brutal, they seemed strong to
her. And she craved strength, finding it preferable to be abused
by the strong than to be ignored. Preferable, maybe; satisfying,
no. Gloria tried to control her world by giving to others what
they demanded, no matter how demeaning, in return for their
love. But she found this a mug's game. The love she got never
equaled the abuse she took.

At this point, Gloria sought treatment to gain some understanding of herself, to see if there weren't some way out of her
destructive pattern. Clearly, it would only be after some successful treatment that she would be able to change scenarios
and develop a more healthy, positive sense of self. At that
juncture, she would be able to start looking for a good mirror
with some real chance of success.

Before we leave this dark side of unmet mirroring needs,

we should take a look at Gloria's lover, Rick, too. One of the manifestations of adequate early mirroring is an adult's ability to protect the self against "narcissistic wounds," or at least to accept them more easily. The secure self can stand to be questioned, doubted, criticized. This was clearly not the case with Rick. He found Gloria's simple questions about their tryst at his house to be criticisms of himself. Though Gloria did not, from her reporting, use words critical of him or shaming him, he took them to be such. His attitude seemed to say: "How dare you question, confront, or do anything except totally accept what I'm saying or doing, accept unquestioningly—for I am perfect. Most importantly, I am in control of you! In no way are you to put a dent into that system." This was, of course, his primitive grandiosity speaking, the vulnerable baby who is now a rageful adult.

Rick's behavior appears much different from Gloria's, but both of them are suffering from early wounding—the lack of mirroring. Rick had to protect his inflated, yet so vulnerable, sense of self by raging and striking out at anything he imagined was an attack on his omnipotence. The last thing such an insecure self can deal with is a mirror that even flirts with the truth. Hence, the bullying.

Beau Ideal: The Peerless Mirror. "A man's reach should exceed his grasp, or what's a heaven for," says the poet Robert Browning, neatly capturing the idea that perfection makes a dandy ideal but a sorry reality. Yet *primitive grandiosity,* the feeling that one is or should be perfect, is a behavior problem that crops up constantly in a number of different ways. We've seen how the adult Rick flies off into childish temper tantrums when his inflated notions of self-perfection are even questioned. Another manifestation of grandiosity, equally destructive, is the individual who seeks perfection in others.

Lisa is an example of this. Whereas the early Greek philosopher Diogenes roamed the streets of ancient Athens holding his lantern to the faces of strangers in the hopes of finding an "honest man," Lisa roamed the streets of her cosmopolitan city looking for the "perfect man." She didn't say perfect, but she meant it. Because perfection is well out of the grasp of mortal man, Lisa's personal history is littered with the ghosts of cast-offs, the discarded men in her life who could not make the grade.

"There's nothing out there. I knew I couldn't get it with my husband. He just couldn't come up with what I needed, but I sure thought I would find it outside the marriage. Goodness knows, I'm not lazy. I've certainly tried hard enough. In these past few years, I've had about half a dozen affairs. They don't last. I begin them with enthusiasm, but within a short time, almost like right at the beginning, things go wrong. I can't put my finger on it, but there's something wrong with every guy I meet."

Lisa's laundry list of complaints could appear justified. Even in an extramarital affair, one cannot expect that every chosen lover will turn out to be "Mr. Right." When we examine the repetitive theme in Lisa's tales, however, it stands out like a man on crutches at a ski lodge. None of her lovers was "perfect."

"We were in bed together and it seemed fine, at first. He was a cop, married like me, but it worked well because he could take time off during the day. I imagined that every time he went racing down a block with the siren blasting, it was to come to me. We met in my studio, my home away from home. I like making love with all my artists' materials around. He was a frisky lover, always ready, with an active restlessness that excited me. The first few times were good. Then he started calling me to meet him when it was convenient for him. He said he had to get away just at special times; otherwise, it was endangering his job. I didn't like that. I had to meet him when I could and when I wanted to.

"He became annoyed and even hung up on me once when I told him that I didn't want to see him that day. He called back a little later, but I was pissed and told him so. After a few more weeks, I decided he just wasn't right for me. Since Ben, I've had a few other affairs, but as I've said, they always seem to do something or say something that really doesn't go down. Then I just get turned off and won't see them anymore."

Lisa knew she wasn't perfect herself, so she sought perfection in others. This is a not uncommon response to flawed early mirroring. Lisa, like many others, was looking for a mirror that would reflect the image of perfection she wished for herself, the image she had wanted to project but didn't. In the beginning, each new affair represented the Beau Ideal, and this was pretty exhilarating for the man. After all, being regarded as perfect is a shot in the arm to anyone's ego. It's rather like riding a tiger, though; the trip is exciting, but getting off may be a problem. One by one, Lisa's lovers were hoisted into the saddle of perfection and then unceremoniously toppled out of it as their all-too-human frailty became evident.

In truth, Lisa's quest is futile. The mirror she is looking for doesn't exist. Self-awareness, however, could replace the desperate search by forcing her to look inwards rather than outwards. A secure self can be tolerant of imperfections—both in itself and in others.

The Inconstant Mirror. Let's suppose you get your act together, do everything right, have self-awareness and a sense of what you need, and run into a streak of luck, as well. You find just the right partner, whose needs and strengths go hand in glove with yours. There's no more to this story than to live happily ever after, right? Wrong.

Ralph, for instance, knew right from the start of their marriage that Llana was a good mirror for him. She was admiring and appreciative of him, especially of his intellectual skills. Herself a high school graduate, she was impressed with his doctoral degree. When he spoke, she appeared to listen in awe. As far as she was concerned, he was a gentleman *and* a scholar, *par excellence.*

At the same time, though, Llana was slowly evolving too. Perhaps in emulation of Ralph, she got the itch to go back to school. There she began to acquire a store of knowledge of her own and to develop her own way of thinking. She now questioned some of Ralph's assumptions, began to make changes in a few of his speeches, which he was in the habit of showing to her. She even did some rewriting. Because of his own insufficient early mirroring, Ralph found it difficult to act as her good mirror and encourage her to continue fulfilling herself. He could only feel abandoned and dismayed.

He sought solace in an affair. Ruth, the "new woman," was Llana of old. Ralph now felt secure in a world that was familiar to him. His anxiety, and the sense of disintegration of self that always accompanies such anxiety, was quieted. His world would stay the same—as long as Ruth did.

Of the Columbus/Leif Ericsson controversy over who discovered America first, Mark Twain said: "Leif Ericsson discovered America first, but it wouldn't *stay* discovered." This is also true of many relationships and affairs. Two people discover each other and the world lights up. But the moment of discovery ends. Time, as it will, alters one or both. After a few years, or less maybe, one partner can truly say of the other, "You're not the person I fell in love with." Extramarital affairs, like Ralph's, may come about not because one's mate has gone stale but because one's mate has developed into someone altogether new. It may grow tiresome waking up next to the same old person year after year, but think of the shock of waking up next to a total stranger, and one you may not be particularly compatible with at that.

The Good Mirror

In mirroring, the really blessed are the ones who can give and receive. A "good mirror" offers a radiant reflection. Listen to Ellen, a young widow, telling of her experience with her child:

"She was lying next to me, this wonderment of the love act. I examined her meticulously. Slowly, carefully, as though they were the most delicate pieces of art, I held her so-so-tiny fingers, wondering how anything that small could be so very perfect, so complete. I then touched her little nose, traced her mouth with my pinky, as though my other fingers would be too coarse, too gross. I gazed into her ears, at the tufts of hair spread across her smooth baby scalp, and finally unwrapped her kimono to fixate on that exquisite little body which would one day be a complete woman—like me.''

This sounds like an adult love experience, but it is the kind of sensibility that provides the positive early mirroring that makes it possible for a child to become a loving adult. Ellen, having received such reassurance and applause in her early life, is now able to extend it to her daughter, the fruit of her liaison with her married lover, John. The secure self radiates outward, fostering security in others. At the same time, Ellen evokes a positive mirroring image from John:

"You have a high mound, like a young girl. Did you know that? Your eyes are hazel but when you are in deep passion, they turn green, slowly, oh, ever so slowly. It is as though figure-ground reverses itself. The light brown recedes into the distance and the strong green pushes forward. And you tremble just so slightly, like a baby's startle, when I nibble on your earlobes. I love the feel of you then. Your trembling is such a turn-on. I never want to leave.''

Unlike the troubled mirrors we've discussed earlier, this relationship offers all concerned the nourishment of good mirroring. Ellen's positive early experiences make her able to both give and take, to both evoke and respond. The power of the extramarital affair is that it can concentrate on the mirroring. Focused, it can become either the vehicle for repairing early wounds or the extension of early pleasures. In either case, the extramarital affair provides for the possibility of a "second chance," the chance for self-fulfillment of one's natural yearning for acceptance and appreciation.

Good mirroring, however, does not always need words to express itself.

"Barbara does these amazingly wonderful things with me. They are little things, but so important. It is as though she thinks all of me is beautiful. While Jane, my wife, teases and calls me 'a hairy bear' and says I 'should be rented out in winter,' Barbara loves it.'' Gerald pauses in reflection, and then goes on:

"She will look at my body, taking a long time. Then slowly, she playfully begins to lick the hair on my chest, looking up at me teasingly as she does so. I can feel the wetness. Then she takes her fingers and makes little curls, the way I imagine women do when they do up their hair, twining each tuft around her fingers and pulling it straight up. When I lift my head off the pillow and look down, I see little curls in a circle around my chest. 'Now you have a natural perm,' she says, 'like me. When I put my head on your chest, our two perms will meet. We'll be the curly twins.' So silly, like two kids playing, but it's such fun. She's making such a fuss about me. My mother sometimes used to do that when I was a kid and trying on something new. I'd feel the pleasure in me and her, and I knew boys weren't supposed to be looked at that way so I'd tell her to stop even though I really didn't want her to. Now Barbara does the same kinds of things, even when we're making love. She tells me about my penis, my testicles, as though they were so special. I feel that, to her, they are. So am I."

More often, though, to ensure good mirroring in a relationship, it's necessary for the partners to communicate their needs to each other. In the movie *Mona Lisa,* the hero/protagonist is with a young prostitute. He urges her: "Talk to me." She gives him a puzzled look. "Do you mean talk dirty?" "No," he insists, "I mean just talk to me."

Being talked to intimately, directly, is a fulfilling form of mirroring. It intensifies our self-esteem. For the male who, like Gerald, is not afraid of the tender side of his nature, mirroring gives a greater sense of his own gentleness and capacity to stay quiet. He doesn't always need to be the "do-er." He can also revel in receiving.

Mirroring reflects the bedrock of our self-esteem. We need the person, the mirror, to share with us his/her joy in us. Some people can give this to each other in marriage. When a marriage goes stale, however, or when one partner changes and mirroring is no longer there, an affair often seems to be the answer. It is the affair, when it is successful, that re-establishes equilibrium.

While seeking an affair in this situation is understandable, another approach for the hurting partner may be to communicate his/her needs to the mate. This implies a good sense of self-knowledge, though. The partner must know what is missing and how to ask for it. It also means taking a risk. Asking for approval involves the risk of being rebuffed. It opens up vulnerabilities that may be exploited rather than soothed. Often it seems easier to turn to someone outside, someone who appears to be offering what is wanted without being asked. Hence the affair.

Affairs, though, are not without risks of their own, as we shall see in later chapters. Not the least of these risks is one we will discuss in the next chapter—the idealization of the partner and the unhappy perch that idols must sit upon.

Chapter Three

GODS OR HUMPTY-DUMPTIES: THE IDEALIZATION SYNDROME

Try this. Think back as far as you can to your early infancy. Do you have any recollection of the first living room you saw? Can you recall any of the pieces of furniture in it? Don't the chairs and tables loom large—even huge—in your mind's eye? Perhaps you "camped out" under the dining table, which seemed to stretch out over you like a cave. It was a world that by turns frightened and comforted you.

For many of us, this early sense of being in a strange world protected by great and good powers (parents, relatives, etc.) represents a kind of personal Eden. We *idealized* those who cared for us because they kept the frightening part of the world at bay.

When we cried and were comforted by our mother, we merged with her calmness and "omnipotent" strength. "Hush, don't cry," she said, and—wonderfully—we stopped crying. We did this, not knowing that some day, because of her steadfastness and soothing, we would be able to do it for ourselves, as if she were really inside us. And, to some extent, she really is,

31

because we internalize the qualities of those we idealize in youth and shape our behavior using those qualities as standards.

When the idealization process is successful, we gain a secure sense of our own narcissistic well-being (we feel whole and powerful). Having thus merged with the idealized person, we are ready for the next developmental step—the recognition that the idealized figure is *not* really omnipotent and that we are not really part of that person but a separate individual—ourselves. Yet, because we have internalized the idealized attachment, we have made it our own. Thus we acquire a set of standards and ideals that we will use to order our world and our relationships.

If, for whatever reason, such an idealized figure was absent from our early years, we will lack the internalized strength we could have gained. In that case, we tend to continue looking for that image of love and power we never had, projecting it onto our mates and lovers. This is the basis of a dangerous game of teeter-totter: gods up, Humpty-Dumpties down.

When early idealization fails, the adult often looks to a partner to take on a super-ideal status—to become a personal god who will flawlessly supply what has been lacking. What is worse, the ideal-seeking adult, despite every evidence that the lover/spouse can't quite pull off playing the super-ideal, will continue to push the role all the harder. Inevitably, the over-idealized partner fails—falls, like Humpty-Dumpty, and can't be put together again. "Oh no, it happened again. I trusted George, believed George, loved George, looked up to George, and just like all the others, he's failed me." And poor George? He never knew why he succeeded and he never knew why he failed. All he knows is that it was one hell of a fall.

That's not to say that we don't need someone in our lives to idealize. Even if we had successful early idealization with an adult figure—parent, aunt, uncle, whoever—we still carry some of the need for idealization with us as adults. After all, it's hard to be a responsible grown-up all the time. We need someone who can put a little order in our lives and protect us from our fears. And who is in a better position to do that than the one we love? It's perfectly natural, then, for us to idealize, to some extent, our loves and our lovers.

With successful early idealization, this need is tempered with moderation, with realism: "He/she is only human after all. I can't expect miracles." The internalized strength takes the heat off the partner to be perfect. No such "sweet reasonableness" is available in cases of failed idealization. For such people, idealization is not just part of the way they love but the totality of their love. The loved one *must* be the ideal, the all-kind, all-wise, all-whatever-they-need. The *less* they got in early life, the *more* of this idealized hero/heroine they'll want in adult life.

In this respect, idealization differs from the need for perfection we discussed in the last chapter on mirroring. There, we found people who were looking for the perfect mirror, the one who would reflect the applause they felt they had to attain. With idealization, though, people are not interested in hearing enthusiastic shouts of "Bravo, bravo." Instead, they are looking for the super-ideal mate/lover to whom *they* can shout "Bravo, bravo" for an outstanding performance. And make no mistake, outstanding performance is exactly what is expected!

These people demand that their mates/lovers *be,* not just *represent,* Prince Charming, Earth Mother, Sex Goddess, and a whole pantheon of super-heroes. How would you like to come home from a tough day at the accounting firm and be expected to spend the evening as Conan the Barbarian or Joan of Arc? Perhaps not . . . But remember, Humpty-Dumpty's always teetering on that wall.

From Disillusion to Illusion: Making Up the Deficit

Lest you think this idealization business involves only glamor and the bon ton, remember that people's needs don't *have* to conform to the glossy men and women you see in the fashion magazines. To some, down-home can be appealing. The ideal is a personal matter. The idealized partner has only to maintain the image—whatever it might be. And the range can be very wide indeed.

Ina, for instance, looked like a lopsided painting; hardly the flashy image you associate with the word "mistress," if that old-fashioned word still has any associative powers left. Nevertheless, she was Carl's mistress, and he adored her and the affair they were having. True, Ina's friends called her "el Sloppo" and teased her about the way she dressed, saying she always looked like she was trying out for "bag lady" roles.

It was just this appearance, though, that Carl most prized. For him, Ina's "hanging loose" style, her shapeless, ill-matched clothes, and her total disregard of anything smacking of chic meant real love and caring. Ina stood in direct contrast to Carl's first wife, Ruth, who had over the years become a—to him—maddening paragon of fashion. Indeed, if you put Ina and Ruth side by side, you'd have no trouble at all in identifying the wife as the lover and the lover as the wife.

Why was Carl so perverse? It was a case of reverse idealization, which dated back some 30 years to Carl's prostitute mother. As one of the "working girls," Carl's mother had spent all available money on clothes, perfume, and cheap jewelry. Food was a "catch-as-catch-can" affair. If he looked hard enough he'd probably come up with something. Carl's father was a shadowy figure who took both himself and his shadow out of sight when Carl was small. His mother would say, "You might as well never have had a father. I don't care if he never comes back."

Stressing that she was their only support, Carl's mother told him that whatever money was around was gotten through her work as a dance-hall hostess. (It was only later that Carl learned she was actually a prostitute.) "In this business, you've got to look good," is how she explained her extensive wardrobe of beautiful dresses. Carl, of course, could not understand why it was so important for his mother always to be dressed up and to go out at night. He wanted, ideally, a woman to care much more about being with him, feeding him, and taking care of him than to care so much about the way she looked. Thus, he soon equated love and caring with a kind of "thrown-together" look. High fashion for him implied the high cost of negligence.

In this case, neglect was experienced by the child (Carl) as a *premature disillusionment*. This premature disillusionment brings in its wake pain and anxiety and also a sense of loss and shame, as if the child blames itself for not being cared about. To overcome the nagging sense of loss and shame, the child as an adult will seek out a partner who appears to offer *constant* availability, an attempt on the part of the two-year-old to recapture the idealized needs for the mothering-fathering figure that was not there. This was the object of Carl's search.

In the beginning, Carl's wife, Ruth, fitted his needs perfectly. She wasn't especially concerned about keeping up with the fashion scene; she displayed a consistent interest in his career as a dentist. It seemed like an ideal relationship and they married, having lived together for a trial period first, as many people do these days.

Then came the revolution. No guns were drawn, no proclamations were read out, but changes came—in Ruth. Prodded by her female friends, she suddenly began to take an interest in her appearance. Turned on by Carl sexually, and "peaking" as many women of 30 do, Ruth no longer wanted to be a dowdy hausfrau. She wanted to be a Cleopatra, to turn Carl on by her appearance, her beauty. Carl had unwittingly triggered Ruth's Venus complex. Now she wanted to be seductive, not only to Carl but to any other man who might glance her way—and, of course, she wanted to impress her female friends cum rivals. Ruth now dressed with pizazz, spending time and money on clothes and, consequently, showing a lot less concern about Carl's work. Carl began to feel that he was back with his mother once again. Ruth was turned on; Carl was turned off. He began looking for another version of Ruth-as-she-was. This Pygmalion, having created a ravishing Galatea, bolted.

He found Ina—jeans, torn T-shirt, and all—perfect. Where Ruth's new-found passion for style reminded him of his mother, Ina's total disregard of her appearance created the needed illusion that all she cared about was—Carl. Thus, the ideal woman and the ideal affair—created from Carl's early needs—

was born. Now all Carl has to worry about is keeping the fashion news out of Ina's hands.

As we can see from Carl's case, keeping Humpty-Dumpty on the wall is a tricky business. He needed Ruth and Ina both for the same reason—to counterbalance the deep disappointment/disillusion with his mother. In a primitive way, his psyche equated high fashion and feminine attractiveness with neglect of his needs. It is also typical of the primitive psyche that it seek no middle ground. "You are either all there for me, or you are not there at all," is the upcompromising message. It is a stance that allows the partner few options.

For Carl, the ideal is no longer what it should be in a healthy growth experience, that is a *guide*. Instead, idealization is now formed into a command, a command so rigorously framed that it invites—almost mandates—failure on the part of the idealized one. As long as Ina plays perfectly the idealized role set out for her, Carl will feel safe. If and when she begins to change, as Carl *perceives* change, the god-into-Humpty-Dumpty pattern will repeat itself. For this affair to remain stable, either Carl must change or Ina must not.

Odd Man Out: The Response of the Non-Idealized

Idealization can also involve figures other than possible sexual partners. This turn of events can keep the ideal-seeking partner in a marriage from straying into an extramarital affair, but it puts a strain on the mate who may find him or herself curiously—inexplicably—neglected. The result may be a kind of dark comedy.

For instance, Joan's mother had been an ideal woman to little Joannie. Then, suddenly, the ideal disappeared, tragically lost in death. Although the family seemed to cope with the great loss successfully, for ten-year-old Joan the scars were there, under the skin. It's hard to speak of such a loss, even to oneself, but one's actions speak louder than words.

Early loss of a parent is always a trauma for a child. When the parent has been idealized by the child the loss is doubly devastating. The death leaves the child bereft, knowing what he or she had but completely baffled as to how to get it back. At four, five, or six, just when the child most needs an ideal, the chosen figure is gone. The world seems empty, devoid of god-like figures who can provide strength, comfort, and reliability. True, in this case the fall of the ideal is not due to human foibles—Humpty-Dumpty didn't fall, he was pushed—but the effect is the same, an ideal is gone and there is a deep-seated need to replace it.

In order to recapture her ideal relationship with her mother, Joan married John. But John was not the person to take the place of her dead mother; it was John's *mother* who could fill that bill. That's not to suggest that Joan deliberately set out to fool John in order to be with his mother. The attraction to John—and to his mother—was very likely unconscious on Joan's part. Yet, like the unseen undertow that tugs at you as you swim in the ocean, the power of such an unconscious attraction must not be dismissed. All Joan knew was the relationship with John—and with her mother-in-law—was a very fulfilling one. Mother-in-law jokes were lost on Joan: she couldn't see the humor in them. She had re-created her ideal relationship, Humpty Dumpty was safely back on the wall, and all was right with the world.

The situation, though, was fraught with comic overtones. For instance, it was Joan who suggested to John that his widowed mother could stay at the same resort with them during their honeymoon! John, of course, was at first pleased by Joan's willingness not to leave his recently widowed mother behind. Yet, he felt it odd and then somewhat irritating to have his mother constantly present throughout this delicate time in a newlyweds' life together. He loved his mother, too, but he felt that Joan was going perhaps a trifle too far.

It was when Joan suggested that John's mother be included in their first trip to Europe that he balked. He told her he was thoroughly opposed to his mother joining them on a Monte Carlo gambol all over Europe. Filial respect was one thing, but really

. . . Still, they were one too many for him, and the three hit the beaches of France together.

On some unconscious level, John was aware of a symbiotic union between the two women that unobtrusively—but firmly— included him out. It was a relationship that clearly called for the talents of a Henry James to delineate properly. John was no Henry James with an exquisite feeling for the sensibilities of others. Baffled, and not knowing why he was baffled, resentful, and not knowing why he was resentful, he was ripe for an affair. He seemed capable of dealing with his problems only by adding to them.

To be fair, how could John know of Joan's early rupture in her process of idealization? Even though he was aware of the facts of her mother's death, how could he know that the loss of her parent was also a loss within Joan of a necessary self-organizing experience? Joan's broken idealization he could not see; he could only sense that, on some level, Joan was on a search—and he was not the target!

The upshot was that John found, on a trip to Yugoslavia, a very attractive woman who was much more responsive to him than to his mother. He was certainly not going to vie with his mother for his wife's attention. The idea didn't cross his mind— probably couldn't have been entertained there if it had. So, although the affair was possible only while he was abroad, it did make him receptive to a concept the French discovered years ago. Every man worth his salt deserves a mistress as well as a wife and a mother. Thus, fully womanned, John was ready to face the future, even if, in all likelihood, he would never be able to explain how things had turned out just that way!

After the Fall: Is Reassembly Possible?

Idealization, while similar to mirroring, goes a step farther. Perhaps more than a step. For instance, we are sure that we can count on the ones we idealize; we know they will be there when we need them. In addition, we are confident that we can rely on the *values* we attribute to those we love and idealize. In short, we often idealize the person we love *and* that person's set of values. A failed idealization here not only deprives us of the loved one, it also leaves us with a broken value system—a rudderless ship at sea. We lose our love and our way.

One response to such a loss can be simply anger—anger proper and anger that covers our hurt. Anger can also lead to action, to our taking "revenge" against the failed ideal's "aggression." For when we experience the failure of something we believe in, we feel attacked. A natural reaction is to counterattack. An extramarital affair is sometimes a wild fling and sometimes a riposte.

Bert, for instance, was having an affair, which was preposterous. He didn't like it and didn't want it; nevertheless, there it was. He was married and she was single. More to the point, the affair lacked—at least on Bert's part—the slightest hint of passion. Now a passionless affair is like an egg without salt; it may be vaguely nourishing but it is bland and without savor. How did Bert get involved with Leila in this unsatisfactory state of affairs? Basically, because the liaison with Leila was Bert's reaction *to* an event, *not* the result of his conscious search for something he wanted. He didn't charge into the affair; he more or less backed into it.

When Bert married his wife, Suzette, one of the traits he most admired in her was her sense of morality and integrity. Like him, she approached the world with clear ideas about how it should go. Everyone and everything had its place. There was no fuzziness in her universe. Bert liked to think that he had known this many years ago when he first asked Suzette to marry him. At the time, they were both only twelve years' old and in a school play. She was the princess and he was the prince. As quickly as she accepted his proposal in the play, so readily did she say "yes" in real life when he asked her again, at 20, to be his wife. For eight years they had lived close to each other, their families knowing each other and everyone assuming that sooner or later they would marry. Bert idealized Suzette *and* the value system she represented. In such a scenario Humpty-Dumpty not only has to sit securely on his perch but has to be placed so high he is above reproach, too.

After marriage, they both had decent jobs and mutual friends, and life seemed to jog right along, with satisfaction for both and no surprises for either. No surprises, at least, until their sixth year of marriage when Bert came home early one day. A sudden teachers' conference had been called, teachers and students were dismissed early. Bert had been eager to get home anyway, because Suzette had told him she was taking the day off as she wasn't feeling well.

Coming in the outer door, Bert hung his coat in the closet and thought he would go to the den turn on the TV and catch the rest of the baseball game. Suzette and a strange man were there. Both dressed, they were, however, in a "compromising" situation, she sitting on the couch with the man lying on it, head in her lap. Suzette had a book in her hand as though she had been reading to him.

The stranger mumbled something, seemed terribly embarrassed, and, quickly thrusting his feet into his shoes, without tying the laces, left the house. Bert, in shock, stayed calm, though he was frozen inside. He asked Suzette, without raising his voice, if she was having an affair. Without raising her voice, Suzette replied, "Yes." A rational man, Bert asked her the ultimate question, "Why?" Her answer, incomprehensible to him, involved some statements like: "We're not communicating. It hasn't been good for a while now. It just happened."

While appearing to listen, Bert shut off part of the colloquy as pain took over. His sense of outrage simmered. He wondered if for all these years he had misjudged Suzette's sense of honor. It was one of the qualities in her that he so much admired. She seemed to have so much spunk, such a secure sense of right and wrong, one that reflected perfectly his parents' and his own family value system. Now the world he had believed to be tight and secure was in the midst of an earthquake. Firm foundations were giving way like the proverbial house of cards.

When Suzette muttered something about seeking family counseling, Bert's composure cracked and he raised his voice for the first time. He shouted that *he* did not need help. There was nothing wrong with *him*. Maybe she should go see a shrink, because evidently there was something deeply the matter with *her*. Then he stormed out of the room. Bert's world was crashing down along with his idealized picture of Suzette. Bert was angry, and not a little frightened.

Bert and Suzette continued to live together in the "gray zone" of neutrality—albeit an armed neutrality. Not long afterward he began his affair with Leila, a fellow teacher who had always been flirtatious with him. In the past, he had felt flattered but had always kept the lid on, saying nothing provocative. Now, he responded. Leila brought her passion into the affair, but Bert's was still centered on Suzette. As often happens when one steps out of character, Bert felt like a poorly chosen actor in a bad play. He just didn't fit the part. He might have been familiar with the role from TV, but try as he would he could never play it convincingly.

Bert still idealized Suzette and his lost picture of her morality. It validated his own sense of what was right in the world. His affair was an almost involuntary response to his pain. It did not even constitute a "getting back," which might have generated its own passion and energy. It was just a halfhearted response, as if he didn't know what else to do. Lacking a plan of action or any real commitment on Bert's part, the affair, like a fire that is not stoked, fizzled. Several weeks later Bert decided to end it and said so to Leila. Reaching out once more for Suzette in a desperate attempt to regain his lost idealization, Bert said he thought they should both seek help. It would be a last chance for them to try to overcome their problems in communication and re-create the good relationship they once had shared. Having overcome his initial denial and his wish for things to magically go back to where they were, Bert is now realistically trying to put Humpty-Dumpty back on the wall.

Bert, unlike many of the people represented in this chapter, had a happy, secure childhood. He had responsive parents who provided him with positive mirroring when it was needed and whom he had successfully idealized. He had internalized their values of constancy, trust, and honesty, which now formed a central core of his character. He felt them to be rich ideals and realistic ones, and it was natural for him to choose a wife who could be counted on to share this value system.

Suzette's affair was a near-fatal blow to this world structure. Leila was Bert's stricken, almost-involuntary response to the blow. As noted, his heart was never in the affair. Shame, the aftermath of his crushed ideals, plagued him. Throughout the turmoil, though, he did not give up believing in what he felt to be of value. It was no false god he had idealized, of that he was sure.

As a sensitive person, then, he redirected his energies, going back to the source—Suzette, himself, and his marriage. Fortunately, Suzette was also willing, to reforge their life together. Very likely she, too, was shaken with the realization that a world that seemed so sound could be so fragile.

Hidden Ideals: What You Don't Know About Yourself

Some affairs have obvious roots in broken or lost idealization; others are not so easily identifiable. In such cases there seems no real reason for the affair, and yet, as with most human behavior, obvious or not, the reason is there.

Judy and Barry seemed to have a good-enough marriage. If she had been asked to look for flaws, Judy would have shrugged her shoulders and said there was nothing particular wrong. If their relationship lacked excitement and zip, Judy would rationalize, "Well, after a while all marriages become somewhat boring, don't they?"

If push came to shove and Judy was asked to define "boredom," she'd probably allow as how she and Barry "just didn't do much." Barry was a pretty sedentary guy—though a good guy—and she, too, would just "hang out" when she wasn't working. Married for only a short time, they were trying to have a child but had not yet succeeded. Even the "trying", she said, had become boring.

One day, Judy, along with others from her work, decided

to spend their lunch hour watching the runners in a mini-marathon race held nearby. The race ended right near the block where she worked, so there she found herself, along with the rest of the crowd, urging the runners on and offering them cups of water. She sensed rather than noticed Lloyd even before he came close to her. He was, like most runners, lithe and slim with a lean, muscular frame, very unlike Barry's large, out-of-shape body. When he quickly took her outstretched cup, quietly said, "Thank you," and pushed on to the finish a short distance away, Judy felt a slight flutter inside her. Something had come awake. She felt a sense of life flowing through her, and, at the same time, thought how silly it was to be stimulated by a man in a race who had only taken a cup of water from her.

A few minutes later, she felt his presence near her again. Sweat still pouring off him, he simply thanked her for the water, saying that hers was the only cup he had drunk from. As he said it, in a low, soft voice, while looking intently at her, it sounded like poetry. The sheer, physical life of the moment struck a responsive chord in her psyche. One thing led to another, as is so often the case, and their affair began.

If Judy had been asked what it was that most attracted her to Lloyd, she would probably have said it was his sweaty body when she first saw him. Raised in a household that put a premium on intellect but set little store on body strength, Judy found physicality intriguing—and foreign. It was a part of her she had always longed to develop but hadn't. Her mother, a frail woman, had been overly protective with her children. While other girls had been allowed to tumble in the snow, ride bikes in the street, and go skiing in their teens, Judy's mother had frowned on all that. "It's for tomboys," she said. "You don't need that kind of activity. Just keep on reading the books you've been reading and stay close to home. Be a lady. You'll have to know a lot to go into anthropology like you want."

As with many parental messages, what Judy's mother said and what she meant were two different things. Consciously, she wanted to keep Judy a "lady." Unconsciously, she wanted to keep Judy close to herself. Keeping Judy shut away at home, reading book after book, was her way of protecting Judy from injury and at the same time seeing to it that she did not become attached to anything or anyone other than her mother. As with many children who are deeply attached to their parents and who are not rebellious, Judy obeyed her parental dictates.

But Judy embraced her mother's idealization of life and relationships more from lack of alternatives than from conviction. Her internalization of those ideals, consequently, was a good deal less than complete. Even as an adult, she still had a need for idealization, but she was not consciously aware of these feelings. In fact, this need remained dormant until she met Lloyd. He, like an idealized parent, was the one who revealed to her a whole aspect of herself she didn't know she knew.

Judy's marriage was the same relationship as with her mother. Barry was "safe." Perhaps too safe. Her marriage seemed to her to be reaching the point of diminishing returns. Yet, as there was no "real" reason to break it apart, she stayed. She sometimes wished she and Barry could "do more things" together, but there didn't seem much chance of that. The "safe" course is not known for its quick changes and sudden veers.

Lloyd came along at just the time in Judy's development when she was ready to break out of the parental/marital mold. That unknown part of herself that she had neglected for all her 27 years now was demanding acknowledgement. She and Lloyd, on their dates, which they kept discreetly tucked away from the world, did a lot of things together. Along with vigorous love-making, they went bike riding and skating. He introduced her to the pleasures of an exercise club, where she learned to love the swimming and exercise rooms. In the past, when she had once tried to get herself in shape, she found the exercising parapher-nalia more akin to a torture chamber. Not any more.

Because Lloyd gloried in the physical side of himself, Judy found that she, too, was discovering a part of herself that she had only been dimly aware of. She had idealized the life of the mind because that's what her parents did, and after them her husband. Now she had something—and someone—new to ide-alize—a new set of ideals to internalize and make her own.

With idealization, you get a second chance to choose a part of yourself, still undiscovered or undeveloped, that you admire. Her spirits uplifted, and in touch with her body senses for the first time, Judy was the child exhilarated with new-found skills. "Safety" was no longer ideal; excitement and joy were the new gods on the block.

The Idealization of Hype

If ever there was a god set up for a Humpty-Dumpty fall, it's the god "Lifestyle of the Rich and Famous." As seen on TV and in the magazines, though, its appeal is enormous. For young people with little or no input from their parents, themselves overburdened with making a living, the pictures of the "good life" are all but irresistible. In a consumer society with a market economy such as ours, consumption—consumption conspicuous and lavish—is raised to an ideal. The young look at the great cars, the great clothes, the great houses—and they dream great dreams.

Patricia came from a family of poor means, and even poorer spirit. She had an emotionally deprived childhood. Economic survival dominated the family thinking. There was nothing left over for emotional caring or sharing; indeed, there was never enough of anything for leftovers of any kind. To compensate, she idealized a lifestyle that came mostly from the media. Young people, deprived of the company of adults and nourished largely by TV and pop records, would have a somewhat skewed set of ideals. How different, for instance, their Madonna is from earlier ones.

Patricia yearned for "the finer things in life." She idealized a lifestyle that included manners, sophistication, and culture. She was quite determined about this, and, as she was bright and very attractive, when the time came for her to marry, she married, in her terms, well. Her husband, Desmond, came from what Patricia considered a suitably high-status family, and she looked forward to moving in the social circles that had been only images on a screen.

Desmond did come from the right social class, but he was

the wrong man. This is always a danger when one chooses a mate on the basis of earlier unmet idealization needs. The individual chosen to meet these needs may be entirely unaware of the role and totally unfit for it.

Patricia soon discovered that Desmond was financially irresponsible—it had never been necessary for him to learn to handle money with care. Far worse, Desmond was unwilling or unable—or both—to protect her from the incessant sniping of his super-snobbish family. High class doesn't always mean high-minded. Patricia's dreams of a cultured, elegant life went out the window. Humpty Dumpty fell, a victim of super-hype and false advertising.

Patricia took a lover who was as far away from the Social Register as she could find. A crude but impassioned man, Leo gave Pat a sense of being overwhelmingly desired—a sense she had never received from her family or her husband, much less from her husband's family. Because of the affair, Patricia came to view her marriage more realistically. Desmond, for all his faults, was not to blame. He had never pretended to be anything but what he was. Patricia, storming up the social ladder, had never stopped to examine Desmond himself. She saw, somewhat bitterly, that it was not so much a question of Desmond's having failed as the ideal as that *he* had never taken on the job in the first place. It was her own "Tinseltown" ideal that had crashed in a thousand irreparable pieces.

Disillusioned with Desmond and the "beautiful life," Pat climbed several rungs back down the social ladder, closer to a world she knew firsthand. It was a retreat into the deficit of her early childhood, with Leo as a lover who could provide some of the missing mirroring she so desperately needed. It sometimes happens that when one unmet childhood need is attended to in adulthood the individual is able to go on to the next stage. This may well be the case with Patricia. Once she has achieved a real sense of self-worth from her relationship with Leo, she may be able to go on and find an idealizable partner based on real values rather than on media hype.

Affairs: Real, Ideal, and Otherwise

As we've seen, such extramarital affairs as we may have—and the kinds of people we are likely to have them with—are often determined by our early idealization experiences. People fortunate enough to experience successful idealization early are apt to have a realistic attitude toward love. Such people are able to appreciate the wonderful aspects of their mates and to cope with and understand the less desirable ones. They love people—not gods—and hence are not in the Humpty-Dumpty-making business.

For those still seeking an idealizable figure as adults, the picture is clouded. If a spouse fails in the role, they are apt to continue the search in an affair. Sometimes the affair can turn into a viable relationship that meets enough of the disillusioned person's needs to keep the thing afloat. At other times, the affair may awaken the person to the fact that he or she is really seeking an unrealizable goal. In the worst case, the process can turn into a destructive pattern of unrealistic demands ending in bitter disappointments.

In any case, an affair is a (more or less) calculated risk. Like the little girl with the curl, when affairs are good, they can be very good. But when they're bad, they're horrid. In the next chapter, we'll discuss some of the risks that extramarital affairs—calculated or not—are likely to involve.

Chapter Four

RISKY BUSINESS

R isks and affairs go hand in hand. After all, if you get caught
there will very likely be serious consequences—some for
which you may not be prepared. On the other hand, some people
want to get caught as a way of bringing up a confrontation.
When Helen didn't erase the revealing message on her tape from
her lover, on some level she must have known that her husband
could stumble into it. He did. "Those nights in Chicago were
the best sex I've ever had" was too specific to be denied (Helen
had just returned from a trip to Chicago). For others who may
be determined to cover their tracks the risks are still there.
Covering tracks always involves deceptions, if not outright lies.
When Gloria instinctively answered the phone in Carl's room at
7:00 A.M., after she had agreed that she wouldn't, Carl was put
on the spot. Would his wife really buy that the sleepy voice she
heard was that of the chambermaid? It was a risky business that
went bad. But unlike business, where you file for bankruptcy
and can reorganize, in "risky business" you are sometimes
forced to file for divorce and it's final. If that's what you want,
the risk can be worthwhile. But if not, there can be great pain
and regret without the possibility of returning to your earlier
life.

Truth and *Consequences*

It happened that way with Oscar. He and Tina had been married
for over 20 years. "Every now and then I took little side trips—

with other women" he explained. "That's just me. I didn't think much about it but it was something I needed. I kept it quiet. But then somehow, a few months ago, when Tina again said that she wasn't in the mood for love and when her busy new schedule with the 'I'm back in school and have to make good grades' seemed to always keep her occupied, I blurted out: 'Well, don't think I've been living the life of a monk lately because I haven't.' She seemed stunned, like when someone you saw yesterday is pronounced dead. About a minute later, after a long stare at me, she said she wanted a divorce. I never expected that. "Twenty-two years, and she's a good woman. Why did I do that?"

Oscar felt himself to be the "heavy" in this scenario. He took his marriage vows seriously and saw his momentary slip-of-the-unconscious as tripping him into a hell of his own creation. Still, not everyone in an affair is a "heavy."

The Grandiosity Syndrome. Despite the obvious inherent risks in affairs many lovers sport a nonchalant attitude. They seem to have a cavalier spirit of "I won't get caught." Ed and Phyllis, both high-powered executives for a large corporation, made love in his office during lunch-time. Their favorite form of sex at this time was Phyllis performing fellatio. The chilling risk was that there was no lock on the door. When asked about this she flippantly replied: "Oh, I think it was pretty safe. Everyone was usually out to lunch or busy with work and phone calls. I don't think anyone would have come into the office. Do you?" She may have been right most of the time—but what if not, even one time? In this instance it was the excitement of the risk itself that was the stimulus for Phyllis and Ed. Safety was tantamont to boredom. Both undoubtedly had the need to make a grandiose statement in their behavior of "Others may get caught but not me. I'm in control and above all that." This type of thinking and need often reflects a profound lack of real control or self-esteem. And with it there is frequently an escalation of risky and outrageous behavior until one is caught; then one can repent and start all over again.

Of far worse consequence, however, is the possibility that

the underlying need for grandiosity can make one blind to reality. All that can be seen is the excitement of the moment. The fact is that if Ed and Phyllis were discovered it could force on them unwelcome problems that they didn't bargain for or seriously consider. It is not uncommon for soldiers in the front lines to exhibit this type of thinking for survival. With his comrades dying all around him, a soldier needs to feel that *he* will survive, if he is to function effectively. A business office, however, is not the front lines, except when the grandiose self takes over.

Johnny left photographs of one of the women he was involved with in an envelope carelessly exposed on a table in his home. Inside not only was there a complete role of developed film but two copies of each picture! In this case it was not so much that he wanted to get caught as his feelings of grandiosity telling him he wouldn't get caught. Further, that if he was somehow caught, it could be explained away because he was different and could not be held to the same constraints as others.

Examples of grandiosity run through the histories of affairs where risk-being is pushed to its limits like gasoline racing through a high-powered engine to generate movement. Sometimes the flow becomes so great that the motor breaks down. So too, in grandiose risk-taking, wives and husbands push the pedal to the floor in their affairs, and their marriages come crashing down, like Humpty-Dumpty from the wall. And, like him, they can't be put together again.

Human behavior, as we have stated, does not usually occur in strict polarities like "I am sick" as against "I am healthy." Rather, it ranges across a continuum, meaning that most of us shift around somewhere in the middle and exhibit both sides of the polarity. It is the balance that counts and that balance is constantly moving. At times we are "here" and at other times "there." Similarly, grandiosity can be healthy or unhealthy. These feelings generally go back to childhood. The child who is made to feel wonderful, powerful and secure knows that his parents will be there to support and/or limit his experiences in the world without rupturing self-esteem. Grandiosity becomes healthy narcissism.

This child and then adult can feel good without having to challenge and conquer the world at every turn. Where the child's early need for grandiosity is not met, however, "archaic grandiosity" emerges and becomes the weed of daily living. The child and then the adult deludes him or herself into an all-powerful position, only to have the power often brutally stripped away, leaving an undefended, frail and vulnerable self burdened with low self-esteem. With the armor gone, the self is no longer the Herculean giant but the tortured dwarf. In the extramarital affair, the "archaic grandiosity" and vulnerability are exposed through distorted, heedless risk-taking.

Sharing The Good News. We often have a great temptation to tell someone about an affair—an old friend, an associate at work, a relative. Not only does it feel good to share our feelings of joy and love but it is also nice to have a sounding board for our pain and doubts. Affairs do have their exciting side, but they invariably pose basic questions about our motives and goals in life. Even when we believe that the affair is parallel play, and don't want it to intrude on the marriage, we find that it can't be totally compartmentalized. Nagging questions come up, especially in times of stress and tension. The affair can serve as a convenient escape—the place where all the good fantasies reside. Reality seems pale by comparison. Still, it is only by communicating with others that we can get the necessary feedback for grounding our experiences in the "real" world and seeing them in perspective. Moreover, the secret often seems even more precious when shared with someone we trust. But who can we trust? Or, to put it another way, is trust also a *risky business?*

"Bill and I were on the college football team and have been friends ever since," says Dick. "He also knew when Barbara and I had problems in our marriage. When I found Gail, I decided to tell Bill about her. I thought he would understand that what she was giving me I could never get from Barbara. He listened and then said to me in an angry tone, 'How would you feel if Barbara were to have an affair?' I was shocked. I always felt that he sympathized with my complaints about the relationship with Barbara. But now I felt totally betrayed and rejected. He was pitching to my guilt. I didn't know where to go with this. I muttered something and changed the subject, sensing his relief when I did so.''

Like children torn between loyalties to parents, friends, too, are forced to make choices when you tell them of your affair. The risk here is not so much that the friend will reveal the secret, but, rather, the blow to your self-esteem when the friend condemns or even mildly disapproves. Instead of getting the stroking and soothing you need, and which draws you closer to your friend, you are suddenly pushed away, feeling like the kid who rushes toward his mama for a hug and is shoved aside with ''Your hands are dirty and you are staining my dress.'' Water douses the warm fire, it turns into ashes, and you are left psychologically out in the cold.

Sometimes a friend disapproves because your action is too close to his or her own need. The difference is you have expressed your need in some way your friend has not. This arouses anger and envy in your friend. You, unintentionally, have hit too close to home. ''Monica always seemed so loving to me. She was like a big sister and a best friend. Then I told her about my affair. I had waited a long time to have one but then I did. I was telling her about my having the 'big O', how fantastic it was—but not only the sex, just being with him, but the more I glowed, the more I felt her moving into the background. Her chair had not moved an inch but she was a thousand miles away. Her eyes, her whole body became mummified. She had left me.''

As Fern was talking to us, she was developing a familiar theme: a good friend, a good friend with a bad marriage, the good friend rooted to her bad marriage as though paralyzed while you have been able, if only temporarily, to break out of bondage. Your actions arouse too much anxiety in her. Her feelings of: ''Why you and not me?'' drive her to move away from you. The "good news" for you strips bare the old "bad news" for her.

Protecting the Children. What hurts children more: stale marriages or affairs? One cannot give a simple answer. There are just too many factors that make each individual situation unique. But almost everyone involved in a bad marriage, separation, divorce, or affair will say that they don't want to hurt the children. Easy enough to say (and most people mean it when they say it) but difficult if not impossible to accomplish. Children are extremely sensitive to what is going on around them, especially when "mommy" and "daddy" are involved. And when the children's emotional security is affected, their awareness becomes like a laser beam.

Parents sometimes conveniently delude themselves into believing that a child doesn't know what is going on because nothing has been said directly. It's as if in order to believe that the child knows, the parent would have to hear something like, "Daddy, I know you are having an affair and it bothers me." It just doesn't happen that way. Also, children's ability to decipher reality differs at different ages. A sixteen-year-old might know the facts but a five-year-old may just sense something wrong; and a ten- or eleven-year-old may know some of the facts but may feel confused and be unable or unwilling to verbalize his or her feelings.

Sara's experience is a case in point. "I hated her [mother] for many years. I think it all started when me and my twin brother were eleven. I never thought that my mother and father were having a good or bad marriage. They were just married and that's the way it was supposed to be. But even though I was naïve, I used to think it was strange that as soon as daddy left for work my mother would get jittery. Then before we finished breakfast or went off to school she would rush off to her room to make a phone call. I couldn't hear what she said because she talked so softly. But as I passed her room, with the door closed, I just sensed that it was someone special. If it were one of her girlfriends, why would the door be so carefully closed and why

the very low tones? I knew I was right when once, needing her
to zip up my dress and worrying that I would be late for school,
I opened the door without knocking. She screamed at me: 'Shut
the damn door I'm talking to someone important.' She was
furious. I started to cry and felt so bad.''

Yesterday's child is today's adult. What Sara experienced
in her mother's affair was the unavailability of her mother. The
message for Sara was simply that when mother was needed, she
was not there. Someone was taking her place in her mother's
world, a someone so important that it caused her usually gentle
mother to scream at her. Sara stayed locked in her anguish, her
eleven-year-old psyche trying hard to make sense of what was
going on but coming up with little. For Sara, the unavailability
continued, as her mother and her lover became more and more
involved with each other. It was almost like a death of a parent.
Her mother was there and, like the women in the movie *The
Stepford Wives*, seemed to go about her business but in a robot-
like manner. The closeness Sara and her mother had experienced before the affair, she remembered, seemed gone forever
and Sara was left with the emptiness, the terror and the desola-
tion of someone orphaned overnight. All of this was unspoken.
Still, while her mother seemed to be blooming, Sara was shrink-
ing.

Because the threads of our childhood are always with us
years later, Sara found herself constantly involved with "una-
vailable" men. She was beginning to learn what that meant to
her and to change some of the "threads" of her existence to
make life more joyous. She was giving to herself out of her own
needs and pain, some of the protection her parent had failed to
provide.

Children caught in a parent's affair are also caught in their
own stage of development. A child of two is different from a
child of sixteen. Protection then, the counterpart of the risk-
taking which must be involved, needs to always relate to the
child and his place in the world. Perhaps protection for the
sixteen-year-old could involve some kind of sharing.

Risk-taking here involves your own sensitive assessment of

the needs of the almost-grown son or daughter, with the risk taking the form of how best to lessen the "split" in the child, how to keep the child from the anguish of divided loyalties. In certain circumstance, the risk may be minimal. For instance, if the child has reached a level of maturity that allows you to discuss the matter openly, or if your case is so extreme that the child can appreciate why you have chosen this course of action, you may be able to lessen the pain of the situation.

On the other hand an older child, on learning of your affair, may choose either to identify with you or your spouse. The child may see you as the hunter, "my aggressive parent out on the prowl for fresh blood," and side with your spouse, or the child may identify with you as the prey, "my victimized parent, easily misled," and offer you sympathy and help. Protection of the child in this case involves attuning the parent-child relationship so that psychological trauma does not take place. (See Chapter 9 for more on the effects of an affair on children.) Uppermost in any risk-taking situation is the need to protect the child from wounds no bandage can cover.

Teaching Your Spouse; When Exhibitionism Takes Over

Some think too much of a good thing is just great, but it can be dangerous. Listen to Debbie's story:

> I had to keep the affair under wraps. I thought I was playing it smart. I knew from school that I had a terrific memory. A straight A student, I could memorize whole pages from a book even when I didn't understand it. It worked well then, and it worked in my affair.
>
> I knew I'd never give things away—not even in my sleep. Whether it was a great, sexy dream or bad nightmare, I'd call everyone by his right name. I was organized, orderly, fully in charge. Risks would be minimal—even non-existent.

Yet Debbie's sexuality, skyrocketing as it did in her affair, had gone through a major revolution. Married at an early age, and with little sexual experience, she was now, ten years later, in sexual high gear, Venus bursting forth. No longer tied to the few sexual positions she and Alex had comfortably settled into, she was experimenting. Her hormones seemed to be working overtime, and she wore her newfound sensuality like a favorite cape, hugged closely to herself. As in the case of sharing with the friend, she wanted to show her new self off—to display it like a dramatic new outfit bought at the newest fashion center. Her "exhibitionism" needed an audience, as is true for those of us who were not permitted to sufficiently "exhibit" early on (the child of 2, 3 and 4 years of age who needs a lot of confirmation from others).

Though her husband Alex had not bought a ticket, and unknown to himself, he was Debbie's sole audience. She did not perceive this as a risk.

"I just thought I would loosen him up a bit—give him some hints of what to do. So I bought these outfits—black lace little bikinis with no crotch or bras with no cups. He just put it down to my suddenly going a little wild—but the night I asked him to swirl whipped cream all over my body and lick it off—his face seemed to crumble, like with old people who have no teeth. It was then he screamed "you're having an affair." I could feel his pain. Nothing I said could make him change his mind. It was like he suddenly went crazy, saying over and over: 'I can't believe it. I can't believe it. What did I do wrong?' Debbie looked puzzled. "I didn't think I was even taking a risk—but I guess I was—wasn't I?"

While Debbie's good mind and memory were under her control, her need for exhibitionism was not. It was this part of her which gave her away. She risked showing off, and, like a bad tire, it blew out when it was least expected. It was a risk not worth taking.

Fatal Attraction

Since the release of the film *Fatal Attraction* a great deal of attention has been given to the type of affair in which rage over rejection takes on obsessive and frightening dimensions. The movie, one of the biggest hits of 1987, had "become a popular password for the quality of contemporary relationships" writes Ellen McGrath. Glenn Close, the female protagonist in the movie, becomes depressed as Michael Douglas, the male hero, attempts to separate himself from her. She, the single woman involved with a married man, reacts with more and more desperation, reaching out for connection and intimacy as he tries to let go of the relationship. Her "crazy" behavior takes on its theme as this push-pull struggle sharpens, while the risks to him and his family intensify with the deepening of what has been identified as her depression, a common symptom for women when relationships with men fail.

While in reality this type of affair is not very common as the dark side of our culture, it still keeps us fascinated.

Unlike *Fatal Attraction's* plot, Dr. Frederick Humphrey in his survey of Marriage and Family Therapists found that only 4% of all the affairs he surveyed were revealed by the affair partner. Undoubtedly, only an even smaller or negligible percent of these involved psychotic revenge. Nevertheless, for those involved in such an affair the consequences are not small.

What is more common are "petite, mini or semi" fatal attractions in which a one night stand, casual affair or parallel play gets out of hand. Some affairs start out seeming to be playful and harmless but then take a sudden turn. These situations can be very painful, if not terrifying. Some people go along with the unwanted affair, hoping to "ease" out of it so that the other person doesn't get angry and turn it into "fatal attraction." "Maybe if I go to bed with him one more time he will leave me alone;" or, "I'll have dinner with her a few times and then trail off;" or, "I'll go to bed with her once more and lay on her all my financial problems and anxieties—that should turn her off." Sometimes these strategies work. At other times they fuel the fires of passion. One person we spoke to thought she would end her "mini" fatal attraction by telling her lover that she had herpes. It turned out that he also had herpes and the disclosure made him feel more comfortable. For the person involved in these dilemmas it can be as scary as a full blown "fatal attraction," for one often doesn't know that it is "mini" until it is over.

When Bob and Helen fell into bed after the out of town business meeting, it certainly seemed harmless enough. The meeting celebrated the conclusion of a big contract for their company so everyone was in a light, up mood. Given a little alcohol, some sexy talk and the distance from home, it seemed natural to fall into bed. The "lets just have some fun no commitment" rap made it even easier. But back on home base, Helen who was single, was not entirely willing to just forget and leave it as a one-night stand. "But you said the sex was fantastic and much better than with your wife." She became persistent in wanting to keep the affair going. Bob did not. He did not want to jeopardize his marriage. When Helen called him at home one weekend he really got alarmed. In this case his anger finally got through to Helen and she backed off.

Not so with Olga and Ira. For Olga the affair was new, glorious and—her first in a so-so marriage but one she wanted to keep together, at least for the present. Ira, still single at forty-two and after many affairs with married women, was now looking for *kinder and kucche*—the home life. Olga was his choice. "You're just what I've been waiting for. I'm not going to let go." Said in a moment of passion, Olga thought it was just that—love-talk. But when he started pushing to the point of leaving messages on her tape (though trying to disguise his New England accent) she knew he was for real—as were the risks. The cork had popped and the champagne was spilling dangerously out. She had wanted a "mini" affair. He had wanted a "maxi"—called marriage. As determined by Olga, the end was "out" for both of them.

As we will see in chapter 6 ("Beyond Parallel Play") affairs often do go beyond their original intentions. This does not necessarily happen because people are lying. In the moment that Helen said that the affair "will not go further than tonight," she probably meant it. But after the initial experience there is new information to integrate with each individual's personality and needs. At that point a new interpretation and conclusion can emerge. "The sex was so great and better than in his marriage." Or, "He really cares for me and makes me feel good—this is really different." And so on. It is, therefore, important to be aware of the possibilities of "mini" fatal attractions and try to head them off at the pass.

Married or Single Partners?

Which type of affair is riskier if you are married? With another married person or a single person? Fatal attraction would certainly seem to pertain more to a single partner, as portrayed in the film. But views differ about which type of affair is less risky. In our interviews with therapists (Chapter 8) we got a broad range of opinions. For example, Dr. Albert Ellis feels that affairs with single partners are often less complicated and easier to arrange because of the single person's greater availability and flexibility with time. And some single people, he points out, like affairs with married persons because it often takes the pressure off them for a commitment which they don't want. But he also notes that he has heard of scores of instances over the years of the single person in the affair telephoning the lover's spouse, but not when both were married. Dr. Marjorie White agrees: "If you have an affair with a single person you don't have to worry about the person getting a divorce or being sued for divorce by the mate who finds out." Dr. Barry Lubetkin on the other hand, feels that an affair is frequently less complicated with another married person, "particularly if there is a kind of unwritten rule. Now look, we are both going to be discreet, we'll seize opportunities to be with each other, we don't really want to disrupt our spouses or our families or our children—and I have seen liaisons like this go on for years successfully with no unrealistic demands or requirements being placed on the other person." But Dr. Lubetkin also recognizes that one can have a very sticky situation in which the single person wants the married person to leave his or her spouse. It has also been found when that happens it causes great turmoil.

Some single people may feel they are rescuing their married lovers by disclosing the affair to the spouse. In one case a young single woman was convinced that her lover really wanted to leave his wife and two children to marry her but that he just couldn't screw up the courage to take his longed-for leap. So she did it for him by calling his wife and revealing the affair. Things did not turn out as she had expected. Her lover was outraged and ended the affair. He and his wife entered marital therapy to save the shaky marriage and deal with the raw emotions his mistress's disclosure had stripped bare.

One Room or Two?

Single people can disappear for a few days without leaving an itinerary of exactly where they will be day by day. This is not generally the case for married people. When a married person has an affair with a single person they can usually take one room on the married person's name. In this way, the spouse at home can be given the name of the hotel or motel. But when both people are married the question sometimes arises of how many rooms to take. Obviously it is best to have two rooms so that each of their spouses knows where to contact them. However this can get pretty pricy in some cities and locations, leading to the temptation to take a risk. After all, "she doesn't have to know where I am every minute—I'm not the president of the United States." Then if it is decided to take the risk, whose name will go on the room? Who will take the risk?

Bud and Joan decided to take the risk. In the resort area where they were traveling the room rate started at $150 a day. It seemed silly to take another room at those rates just to have a phone number where someone could call. Joan thought she could get away with it since her husband, an accountant, was busy with the tax season. So Bud's name went on the bill and his wife could call him. On the second day Joan called her husband from a phone booth to explain that she was on the move because of business meetings and had changed hotels. It was too late to call him after the dinner meeting that went on into the wee hours. If she could check into the new hotel at a reasonable hour she would call him that night and let him know where she was staying. Despite accounting figures spinning around in his head, her husband had other images as well. Perhaps based on previous suspicions, he accused her of having an affair and they had a heated argument over the phone. Joan promptly took her own room and she and Bud swore that they would never take the risk again—it just wasn't worth it. Fortunately for her, the incident "blew over" and did not escalate. Penny wise and pound foolish may have very real meaning when it comes to the finances of an affair.

Risks in the Age of Electronics

In this age of fast checkouts, computerized printouts and information storage, the old adage of "put nothing in writing" can get out of control. Mike found this out when his wife asked him: "Who was that second driver on the statement that came from Hertz today?" Mike and Sheila had barely enough time to drop the car off at the Los Angeles airport to catch their plane back to New York. Thanks to "quick check out" he could just leave the car, jump on the shuttle bus, and check the statement when it arrived in the mail. Now he had to do some fancy footwork to explain Sheila, the second driver, to his wife.

Almost no payment is safe from the computer and the wealth of information it can store and then spit out at the most unexpected times. For example those elaborate statements some credit card companies provide summarizing exactly where you have eaten, drunk, driven and slept can suggest a suspicious trail for a "strictly business meeting weekend." Then those wonderful hotel printouts, that are so useful at tax time for itemizing expenses, also record a revealing list of actual phone numbers called. Telephoning your lover frequently when you are on a trip opens you up to this electronic risk. "Who did you call in Santa Monica twice a day when you were in St. Louis?" What if the question isn't asked but rather the number is dialed to discover who that was? Many people deal with their electronic shadows by having their personal bank, credit card, and other financial statements sent to their office addresses. After all, it is easier to go over these statements with your accountant when you have them in the office, right? Maggie didn't buy that explanation and it aroused her suspicions. Her closer attentions to her husband's movements eventually uncovered his affair and led to a split in their marriage.

Even one's junk mail is not above giving a not-so-innocent filing away. An airline decided to promote its business flights by offering to fly for free the spouses of those purchasing a full-fare business-class ticket. The promotion was a success, with quite a number of business fliers taking advantage of the offer. The airline, not content with that, decided to send a follow-up letter to the *spouses* of the business fliers. The letter said the airline hoped that the spouse had enjoyed his/her trip and would choose to fly with them again. People who had brought their lovers on the trip—instead of their spouses—had a lot of explaining to do when a curious or furious mate met them with: "And just who the hell *was* with you on that trip to Chicago that the airline thinks I took?" Doubtless, there were some changes in the advertising and promotion department of the airline after the flood of hate mail from enraged—and embarrassed—patrons subsided.

Overall Risks: From The General to The Specific

Freud wrote that fidelity in marriage is only maintained in the face of continual temptation and suggested that little excursions in the directions of unfaithfulness can have a salutary effect on a relationship by reawakening desire between partners. Along the line, however, he omitted the factor of risk. And while our views of extramarital affairs have progressed from the ancient Roman, Christian, Hebrew and Arab views that considered women's sexual desire insatiable and proposed circumcision to curb appetites, to the lure of Playboy bunnies and heterosexual male strip shows, we still frown on open admissions of infidelity.

To be found out or even to be suspected invites entry into the leper's colony of infidels.

Risking What You Have. A clergyman who strays can lose his parish; a politician who flaunts his liaisons can lose his voters; the employee who is found out may be considered "unreliable." Marriages, says society, are *the* only ties to be sanctioned. Good or bad, they are a government-approved/stamped/sealed way of adult living. Defying this brings heavy risks—losses that can not be recouped. Yet, while the risks are real, the real risk, above all others, is the risk of you losing yourself—to yourself. When your view of yourself, your self-esteem, is open to damage, that, more than any other, is the ultimate risk.

Losing the Real You. "I felt like a sleaze. What was I doing in this dingy, stinky hotel room with a man I'd just met a few hours ago? Everything about the place looked like old-time movie whorehouses what with the cruddy blankets and dead-yellow wallpaper. It was like everyone in the world had gotten laid here." Zena was full of disgust for herself and the impulsiveness which had driven her into this "petite" affair. She was also aware that there was a desperation to her need to make contact with someone after leaving a party where she had felt like an alien. But riding along this conflict was her own self-loathing where she felt that the "bad-me" had overtaken the "good-me." The split was too much for her. "I can't go around doing that to myself. I've got to take my brains out of hock and change my life around." A noble effort which paid off! A critical loss turned to gain where one risk too many, the risk of losing one's self, was the turn-around point.

Overall Risks; From the Concrete to the More Concrete

Here are eight helpful hints collected from people who have repeatedly told us that "this" was the way they got trapped. Not to be taken as the end-all of caution, these points seem to come up again and again, and they constitute a set of "golden" (or as one man said "slightly tarnished") rules. They are included here because there are really no self-help groups for adultery as there are for almost every other human condition that affects a large number of people. The collective folk wisdom here represents the painful lessons of a multitude of risk takers. A word to the wise is sufficient.

1. No picture taking or receiving. We have heard stories where pictures were given to best friends, placed in drawers a skilled robber himself couldn't search, given such identifications as "picture of Cousin John taken at a chance meeting," and on and on. It didn't work. Somehow, somewhere, they were found and the cover was blown.

2. Nothing in writing. Same type of problem. Letters received were hidden, disguised, given to others to keep. Letters to be mailed were sent from another county, and so on. But what if you put one down for a moment and then you forget to mail it? Affairs are allergic to anything in writing. That goes double for diaries, strictly a no-no.

3. No souvenirs. Pack rats as we are, we want mementoes of everything. Definitely *not* a good idea for those engaged in liaisons.

> I just took a matchbox from the restaurant as a souvenir because the place was so darn good. I never thought to look inside the thing because I don't smoke. I forgot that my wife did. She opened the matchbox, turned it over just by chance—and there was a little note from "her." It was only a phrase thanking me for everything. It was one "thank you" I could have done without. Five years later I'm still hearing about it.

4. Not in the neighborhood or in public. Restaurants, hotels, borrowed rooms should all be far, far away—for obvious reasons. Also, never, never, display affection in public places, no matter how far away from the neighborhood. One inveterate risk-taker told us he not only doesn't bill and coo with his *amour* in public but he takes pains to travel in threes.

> I have a "beard"—someone who acts as a cover for me. If the three of us are seen together they'll think I'm with one or another of them. I might be just a friend—either of him or her—certainly they won't think I'm the main event. It's only at night, when we're alone together in a room that I'm actually with her. For the rest of the time, it's the three of us. Three's a crowd? Not here.

5. *No thoughtlessness.* Just a moment of incaution can bring down the whole world of risk. You may throw a bra or panties into the glove compartment of a car—to be stored for just a little while. Ditto with other evidences of intimacy: prophylactics, sexual aids, and the like.

6. *Never in the home.* Possibly the most inviolate rule of all. Never, not even once, consider using your home or apartment for a tryst. Even if you know your spouse is away until next week, there's always the overbooked plane, the ticket left home, the sudden illness—the million and one things that can bring a person back at an unexpected time. Explaining this away is a real trial, and while the excuses we have heard run from the tragic to the hilarious, few spouses have bought them.

7. *Never forget to keep track.* From the males particularly comes the suggestion to check out all your pockets before going home after a tryst. This also includes briefcases. And check your jacket/shirt for stray hairs. Long red hairs around your collar won't sit well with your blonde wife. Said one man: "My wife never checked my personal stuff, but let me tell you, as soon as I began my affair she became Sherlock Holmes incarnate—a real bloodhound."

He also suggested that men should ask their lovers not to wear perfumes or scented cosmetics that leave traces for hours. There's a limit to the number of times you can blame a new scent on those aggressive perfume sellers who spray everyone in department stores. Also, as mentioned earlier, be careful of presents or phone calls that appear on credit cards or itemized phone bills.

8. Never change your style. For better or worse, each marriage has its own style. Your spouse knows how you act and respond. Don't change your style because you feel different. As we showed earlier in the chapter, bringing your newfound sexual hijinks into the connubial bedroom can arouse suspicion in the most trusting heart. Suddenly showering your spouse with love, attention, and gifts, if that's not your normal style, can be a dead giveaway. Keeping consistent is the trick, but it's not always easy. One woman said:

> I come home from my lover's, and I'm really too tired for sex again. Or, when I'm not too tired, it's just that I've had such a terrific time and still feel him inside me. But I don't give that away. I try to enjoy my husband as much as possible and keep my real feelings to myself. It seems to work.

In short, the message is, don't change your ways if you want to hold onto your marriage and minimize risks. Keep your cool and your cover. You'll need them. Complex? Difficult? Is it worth it all?

Is a double life twice as much fun? We'll have more to say about this in the next chapter, "Parallel Play."

But keep in mind that while these guidelines may serve as some self-protection, they are not a substitute for determining whether the risks are worth it. If you decide they are, self-protection is always advisable so there is not unnecessary pain for you and the others involved.

CHAPTER FIVE

PARALLEL PLAY

Mark by his own description was a fuckaholic. Married just one year to "a beautiful and very intelligent woman," he had no complaints about the marriage. On the contrary, "sex is great and I love to be with her." At the same time, Mark could not resist other women, and the opportunities always seemed to be there. As the administrator of a professional association, he traveled at least once a month. During these trips he hardly ever spent a night alone. His extreme good looks and attractiveness to women made it easy for him to have affairs. "Even when I try to go on the wagon, women come on to me and I can't resist." Mark was always up front about the temporariness of these affairs. He always told his partners that he was married and that the affair was recreational sex. If he felt any guilt it was quickly rationalized with the familiar arguments: "I'm discreet; who am I hurting? I feel I need it and it doesn't affect my commitment to my marriage."

Side by Side—But Separate

In Mark's mind the affair was *parallel play*. It existed side by side with the marriage but didn't touch it, or, at least, he believed it didn't. A lot of questions can be raised about the psychological motives behind Mark's behavior and his addiction to sex. Perhaps the ease of these affairs and his skill in managing them helped maintain his defense against looking honestly at his

own behavior; that is, until the whole thing fell apart. News of
one of his affairs got back to his wife who then started looking
more suspiciously at his activities and "stories." With someone
as active as Mark it's difficult if not impossible to cover all
tracks. In the curious geometry of affairs, parallel lines have a
fightening tendency to meet. So when Mark's wife ran into his
ostensible dinner partner some 600 miles away from the dinner,
a confrontation was inevitable. The pain on both sides was too
great to surmount, and the marriage ended. Now at age 38 and
recently remarried, Mark still has affairs but not on the previous
scale. Five years of therapy has at least made him see his earlier
behavior as obsessive and a problem.

The world is full of so many things. Most people who are in an
affair and who are not thinking about splitting with their mates
view the affair as parallel play. People give many justifications
or rationalizations for the affair of parallel play. "I need variety"
says one 35-year-old married man. "There's nothing wrong with
my wife but I don't want to feel later that I missed out on things
and then it's too late." This is echoed by a 28-year-old married
woman: "Al is a great guy and a terrific father. But I have to
deal with the fact that he's a lousy lover—he couldn't make
Linda Lovelace come. So I have affairs but I'm careful. I don't
think I could deal with the idea that the prime of my sex life
would be all Al. Would I be a better wife and mother if I were
frustrated and depressed?" Another 34-year-old married man
just talks about his need for variety. "It's not that my girlfriends
are better sexually than my wife. They're all different. I had a
lot of sex when I was younger and thought I got over the hump,
so to speak, when I got married. I was ready to settle down and
have a family—and I loved Ellen and loved fucking with her.
But after five years it got to be routine. It was really getting me
down. I missed the variety and the new experiences—fucking
someone for the first time. So I gave in and started having
affairs."

Parallel Play—Adjustment or Maladjustment?

In Mark's case, we can clearly see the destructiveness behind the parallel play. We could talk about his insatiable need for attention and confirmation of his grandiose self. We could cite his repeated futile efforts to make up through sexual behavior what was lacking in his early relationship with his mother. Parallel play in the case of Mark can be unmasked as a cover for deeper emotional frustrations and longings. But there are other cases in which parallel play seems to represent a more positive role in people's lives. For instance, behavior is often not clearly right or wrong, good or bad, destructive or constructive. Parallel play can be the safety valve in a relationship. Should a safety valve be necessary? Should all dissatisfactions be met head on? Should a marriage be all or none? What follows are descriptions of parallel play. These affairs are not as one-sided as Mark's and therefore will raise some painful issues about the value of and justifications for parallel play. You make the judgement.

Great and Good Friends. Craig and Alice met in an executive training program for an advertising agency. Both were 28 and "happily married." Alice's husband was rising fast in investment banking so they could comfortably afford the full-time housekeeper to care for their three-year-old daughter. Since both Alice and her husband were trying to make it in the business world there were many pressures on them and not that much time to be together. Nevertheless, Alice felt that their relationship was good and that the time they spent together was quality time. While they didn't have as much sex as a few years earlier, sex was still good and they were turned on to each other. She said that sex was not an issue in her marital relationship, because what she had was satisfying and there were other exciting things going on in their lives. Alice felt she was more focused on her career than sex.

Craig's wife was on a one-year leave to care for their daughter who had been born six months earlier. Craig, too, was committed to his marriage and described his relationship and sex life with his wife in fairly glowing terms.

So it came as quite a surprise to both Craig and Alice when they fell into bed with each other and started a long affair of parallel play. The first time happened at a regional conference in another city. They had a few drinks at the bar with other executives and trainees. The mood was loose and very up. Subsequently, they stopped in Alice's room to go over a report for a meeting later that day. What with the drinks, the camaraderie and the joking, they ended up taking a shower together and then going to bed. They laughed about it later because it appeared more funny than erotic. It just seemed like good harmless fun that wasn't hurting anyone. They felt more like buddies than lovers. Neither of them even thought about it as an AFFAIR. Yet once started, it was all too easy to continue. They really liked each other and had a clear understanding that their relationship would not jeopardize their marriages.

Their jobs, once they were out of the training program, became very high pressured, generating a great deal of anxiety. It felt good to have someone right there who was in the same boat, someone to trust and lean on. The afternoons they spent together in a nearby hotel were an important depressurizer for both of them. Sex just seemed to be a natural part of the whole package. The occasional marijuana cigarette made it all even easier. Although they had a lot of sex together, they both felt it was not the most important part of their relationship. Sometimes they would even fall asleep without having sex—and not feel disappointed. Although sex was fun and enjoyable, they could not rate it higher than sex with their spouses. It was just different and, they felt, vital for maintaining their sanity on the job. The affair was very much tied to their jobs and the office. While it occasionally spilled over into the early evening when pressures were particularly high and they worked late, it was kept strictly separate from their home lives. There were no long laundry lists of complaints about their marriages that they would drag out. Nor were there late night or weekend surreptitious phone calls.

Their affair lasted three years until Alice and her husband

moved to another city. He had an opportunity for a big promotion that they both felt they couldn't afford to turn down. She was able to get a good position at an advertising agency in that city that paid even more than her previous job. Craig and Alice ran into each other at a conference seven months later. The good feelings and friendship were still alive, but there was no expectation or suggestion that they have sex. The parallel play was over and sex had been just a part of it. On reflection they had no regrets. They cherished their memories and considered the affair as a major part of their personal growth.

In truth, Craig's and Alice's affair was not as neat or simple as it appeared on the surface. There were times when each was tempted to turn the relationship into more than parallel play. During a lengthy period when Alice's husband, Marv, was putting in long hours and was totally absorbed in his work, Alice was depressed and grouchy much of the time. She felt that her marriage and home life were becoming all work and no play. The fun-filled afternoons with Craig seemed so much more real and so much more what she wanted. She longed for the light and easy intimacy she had with Craig.

Craig and his wife Judith also went through a "distant" period of high tension. Judith started resenting her decision to put her career on hold for two years to care for their child. Although she firmly believed in the importance of mother-child bonding in the early years, she was feeling isolated and lonely in the full-time role of "Mommy." She found little in common with the other women with small children in the neighborhood. She also worried about losing her professional skills. And she could not contain her envy of Craig going off to work every day seeming so enthusiastic. Craig sensed her hostility and pulled back emotionally, making their distance even greater. During that period, he fantasized about Alice a lot. On a number of evenings and weekends he almost called her.

Why did this couple restrain themselves and not cross over the boundaries of parallel play? First, they loved their spouses and valued their family life. But more importantly, they probably sensed the limited safety-valve nature of their relationship.

In the affair they could be themselves without having to deal with the problems and conflicts of daily life. They could support each other and vent their feelings without any implications of blame or need of expectations. There were no demands other than to be supportive and to give each other physical pleasure. At the same time, they could preserve their images of independence and competence at home because they were fulfilling their dependency needs in the parallel play. Perhaps they felt that outside of the parallel play they would not be loved as adults if their dependency needs showed. So they found a relationship in which their child-part could thrive while their adult-part could grow and gain confidence.

Should they have striven to resolve their emotional conflicts *in* their marriages rather than using parallel play? The issue can be debated endlessly without any definite conclusion. But if outcomes mean anything, both Craig and Alice seem to have stronger marriages after their affair, and they have apparently grown beyond the need for parallel play.

Bedside Manner. Betty was very lonely and depressed since her husband Al had a stroke six months before she started her affair. Betty and Al had a good marriage for 39 years. Al was 64 and Betty was 59. She was married at age 20; and Al was the only person she had dated more than twice and he was her only sexual experience. This was not uncommon for women of Betty's generation. At 59, Betty was still very attractive and trim. Her friends called her a health food and exercise nut. She read *Prevention* magazine, went to an exercise class, and swam three times a week at the neighborhood community center. People described her as a handsome and elegant woman.

Since Al's stroke, Betty's routine had become pretty fixed. First the daily visits to the hospital, and then to the nursing home. At first there was hope for Al's recovery, but now she wondered. He had no speech, was partially paralyzed, and periodically drifted into a coma. Betty was very devoted to Al and prayed that he would recover enough so that she could care for him at home.

Betty had many friends in the neighborhood and in the apartment building where she and Al had lived for twenty-five years. But their friends were coming around less and less frequently and staying for shorter and shorter periods of time. Moreover, she was never invited out any more by the couples with whom they had socialized. This is a phenomenon very well known to widows and other single women.

The nights and weekends seemed to get longer and longer. Many times Betty cried herself to sleep, feeling that her life was hopeless. But Betty was a survivor, like so many women of her generation, and she knew that she would hang in there and do what she was supposed to do. Her two daughters, aged 35 and 37, lived in distant cities. They talked with Betty a lot on the phone but that was not the same as someone being there for you. Also, they had their hands full with their careers and teenage children.

Then one Saturday afternoon when she was returning from the nursing home, she ran into Phil in front of her buidling. He lived in another building down the street. He was a 68-year-old widower whose wife had died of cancer two years earlier. Phil was semi-retired from his law practice, although he continued to service some of his old clients. The two couples had socialized from time to time before Phil's wife died.

Phil called a few times when he first heard about Al's stroke, but Betty hadn't heard from him for months. They chatted for a while, then Phil invited her to continue their talk over coffee in a neighborhood restaurant. She felt a little uncomfortable but accepted. It felt good to talk to someone one-to-one, and they had a lot in common. Phil was a sensitive man who genuinely sympathized with Betty's pain. He suggested that they meet again to talk. She agreed. He called later that week and they met over coffee at the same restaurant. Then one thing led to another, and she invited him to her apartment for dinner.

Betty didn't think that his visit would attract any special notice from the neighbors since they were used to people coming to Betty's apartment for sympathy calls. After dinner Betty responded to Phil's affectionate overtures, and they wound up in bed. It was a tender and warm experience for both. Phil was a good lover and was sensitive to her embarrassment and nervousness. She enjoyed the attention and physical contact that reminded her that she was a woman and alive. It was a terrific release for the tension she had built up over the past six months. Much to her own surprise, she had an orgasm. She then realized how frustrated she had been and how much she missed and needed physical contact and sex. Tears came to her eyes.

But the experience was not without an aftermath of guilt and ambivalence. "Was it fair to Al? Was she a terrible person? What if the children found out?" These and many other questions confused her. She shared these feelings with Phil. He reminded her how tolerant she had been when her older daughter moved in with her boyfriend in her senior year of college. Yes, they eventually got married, but Betty and Phil had to suppress their own standards for the new generation of morality, and she could not see that it was bad in the long run. Well, she concluded, older people have needs too, and fewer opportunities to satisfy them. And who is she taking anything away from?

Betty's affair was parallel play only in the sense that she was married and committed to her marriage. Her needs as a person and as a sexual being were not fulfilled and had little hope of fulfillment in her marriage. Her feelings of self-esteem were fading. She was becoming more and more isolated. Her relationship with Phil changed all that. She had renewed vitality. She felt more energetic and enthusiastic in her visits with Al despite his apparent lack of progress. But she was aware that at times she cut her visits short. She previously stayed all day on Saturday. Now she would leave in time to get to the hairdressers and prepare for seeing Phil.

Constant questions ran through Betty's mind. What if Al recovered somewhat? Would she continue the parallel play? Would the affair take on a different meaning? Was she perhaps wishing that Al not recover because he would not be the same person and she would be stuck with a cripple? Was she really still committed to Al even though she continued to do all the right things as well?

Should you only engage in this form of parallel play if there is no hope of your partner's recovery?—and how can you be sure? These are questions to answer that would defy a King Solomon.

May and December. A very common type of parallel play is the older-man younger-woman combination. These affairs usually invite speculation about the younger woman's unmet needs from her father or competition with her mother for her father's love and attention (Electra Complex) and the older man's quest for rejuvenation. They frequently are very loving relationships that can be mutually beneficial. In the case of Fred, age 62, and Paula, age 29, both married, it turned out that way.

Fred was the founder and president of a computer training school with offices in a number of cities. Paula was his executive assistant who actually ran much of the business. In fact, Fred considered her indispensable for the day-to-day operations. She was extremely bright and efficient and had an incredible memory for detail. Paula had been with Fred's company for seven years. It was the first really steady job she had since graduating from college. She married Frank, a young corporate lawyer, when she was 23 and he 27. They had a daughter, Lisa, who was now four-and-a-half years old. Paula went back to work for Fred when Lisa was a year-and-a-half old. Her employment was a source of great tension between Frank and Paula. Frank, despite all his liberalism had very traditional ideas about his wife and home life. Also, he felt that he earned enough money so that Paula didn't have to work. Money was not the issue for Paula; her sanity and self-esteem were. The fact that the job at the computer school was, at first, of the secretarial, "Girl Friday" type, did not serve to ease tensions. Sex during this period was "dismal." During the first six months on her new job, Paula and Frank had sex about four or five times. Paula describes the couplings as quickies in which she felt like a seminal spitoon because emotion and sentiment were totally absent. It is ironic that during these tense times just when young couples need each other most for support, they often tend to drift apart. Sex is usually the first thing to go, because it is so intimate and carries such a freight of meaning and need.

Wisely, Frank and Paula sought marriage counseling to see if they could restore the good things they had going before the disruption. Paula wondered if she hadn't made too many concessions in marrying Frank, but she felt that she loved him and that they shared the same interests and friends. She also felt a strong need for a stable family life. She did not find the lives of her single friends very appealing. She had been through that scene and didn't want to face it again. Although Frank wasn't the greatest lover, he was attentive to her needs. If she didn't come during intercourse, he wouldn't leave her hanging. He would patiently use oral or manual stimulation until she was satisfied. Frank was also willing to experiment and had a strong sex drive. Before their conflict, they had sex four or five times a week.

When Fred made his proposal of an affair to Paula she was ripe for something new. She had risen rapidly to executive assistant as her talent had become quickly evident after her first six months on the job. In fact it was her excitement about the job that kept her spirits buoyant during a very difficult time of her life. Now she traveled with Fred once a month to one of their other locations in different cities. They usually stayed overnight. At first it was strictly business and certainly Paula had no other ideas. She enjoyed being away—the fine restaurants and hotels, being served, and perhaps above all, feeling important and good about herself.

She was really quite stunned when Fred first came on to her. Many things went through her mind. It happened at dinner after a long day of meetings and nitty-gritty facts and figures. Fred simply told Paula how he admired her and was attracted to her. At the same time, he reassured her that if she didn't have sex it would not affect her job and he would drop the issue. He also emphasized that the affair would not disrupt his or her marriage. He described his marriage of thirty-eight years as loveless—although there was no open warfare. He wouldn't consider leaving his wife, because he felt it would be too devastating for her and his two children (both now married).

Paula was confused. On the one hand, she considered Fred a very honorable man and believed what he said. On the other hand, she was afraid that a refusal might affect her job and she didn't want that to happen. It was an important refuge for her. While she was not especially physically attracted to Fred, she was not unattracted. Although he was older than her father, he was trim and athletic looking. He kept in good shape with his avid tennis playing. At the same time, Paula had been thinking a lot about possibly having an affair, but she didn't know with whom or how it would come about. Maybe an affair with Fred would be a safe and sane way to test the waters. She really missed the frequent sex she used to have. But she also remembered all the warnings she had heard about mixing sex and work—would an affair mess things up? With all these thoughts thrashing around in her head, Paula made a quick decision. She said yes.

Paula was very nervous when they went to her room. It was decided to use her room in order to protect her in case Frank called at some odd hour. She couldn't imagine how it would feel to get undressed in front of an older man and then have sex with him. But it all seemed very natural and tender once they were making love. Fred was much more skilled than Frank. And he loved to touch and explore her body. She was aroused more than she had ever remembered. Fred had some difficulty getting an erection but Paula helped him and they had intercourse. But that part almost seemed an anticlimax to the seeming hours of touching. Their affair continued and did not disrupt either of their marriages. In fact Paula's marriage got much better. Frank began to accept her career and this eased much of the tension. Perhaps the fact that Paula was now an executive made her position more acceptable to Frank. Their sex life resumed and Paula welcomed it. It was a more intense and physical sex than with Fred. But she also loved the quieter, more sensual sex with Fred.

The affair with Fred, far from creating problems on the job,

made her feel more secure. They would also now take longer
and more luxurious trips that would not arouse suspicion; all
were job-related and appeared to make good business sense.
Their sex was always confined to their trips. Fred adored Paula
and genuinely appreciated her presence in his life. He even
talked about making her a partner since he planned to retire in
the not-too-distant future and none of his children were interested in the business. Certainly, neither felt used or abused.
Here is another instance of parallel play that seems to have
worked well.

Forty Carats. While parallel play has many variations, some
have the quality of "crisis intervention" in psychotherapy treatment: they are necessary, short-term and intense. The best of
them are successful. Nina's was like that. Unlike the not uncommon younger woman/older man theme in Fred and Paula's case,
Nina was the "older woman" in her love affair with Eduardo.
Though only 40, she was fifteen years older than he. "I was
fifteen years old when you were born," she would playfully
tease as they were making love, and "Do you know that when I
was your age I was already married. How come you're not?"
Responding to the play, he would pull her closer toward him
and, running his tongue in outline around her open mouth,
respond with: "Because I haven't met anyone as wonderful as
you. When I do—watch out."
　　Tony, Nina's husband, was close in age to her, the typical
American style of two or three years her senior. When she was
25 and he 28, they seemed to have a lot in common, sharing
interests and values. Sports devotees, they had fun together,
enjoying both participating in activities and being enthusiastic
observers. Then somehow, a few years before the affair, Tony
started to change. It was nothing Nina could put her finger on,
like the beginnings of an allergy or a disc which slips out of
alignment. It was subtle and ambiguous but she felt him moving
away from her, from the world, and from people around them.
She had been aware that, before meeting her, he had problems.
He had told her about "doing drugs" and the fact that, at times,

he just could not seem to function. But he said he had overcome
it all. He seemed fine when they met and during the first few
years of their marriage. Like many situations where one cannot
pinpoint an exact time, day, or date of the happening, Tony
seemed at one moment in time, to be slipping away, "shriveling
up" as Nina said. Thinking much of it was due to depression,
they sought help until their therapist suggested that Tony begin
coming for sessions for himself. He did and was still in treatment
when Nina met Eduardo, in the lobby of the theater to which
she had gone to see the play she and Tony had bought tickets
for but for which Tony had said, as on many occasions: "I'm
not in the mood. Go by yourself."

Walking around in the heady ambience of the magnificent
lobby, she had felt isolated and alone. The drink in her hand,
purchased at the crowded bar, was her pacifier and gave her
some reassurance. Eduardo had been one of the bartenders. His
smile, as he poured her drink, had intrigued her, as did his
warmth and opening comment: "Was that one drink or two?"
while he seemed to be genuinely scanning the people pressed
around her as though to see who her companion was. He later
told her that it was her look of loneliness, along with her dark
beauty, that prompted him to ask for her number during the
second intermission when she again asked for one drink of wine.
Both his poise and sincerity appealed to her and though she felt
like the 14-year-old who "goes too far" she allowed her impul-
sivity to run its course. She gave him her number and their love
affair began.

Like many women who are caring and nurturing, Nina did
not want to leave Tony and their marriage when he seemed to
need her so much. Though her women friends had said he had
become "a yoke around her neck," she could not cast him off.
It would have been easy, she said, if he had "done something
terrible—had a drinking problem, been abusive, or engaged in
some behavior that was outrageous." He had done none of that.
He had only become more and more childlike in his needs, more
dependent and clinging. She found herself in the same position

she had been in during childhood when she, as the oldest of four, had taken care of her siblings. It was all familiar material.

Her reversal was being with Eduardo. Though fifteen years her junior, he, unbelievably, took care of her! Tender, he was nonetheless strong within himself. Life, to him, was uncomplicated: you simply lived it, enjoying every minute. His mastery of himself gave her strength. He could be relied on as much as his "reliable erections" as she learned to call them. In one hour, they made love two or three times within a short time span. He always seemed to be wanting her but when he left, it was a clean separation. She did not feel, as she always did about Tony, that he could not manage without her. Nina and Eduardo could be separate and they could be together. It gave her the strength to stay with Tony without either fragmenting inside herself or becoming a merged part of him out of his need for her.

It was parallel play that seemed to be successful for the players caught up in it. While Tony was solving his own problems in regular psychotherapy, Nina was coping with hers through Eduardo. As with many people, therapy often takes place in the real world in situations that prove to be therapeutic. It was that way for Nina and Eduardo. And what would happen when the "crisis" was over? It's anybody's guess.

To Play or Not To Play

Despite the reassurances that parallel players give to themselves and each other, there are usually nagging doubts and recurring feelings of guilt. Remember, these are people who believe they are committed to their marriages. The play is only meant to fill a small hole, to provide needed variety or compensate for a stale piece of the marriage. But the contradictions and moral dilemmas are not easily swept aside. There are risks. One may get caught and lose the marriage. The play looks different when that happens.

Would you readily accept your spouse having an affair? When Dick posed that question to Bill, Dick was disappointed by Bill's lack of support. Yet his anger masked the fact that the same question had often occurred to him. Is it possible that for some people who are committed to parallel play there is a need to maintain or find stale pieces in their marriage and exaggerate them? Without the stalemate, it is difficult to justify an affair without recognizing that you just want it all on your terms. How many are willing to do that?

Sometimes, though, you can get so involved in an affair that it doesn't seem possible to go back. A new course seems to be warranted. Perhaps one that is even better, or so you might think. But what actually happens when affairs go beyond parallel play? This will be discussed in the following chapter.

CHAPTER SIX

BEYOND PARALLEL PLAY

Few affairs—and definitely no long-term ones—can avoid the QUESTION: "What do we do now?" At the beginning of an affair—and the beginning is often childishly simple—the Question is set down next to the players like a time bomb. Sooner or later, it will have to be dealt with. Meanwhile, it goes on ticking.

The players have a number of options. They can end the affair long before the Question gets critical. They can disarm the Question, muffle it, even bury it; what they can't do is continue to ignore it—the timer is set and it can and will go off.

As discussed in the previous chapter, parallel play is one method of defusing the Question. Both parallel players take the charge out of the bomb by agreeing ahead of time that they will *not* let the affair change their lives. "We don't need to *do* anything," they say, "but keep things just the way they are." Good thinking this, but they will need plenty of skill and luck to make it work.

For instance, the amount of care and commitment required to maintain a parallel play situation over any length of time puts extraordinary demands on any affair's partners. Pauline Reage in her introduction ("A Girl in Love") to her novel *Return to the Chateau* depicts the girl's meeting with her married lover this way:

85

It was already a stroke of luck that he had been able to get away at all. Otherwise she would have waited for an hour and then come back the following day at the same time, the same place, in accordance with the classic rules of clandestine lovers.

Oh, those "classic rules of clandestine lovers"! Even the best managed affairs have their full share of frustrations. And over time these frustrations take their toll. Seeking relief from tension, the partners in an affair may just decide that anywhere is better than where they are. If nothing else does, a fatigue factor may set off that ticking bomb, as in the time-honored Hollywood dialogue:

> Darling, we can't go on meeting like this!
> I know. But what do we do, what *can* we do, now?

A Double Life is One Too Many

The early Egyptians experienced the heart as an intrapsychic structure, separate and apart from the rest of the personality. Translated into contemporary psychological thinking, this means that for some people there is no difficulty in functioning well with a "split-object," a focusing on just one part of themselves and the beloved "other." For many, though, the tension of maintaining two lives—an affair and a marriage—becomes too great. The most obvious solution is to end a faltering marriage and escalate the affair into a permanent relationship. The problem here comes when what once had been a separate, split-off life—the affair—must be integrated into the real world.

As Julie put it:

> I felt like a combination of Aphrodite, the goddess of sexual passion, and Eros, the god of love. My marriage was an OK one—not terribly high, not terribly low—OK. Daryl was a woman's version of a wet dream. Lucky for me he felt the same way and our affair began. Of course, he was also married, but as we both said, "So what's new?" I was

almost always out of control when I was with him, feeling total abandonment of my inhibitions. I rationalized my outrageous behavior with, "I can't help myself," much as Helen of Troy did when she excused her behavior by blaming her husband Menalaus for leaving her alone with the stranger Paris.

Daryl and Julie met regularly twice a week for five years. Julie said she felt continuously interested, always aroused by Daryl. He was the high of her life. She couldn't think of a world without him. As she focused more and more on Daryl, and he on her, her other world started to distance, moving into the background finally only becoming a place to be in between the liaisons with Daryl. She felt robot-like at home and an enchantress outside. Pushing against this split inside herself, her self-awareness propelled her to move toward divorce and marriage with Daryl. It seemed to make sense to him, too. They married.

Daryl, now in his mid-forties, had a married son who lived in another state. Ties were close as far as emotional bonding was concerned, with calls once a week or so, holidays spent together, but little physical proximity. He loved his son, enjoyed and was very fond of his daughter-in-law, and all seemed well. Julie, nine years younger than Daryl, had two teen-aged daughters, who lived with Julie and Daryl, with the usual week-end visits to their dad. It all seemed to work out. Tina, the older daughter, seemed happy in her adjustment to the new situation. Laurel, the younger, also seemed fine.

It was Samantha who broke the bubble. Samantha was Laurel's cat, nurtured and loved by her since kittenhood. It seemed like no big deal until it was discovered that Daryl was allergic—especially to very long-haired cats, and that's what Samantha was. Julie, a sensitive, responsive mother was delicate in her approach. "Honey, I know how attached you are to Samantha, but Daryl can't breathe when the cat's in the house. You'll have to get rid of her." Julie didn't miss a beat. "Why don't you get rid of Daryl? I've known Samantha longer." The scenario, almost predictably, seemed to be writing itself. Compromises were suggested: shots for Daryl over protestations of, "I'm not taking drugs just for a cat. If you really cared about me, you'd. . . ." From Julie: "If Samantha goes, I go. If you really loved me, you'd. . . ."

Cajoling went into suggestions, which went into demands, which went into feelings of being unloved and, finally, the breakup of the marriage. The beloved can manage an existence split off from the rest of the world. It's in the integrating of the loved one with the real world that troubles come. It makes one almost believe, for a moment, Bernard Shaw's dour pronouncement: "There are only two tragedies in life; one is to lose your heart's desire, the other is to gain it."

Yet a deeper look into this case would doubtless lead us to an examination of the psyches of all the players—particularly Daryl's and Julie's—when they were being formed. That Daryl was subject to asthma attacks, considered highly psychological in nature, seems to indicate that he had some deeply unresolved problems, though these did not get in the way in liaisons where no cat was present. Daryl's need for idealization (see chapter 3) may have been punctured when it was suggested to him that he take shots, i.e., that he was less than perfect. Likewise, Laura's need for mirroring (see chapter 2) may have gone unmet because in their new marital situation Daryl was not able to focus on her as in the past. In other words, the underlying dynamics of each partner's participation in the affair also help determine the development of the affair. Where unmet childhood needs for mirroring or idealization create unrealistic demands, the course of an affair, continued beyond parallel play, may not be very promising. The same forces that led to a breakdown of the marriage are likely to lead to a breakdown of the affair—or of the second marriage if the affair leads to that.

Marriage counselors caution people about this when they cite examples from their casebooks of second and even third marriages repeating a negative pattern. Statistics show that second marriages have as high a divorce rate as first marriages. True, these statistics do not show how many of these second marriages are the outgrowth of parallel play. But some of them may be.

As psychoanalyst Martin S. Bergmann points out in *The Anatomy of Loving*: "Extramarital relationships often derive their intensity from the mother-child model, undisturbed by reality considerations, be they financial or problems of parenthood." Later on, he writes: "Different people love differently. Childish people love childishly and mature people show maturity in the way they love."

One should not conclude from this, however, that all marriage breakups result from distorted needs or psychological problems. Often there are real external problems or basic incompatibilities between the couples that will bring a marriage to an end. Still, for those contemplating going beyond parallel play and turning an affair into a marriage, these statistics flash at least an amber "Go Slow" light. Such couples may be well advised to think about changing themselves before they consider changing their mates. The danger in going beyond parallel play often lies not so much in radical change as in not really changing enough.

What You Can't Learn in Parallel Play

Lainie and Monty had been lovers for over eight years—a solid, parallel-playing couple. She was married, he was a young widower of 37. Lainie described her husband, Ethan, as a "hyperactive adult."

"He's always on the move. He has this tall, awkward body that pushes out in all directions at the same time. He makes me nervous.

"I didn't notice at the beginning of the marriage; I was tied up with the kids and all. But he was always, always so busy. Lovemaking was like we were on a speeding train. I had no experience, though, so I thought that was the way it was supposed to be. I even learned to speed up my orgasm.

"Ethan didn't have time for leisure—in or out of bed—and I had to run like hell just to keep up. At a restaurant, for instance, he'd eat a full meal in about twelve minutes flat. I didn't say anything because I didn't want to be a nag, but it embarrassed me—and nearly ruined my digestion, too. I realized our tempos were different, and I thought it was up to me to be quicker. That is, until I met Monty.''

Like many women of her generation, Lainie hadn't developed a strong sense of her own identity. She tended to seek herself in the men in her life and fall into step with whatever image they seemed to want. With Monty, she found a man who seemed to be what *she* wanted. Of Monty, she said:

"He was that slow and methodical that I felt like a supercharged kid with him. But I loved his slow, even pace. There were long pauses when we talked. He seemed to need time to think and weigh things. When I'd ask him a question, he'd look at me for a long second or two, then say something like, ''I'd have to think about that,'' or, ''I'll let you know.'' I felt finally at peace. It was like having your own yoga master. When I was with him it was like being in an Alpha-relaxed state most of the time. With him sex was massage therapy mixed with scent therapy and plain good screwing. No more, ''Wham, bam, thank you ma'am. Life was sublime.''

In this affair, it was Monty who continually urged Lainie to get a divorce so they could marry, but, even though life with him looked ideal, she was reluctant, and would say, "Wait at least until the kids are old enough to understand. I don't want to create problems for the children." Lainie complained that her husband was too busy doing, doing, doing to notice if she were there or not. Her leaving wouldn't cause a problem for him.

Finally, one day, as all fairy tales go, the waiting ended. Her two sons were teenagers, Ethan was, as usual, charging off on new tacks and Lainie was tired of an unfulfilling marriage. Lainie told Ethan her plans and explained everything to the kids. Shortly afterward, she and Ethan were divorced. After eight years, she stepped over the imaginary chalk-drawn lines of parallel play and into a new marriage with Monty.

For the first month, life seemed to flow right on—at an *unhurried* pace. It was summertime and Lainie's sons were away at camp, as counsellors, so it was a perfect way to begin a new life. As far as Lainie knew, Ethan was off climbing mountains, flying planes, moving, always moving, at a dogged trot as she had known him to. The whole thing had been managed with the least amount of pain possible.

Then real life commenced. The boys returned from camp and got ready for school. To Lainie's surprise, Monty began to complain bitterly over, "the boys making noise." In Monty's view, "noise" was just about anything that wasn't deep, silent dreaming. Her sons' friends coming over was "noise." Playing music was "noise." Opening/closing doors was "noise." Up/down moods were "noise."

Lainie realized, too late, that Monty was basically a loner. As long as there was just the two of them—as in parallel play—things were fine. They could form exactly the low-tense, uninterrupted environment Monty thrived on. However, having never had children himself, he was totally unready for the kind of commotion even the best behaved teenager generates naturally.

Moreover, as an essential loner, Monty was an autocrat at heart. There's no need for democracy in a kingdom of one. He ordained that peace and quiet were *the way*. He, of course, was the one who determined what constituted peace and quiet. Children, friends, relatives did not; Lainie and Monty—his Romeo and Juliet—did. All others had to leave. Which, after not too long, Lainie and the children did, as the marriage ended. In this case, unlike that of Daryl and Julie, it wasn't a cat whose claws pierced the cloud, yet the dynamics were similar. It was the "outside world" itself that was the culprit. In both cases, parallel play shielded the players from finding out what each was truly like in the rough-and-tumble real world. Insulated as in a womb, the lovers in an affair often breathe in step with each other in a prenatal way, recapturing the lost mother of early symbiosis—that early blissful tie of mother to infant when life is perfect.

When the affair is pushed out into the harsh light of reality, the lovers experience a kind of Rankian "birth trauma," an idea put forward some years ago by psychoanalyst Otto Rank. The insulation of the affair allows and encourages the lovers to focus only on each other. When they are forced into integrating themselves into the real, "other" world, they often find themselves overwhelmed. There's too much to cope with, too much going on, too much . . . of too much! The clandestineness of the affair, risky and fragile as it may be, is often its most durable quality. Knowing this in advance can help you avoid pitfalls. And so can, in another way, a less romantic and more realistic view of the possibilities of relationships.

On Settling for What You've Selected

Lois and Pete were married when Pete was 23 and Lois 22. The marriage was a good one for the first ten years. After that it turned stale, at least for Lois. Later it got crusty and finally broke.

Their relationship was pretty good for the first five years. Or, perhaps it was just that they were so occupied that they never looked at or evaluated the relationship. In any event it seemed to work just fine. Their major complaints were about fatigue and the lack of enough time in the day to complete all their chores.

Although Lois had a college degree, with a major in Art History, she slipped unhesitatingly into the role of housewife when their first daughter was born one year after their marriage. In the early '70s, that was still not so unusual. Like many women, she planned to "go back" to work, even though a time to "go back" had never been established. Pete was under such intense pressure at his accounting firm, which had been acquired by an aggressive large corporation (everyone was under the gun), that subjects like relationships, sex, and the quality or frequency of orgasms suffered what can most kindly be called "benign neglect."

Both were committed to the belief that their future rested

on the success of Pete's career. They had fallen into a pattern of very little sex. Most of their conversations were about finances, work, and the children. This didn't seem unusual since that's what everyone talked about in their small circle of friends. Occasionally with their friends they smoked grass and giggled a lot—enough to make them feel "with it" and avant-garde. Lois had her routines and Pete had his.

All that seemed to fall apart when Lois registered for a painting class at the museum. There she met Clyde. It was the beginning of what she later called "the awakening from a long hypnotic sleep." She embraced the relationship hungrily. This made her acutely aware of how deeply anesthetized she had been. More important than the discovery of multiple orgasms— she rarely had an orgasm with Pete—was the discovery of multiple communications—intimacy that transcends superficial masks and chitchat. Her joy triggered a profound despair as she realized that what she had and craved for with Clyde she could never have with Pete. What was she to do? Could she just walk out on innocent and loving Pete? And what about the children? She never thought that anything like this could happen to her.

Predictably, the relationship with Pete became strained. Everything seemed wrong. Lois was constantly edgy and critical. Pete didn't quite know what was going on. Finally, they decided to see a marriage counsellor. Pete was hoping that the counsellor could somehow wave the magic wand and give him back his idyllic little paradise. Lois felt dishonest and guilty about the fact that neither Pete nor the counsellor knew about Clyde. She felt that Pete would be totally destroyed by that information.

Pete really tried and did make some changes, and Lois tried to be more understanding and less critical. He became more attentive to her orgasms and made real strides at being more flexible. But Pete would never be Clyde. Deep down Lois knew that she would either have to break away or accept a constricted life. But she dreaded leaving. She didn't hate Pete, only the limitations of their marital relationship. She felt she could be perfectly good friends with him but not his lifelong partner. Finally, she couldn't bear the tension any longer and left.

Pete was devastated and very bitter. He felt betrayed and didn't understand why. Because he didn't have anything else to lean on, anger and revenge became his crutches. He fought for custody of the two girls. Finally, Lois agreed in order to avoid a painful and costly battle in which only the lawyers would win. She also thought it would be best all around for the moment. But she paid for that decision with enormous guilt.

She rented a small apartment and enrolled in a graduate program in Art History. After a year she married Clyde. They moved into a larger apartment in Greenwich Village and opened an art gallery. She felt reborn.

After the divorce, Pete accepted the finality of the split and started dating Gwen, a secretary in his office. She was 32, never married, tall, very attractive, and as conservative as Pete. She adored him for his education, achievement, good nature, and kindness. She considered Pete a miracle in the dog-eat-dog, meat-rack singles world. They were married three months after Lois and Clyde got married.

As this is not a fairy tale, everything did not end in bliss. But as Lois ultimately concluded, 80 percent is better than 30 percent. In some respects, it is the difference between psychological life and death.

Although Clyde was very loving and exciting, having introduced Lois to a whole new self and a new world, he was, at the same time, very demanding. He demanded a great deal of attention to his every emotional and sexual need. At times this was a strain. She even occasionally longed for the quiet times with Pete in which nothing was demanded and she had her own internal private place. But then she remembered how empty that really felt.

Also, Clyde never had children of his own. When Lois's two daughters visited and stayed over, Clyde tried to be friendly but often it was forced and even grudging. He did not welcome the intrusion. He didn't want any wedges in his relationship with Lois. She wished he could display more genuine warmth toward the girls. She feared that his coolness would influence their feelings about men during these important years of their development.

While Pete and Gwen functioned like a well-oiled machine, Pete sometimes missed Lois. Despite Lois's complaints, he missed her warmth, impulsiveness, and the cozy intimacy that they had as a young family. On the other hand, he knew that he and Lois could not make it together at this point in their lives. With Gwen he was assured of much smoother sailing even if some depth of feeling was lacking.

Love—the blissful experience or the "pleasure ego"— changes as we change. Some pieces of Pete were those he found in Gwen; others he found in Lois. Since compromise is part of life, we make a choice in what we give up in *ourselves* when we choose one particular partner. Choices change when we ourselves do; our partners are only reflections of our re-arranging of our own selves.

Escalating an affair into a second marriage can be risky, as documented here. If the people involved in the affair and the failed marriage(s) have come to a better understanding of themselves, the chances of a successful second relationship are enhanced. If, however, the affair was mostly a way of *not* learning about themselves, their chances of a successful change are gravely diminished.

Nor is escalating an affair into a new permanent relationship the only way to go beyond parallel play. Affairs can deteriorate, too, with the partners breaking up and each going his own way. Even when an affair does escalate into a new marriage, there's always the chance that it can go sour. A previous marriage can also prove more durable than anyone of the partners thought possible. Pete and Lois, for instance, felt a very strong attraction to their old relationship even while working hard on their new marriages. At times guilt, familiarity, or a new realization of what one feels is truly important, work to undermine the new marriage and return the previous partners to each other. In this case, it may be said that the affair helped to build a stronger marriage—albeit, the hard way.

You Can, Too, Go Home Again

Bob felt his marriage was going along pretty smoothly; that is, until he found out that his wife was having an affair. Once again "risky business" reared its ugly head; this time in the form of an airline ticket. Amy was going to a nursing convention in San Francisco. Her airline ticket from the travel agent was made out to Erik Simms. Innocent mistake? No, Erik was someone they had met at a dinner party three weeks earlier. He was neither a doctor nor a nurse nor a hospital administrator. He was in the construction business and had, as Bob now relfected on it, an open, breezy, masculine manner that some women would probably find attractive.

At any rate, Bob knew the truth instantaneously. He remembered how chatty Amy and Erik were at the dinner party. He had paid no particular attention to it at the time. He was never suspicious. Now he wondered and thought back to all the other people with whom she might have had an affair.

When confronted, Amy could not deny the situation. She had ordered both tickets, and asked that one be sent to each of them. The travel agent had made a mistake. Bob went berserk. He was not ordinarily an angry or violent person so his revenge would take a different form. He decided he would go to bed with every woman he could find, making up for lost time and lost opportunities. But before he could set his plans into motion, he met Simone.

Bob had his share of sex before he was married, but that was more than 12 years before. Now at age 36 he felt he was a babe in the woods again, especially when he was with Simone. She knew things he had only read about; yet she was such a sensual person that just looking at her gave him a firm erection. This came as quite a surprise to him since for the last two years of his marriage he needed a lot of foreplay to get an erection and would often lose it while having intercourse. At times he would have to concentrate on "dirty fantasies" to keep his penis stiff. He hadn't been able to come more than once a night since the early years of his marraige. With Simone, however, it seemed easy and natural. He never lost his erection, and one night he came three times. The three weekends he spent with Simone, one in Las Vagas, one in Los Angeles, and one in London were the most exciting times of his life.

Amy knew he was having this fling but felt she wasn't in any position to say or do anything. She hoped that things would blow over and their marriage would return to its usual state. She also wanted to keep things as calm and as normal as possible for their 11-year-old daughter. Things didn't work out the way she had hoped. As soon as Bob returned from London, he announced that he wanted a divorce and was going to marry Simone.

When Bob and Simone settled into their married life, it didn't turn out as Bob had envisioned. More likely, he had not realistically envisioned the situation at all, nor had he seriously considered its potential liabilities. All that was ignored in the service of his excitement of the moment. As it turned out, Bob was hardly Simone's first lover, nor did she want him to be her last.

If Bob was distressed by Amy's affair, Simone's endorsement of open marriage was a shattering blow to his ego. After six months, the marriage fell apart—and he only hung on that long to save face for having made the decision to marry Simone.

Amy hadn't dated at all since the separation and divorce. Her affair with Erik really was her first and was intended strictly as parallel play for both. Bob's overreaction and remarriage were crushing blows to bear and she sought help for her deep depression.

When Bob called her after he left Simone, Amy was elated, but wisely contained her feelings. On the advise of her therapist, she proceeded slowly with Bob. They dated but did not sleep together. She did not want to open herself to another deep wound. First, she wanted to test the prospects of their getting back together again, which is probable. For all their pain, their marriage just might be stronger and their communicataion more intimate and honest than it was in the past.

Some people don't really mean to use parallel play as a new

way of life; some just want to experience the world a bit and then return to the way it was. This is similar to what the psychoanalyst Margaret Mahler termed the "rapprochement subphase" in the child. Here, the mother waits for the child to come back, as he plays or focuses elsewhere, for his "refueling." It makes, so the theory goes, for a secure adult who feels that he/she can wander out into the world, create and carve out his/her own experience, and then "refuel." The steady person will be there.

It's not at all uncommon to see this "rapprochement" cycle repeated many times in a marriage, where one partner continually embarks on new affairs, only to break them off and return in due time to the marriage. For such people, affairs are only satisfying when they are secure in the knowledge that "home base" is inviolate. The patient partner, in turn, learns the satisfactions of patience, martyrdom, and forgiveness, with the occupation of the moral high ground making up for the humiliation of the infidelity.

From Womb to Tomb: The Death of an Affair

"Had we but world enough and time," the poet Andrew Marvell begins, setting forth the ultimate parameter of all affairs.

Donna and Seth, for example, had been in an intense affair for ten years. Both were married and both found their marriages "comfortable." This is not surprising. To keep up an intense relationship for ten years, one has to have a "comfortable" sanctuary to repair to now and then, if only for a little R and R and a recharging of emotional batteries. Like "rapprochement" children, they used the marriage to help their affair.

For Seth and Donna, the affair had not begun in their salad days when they were green in judgment; rather, it was a product of their maturity, having begun when Seth was 52 and Donna 46. Both had been married for over 20 years, had grown children out on their own, and understanding and, to their best knowledge, unsuspecting spouses. Life consisted of work, marriage, and—the affair.

Naturally, one of the iron rules of this arrangement was discretion. No phone calls on weekends, no writing of letters, no sudden emergency calls, no stealing quick kisses or cuddles in dangerous places, no telltale clues of any kind. They were beyond that kid stuff.

If maturity brought them some advantages, it had its perils, too. During a routine physical checkup, (part of Seth's characteristically sensible approach to everything) he was told by his physician that he had, without knowing it, suffered a "silent heart attack." The test results were unmistakable. According to his doctor, though Seth was in no immediate danger, he should now, nevertheless, "slow down a bit," take it easy, be especially attentive to good diet, and so on. As yet it was only a warning tap on the shoulder but stock-taking and prudence were in order.

The diagnosis sent a chill through Seth despite all the doctor's reassurances. No one wants to be reminded of his or her mortality, and all such reminders come—no matter how mildly—with a kettledrum thump and an ominous growl in the double basses.

Seth, of course, shared the news with his wife—and with Donna. Not a hypochondriac by nature, Seth reacted to the situation by following the general rules laid down by the doctor and by trying to keep things pretty much the way they were. It was Donna who felt the brunt of the new situation.

A nurturing woman, she wanted to fulfill her role as healer, lover, wife/mother to the man she loved. Suddenly she saw a way to meet her own needs for having someone dependent on her. She wanted to cradle Seth, hug him to her, bring him hot tea, ask him how he felt, and watch over him as a parent does with a frail child—to excess.

She pushed old rules aside. She began making calls to Seth's house. If his wife answered, she would hang up, or blurt out in a changed voice that she had the wrong number, or she would claim she was a telephone solicitor, or she'd ask if they were selling their house. Anything. The wife stayed unsuspecting, mostly because her energies were now directed on Seth and his "condition."

Seth became more and more irritable with Donna. He told her that when he needed her, that is, if there was an emergency, he would call her. If he had any pain suggestive of "heart," he would let her know immediately, but that, no, she could not go with him to the doctor for his next checkup. She was, he said, only adding stress to his life with this behavior, and stress was the one thing he didn't need at the present time!

Donna felt hurt, rejected, abandoned, and dazed. What had she done wrong? She was only playing the part any good person would play if a loved one became ill. She could not understand Seth's annoyance with her. Couldn't he see it was for his own good? Would he want her to be hard and uncaring? She wanted to play by the old rules, but, as she explained, the situation had changed. Shouldn't they change, too? Time had popped the question.

Seth could logically appreciate Donna's need, and, on some level, even applaud her caring for him. Yet, as things were, he really needed attention from his wife. It was she, after all, who was with him all the time. Should anything happen, he would necessarily have to turn to her. He wasn't even sure that if anything happened Donna would find out about it—except perhaps in the newspapers.

In addition, in the back of his mind, Seth had that lugubrious fear of being "caught in the saddle." Sniggering stories about famous movie stars, politicians, and such "whose heart had stopped before they did" floated in his mind. To be stricken while he was with Donna would ruin both their reputations and make a snide, bathroom joke of what they spent ten years of their lives creating.

The affair had gone beyond parallel play, and a decision had to be made. Seth felt there was only one choice, he had to end the affair. He explained his reasons to Donna and pleaded with her to understand that it was nothing *she* did; they were only players who had to play the hand they were dealt. There was no real possibility of future life together for them, and they could no longer continue their prior arrangement. But they could keep intact the memory of what they had shared.

Different people are needed at different times in our lives. While Seth was in a state of good health, the bliss he shared with Donna in their affair was the dream world most affairs are made of. However, as stated in psychoanalytic theory, since love is not only a "finding" but, more importantly, a "refinding" of that original state of bliss in infancy, bliss may take on different meanings at particular times in our lives. Bliss for Seth may be having the original wife/mother take care of him at times of illness and stress. This may be a re-creation of the healing of Seth's "early wounds" of childhood, to be accomplished only with the wife, and a throwback to the splitting of Aphrodite herself, when in the 4th century B.C., there was both the celestial (higher form) Aphrodite and the lower one, a goddess of "sexual life and patron of prostitutes." Like the "split" Aphrodite, Seth may have needed two women to fulfill his needs. When Donna tried to be one, wife/mother/lover, he rejected her. Though Donna felt crushed, had she been aware of the psychological theory, she would have known that we do not love a person, but remain always under the spell of a fleeting image of our own creation for which we search for throughout our lives. Seth's vision of a nurturer for his illness was only his wife. Needing different people at different times may be one revelation of an affair, even a parallel play one.

When Parallel Play Simply Won't Do

Chic is chic and satisfying for a time. Then, despite all the sophistication of Yuppiedom and the "me" generation, a primal urge awakes, yawns, stretches, and slouches off to be born. Children. Family. Home. These are quiet and dignified ideas that can shake the foundations of the most solid parallel play. The umarried partner in an extramarital affair is acutely vulnerable.

Laura, for instance, had been waiting around for Henry to leave his wife. She was single and dedicated to her career. The waiting was no big deal to her. By her own admission, she was not ready for marriage when she met Henry. If anything, his being married was a big plus for her. It took her "off the hook" she said. She could have her freedom, live her own life in her own apartment, keep seeing her friends, pursue her work, maintain her privacy—and still have Henry. Parallel play was a perfect answer to her needs.

Henry was pleased with the situation, too. He did not want to break up his marriage, and though he referred to his wife as a "pain in the A," he said it without malice. And the "pain" seemed less as the affair with Laura grew. A delicate balance had been struck.

Then it all went askew. He related his problems to Laura's last birthday—thirty-eight. As was their habit, they celebrated in a cozy place an hour or so from where they lived. Henry had tucked away a small but expensive gift, preordered an elaborate dinner, and carefully chosen the wine. Laura, generally buoyant and "up," did not seem like her usual self. Henry sensed there was something wrong but waited until after the dessert to ask her.

She told him in only four words. "I want a baby." He took a minute or two to gain composure. What came out next sounded ridiculous to him, but all he could do for the moment was stall for time. "What do you mean?" he asked.

She played with her dessert, licking the spoon in a concentrated way, as though it were important to clean it thoroughly. "I'm 38, right?" "Right," he responded. "And so?" "And so," she said, "I'm running out of time. I mean, if I'm going to have a kid, I have to do it before I'm 40, right?"

Feeling like he was in some crazy quiz game just beyond his understanding, Henry mindlessly repeated, "Right."

Laura plunged in. She told him how, when they had first met, "just an affair" was okay. She went on to compliment him and tell him how great it had been for her—how wonderful he is as a lover, how sensitive as a person, how exciting a companion, how instructive as an older, wiser person, and much more of the same.

She took great pains to emphasize that she was in love with him, and was prepared to wait it out until he left his wife. *But—*

oh that "but"—she wanted a baby. She needed to be "fulfilled as a woman," and, because her biological time clock was ticking, it had to be—now. She backed this up with what her gynecologist had recently told her. "It's best to try motherhood before 40—for all the obvious reasons." Laura said she had given the matter serious thought. The baby, of course, could not be a by-product of an affair. It needed parents. There was no alternative. So there it was. Biology had tripped off an unexploded mine. What Laura wanted was aeons old. It was to settle down, settle in, and go the whole traditional route. She wanted the baby, and she wanted Henry to be its father—not just to father it. "I don't want just your seed," she said with tears in her eyes. "I want you. I know what you've done with your own kids and I think you'll be just terrific. We'd be a knockout team."

Henry felt like the actor who's suddenly faced with a closing notice on the backstage bulletin board. He could not possibly leave his marriage. He thought that had been accepted by them both at the start. (It had been, but who reckons with life forces at such a time?)

What's more, even if he felt, for one slim minute, that he *could* break up his marriage, he couldn't imagine having more children. He had had his two kids, loved them, done the parenting bit—and done it well. He didn't want to begin again with infant needs, school plays, the whole lot. He served his hitch and was not about to re-up.

He told Laura just that. She said she had sort of expected it, but still—she hoped that. . . . They kissed and parted, covering up their loss with words like, "If you ever need me. . . ." Theirs is an example of the painful fact that there are needs—deep and abiding ones—with which parallel play cannot begin to cope.

It's not only women, with their built-in biological clock, who face this problem. Men, too, for all their vaunted machismo, have a powerful nesting instinct. Many men feel that a home which is childless and wifeless is a cold one—even when it's done up in perfect taste. That's why psychiatrists' and therapists' phones ring endlessly around holiday time. Lonely men and women—sometimes the single partners in a parallel-play situation—find themselves beggars at everyone else's feast. What they have is so near—yet so far. For them, the parallel lines seem to stretch away into infinity.

Laura had found true love. It was ripening love that pushed toward maturity, toward taking care of others, toward founding a family. This is another aspect of the "love bliss,": i.e., in the service of refinding the paradise of lost childhood and in undoing the boundary that separates the self from the other. In Laura's demands for a child there was, no doubt, the vision of the family as a unit: "You, me, and our child will be one and the same," the extension of the "togetherness" ideal. In this form of love, the feeling of generativity exists—that one will continue in the next generation, that of the children. Though Laura's desires were healthy and mature, her lover was not able to fulfill them.

The Margaret Mahler Child: When You Can't Take the Big Step

Bernice and Chuck have been parallel players for almost fifteen years. The relationship is still going strong, and even though they've talked about getting married from time to time, they're no closer to doing it than when the relationship began. Both are married and forty-four years old. Bernice has three children—two boys and a girl. She's a writer for a national magazine. Chuck has two boys. He's an investment banker—a pressured and pressuring business.

They met for the first time when they both attended a convention on women in banking. At first, it had all the earmarks of a harmless weekend interlude. In short order, however, it became much more than that. Even beyond the intense sexual experience, they related to each other and touched each other in ways that were totally foreign in their marriages. Friends and relatives thought their marriages looked good, even admirable. Chuck and Bernice felt a little this way, too, and yet . . . parallel play filled some emptiness in their lives. Perhaps each was the perfect mirror for the other so right did they feel together. Deep and genuine as these feelings were, they still couldn't bring themselves to the step beyond parallel play. They were quite certain that their intimacy and commitment to each other could have overcome any difficulty if put to the test. But they were never able to get to the point where they dared the test.

There were times when it almost happened. After attending another industry meeting, they spent a week together that was particularly real and satisfying, and going home was tough. At the meeting, they had spent many leisurely hours together, some with other people at parties and dinner. It was like being a real couple, and it felt just perfect. Re-entry to their normal worlds afterward was particularly difficult for Bernice. Her husband chose just that moment to show real hostilitiy and anger at her being away (even though he fully accepted it as a legitimate business trip). Bernice went through some very tense moments with her husband then; they even talked about separating. She went so far as to call a real estate agent and look for a place of her own.

Chuck got very anxious at these unexpected developments. He, too, remembered the splendid week, but he wasn't in the same place as Bernice in his home relationship. In fact, he was moving in opposite directions. He was busy trying to keep things calm with his wife to avoid any eruption. He had done this rather successfully, and was now appalled at the prospect of doing just the reverse, that is, creating stress so as to justify his leaving. Psychologically, he couldn't bring himself to about-face so abruptly. For two married parallel players to take the big step requires the most delicate timing.

Despite Chuck's waffling at this juncture, Bernice's trouble at home blew over. Bernice herself got cold feet when she looked squarely at the financial problems of living in a big city on her own. Faced with managing a career, a lover, three teen-aged children, and an angry husband, Bernice dropped the idea of separation. Parallel play with Chuck began again, and both of them were relieved.

At another time, when Chuck was on the verge of leaving his wife, he backed down because he couldn't be sure that

Bernice would be able to leave at the same time—and he knew he would only leave for her. And so it went. Whenever they got close to taking the big step some uncertainty or other would crop up: a crisis with one of the children, a death in the family (how can I leave her when her father just died?), a business problem that couldn't be ignored, an assignment that couldn't be refused. So up came the Question like a jack-in-the-box, and down it was pushed again with a "Some day, when this is over . . ."

Oh yes, there was anger about the limited relationship and about what they came to call "phonication"—a relationship confined largely to telephone calls. They'd call each other from all over the country when they traveled, and they each had their usual telephone booths in the city where they lived. Chuck once jokingly suggested they make a montage of photographs of their favorite phone booths for erotic purposes. "Remember that phone booth I called you from in San Francisco? Wow! Or that hot box on 34th!" Bernice gave her favorite forms of sex in the following order: oral sex, intercourse, phonication, and masturbation. Said half in jest, it was equally half true. Sometimes parallel play is sustained because the partners cannot mount a concerted effort to go beyond it.

Why do some affairs remain parallel play while some go beyond this stage? There are many theories. One, from traditional psychoanalytic theory, suggests that the lover can be like the "original object" (the opposite-sexed parent) but not come too close. When it does appear too close, the incest taboo raises its head. In an affair, it may be permissible to stay with the lover as parallel play but marriage may be hitting too close to incest.

For those who attempt to go beyond parallel play into marriage, the partners' children may threaten the lovers' own needs for exclusive attention. Often people with such intense needs grew up in homes where disharmony made it difficult for them to integrate multiple love objects, such as mother, father, siblings, etc. Later in life, they constantly crave, compete for, and seek center stage in relationships. For them, sharing means being uncared for.

Where affairs stay parallel for many years, it is probable that one of the partners needs the "constant mother"—be it wife or husband—to be there, in the background, while new territory is explored. When the affair leaps into marriage, what appears to puncture the rapture is the intrusion of the real world into the cocoon of bliss. Again, a child of either lover may be seen as an intrusion, particularly when that love has been in the service of healing a past injury and the partners are replaying for each other the role of parent and child.

For some parallel players, along with the need for a "constant mother" (male or female) to stay in the background is a fear: that loving one person will make them too dependent on that person, causing them to lose their sense of self. Safety is then found in dividing their love between different persons. For them, love is a state of indecision between two or more lovers. This love for them is experienced as profound and real but its character is that they can only love when they love more than one person at a time. As psychoanalyst Bergmann suggests: "Love is a compound of many emotions, diverse memories and many needs that remain ungratified in childhood, that seek resolution in adulthood." A person's ability to love is based on one's developmental level, regardless of age. Insofar as we had a happy childhood, with good symbiosis we can then go on to try to recapture that in the love experience by some idealization of the partner and love itself.

As for our parallel players, the transformation of falling in love into a permanent tie depends significantly on the ability to establish an inner peace between the idealizations we bring with us from infancy and our capacity to accept the limitations of reality. Love is then as much a state of the self as it is an adoration of the uniqueness and personality of the beloved. That state of self either is fulfilled in parallel play or pushes beyond its boundaries.

CHAPTER SEVEN

SEXUAL PRACTICES IN THE AGE OF AIDS; AND QUIET FLOWS THE DON

In Mozart's opera *Don Giovanni* the Don's servant Leporello gives a catalogue of the Don's conquests that includes 1,003 in Spain alone. Pretty impressive. However, Shere Hite recently suggested that 70% of women married five years or more had had affairs. One gets the feeling that the Don had better look to his laurels as we are creating a race of Donna Giovannas bent on equaling his exploits.

But amidst this new-wave Roman orgy of current sexual activity, there has appeared a cloud. At first it was no bigger than a man's hand but it has, as clouds will, grown larger and larger, until now it threatens to blot out the sky. AIDS and other sexually transmitted diseases (STDs), like an unwelcome guest at a rendevous for two, have dampened the party. The wonderful promise of "having it all" suddenly rings hollow.

Harold, age 48, on his recent separation from his wife of 23 years, said:

"I got married before the sexual revolution and stayed married and faithful all through the hot times. 'Do your own thing,' they all said. I did nothing. Now that I'm unattached and have all the running room in the world, what do I find? AIDS, herpes, God knows what! How's that for perfect timing?"

While Barbara sees even her affair as a constraint (is the Don taking his revenge?):

"I'm staying in my affair *and* my marriage. With all that's going on out there, I'm not taking any risks. I don't think my husband is having an affair; he's so passive he hardly does anything. That's what drove me into the affair in the first place. The sex with my lover is good, but best of all he says he's faithful to me and has no need of anyone else. He knows what the score is out there, and he knows he's safe with me. The truth is, even if both my relationships were unsatisfactory, I don't think I'd leave either my husband or my lover. 'Safe sex' means knowing who you're with—and staying there."

Both Barbara and Harold are coping with today's sexual "counter-revolution". The sixties' garden of earthly delights seems to be sown now with tares and bitter vetches. Indeed, some people feel such intense fear that they are almost phobic. Their comments are similar to those of the male who said to us:

"I'm not sleeping with anyone—period! In the past, when I was single, I had it all—singles and a few married women. Now, if you listen to the statistics, each person has been with X number of people, multiplied by the X number of people they've been with, and so on. Soon you feel like you've slept with half the world—and whatever they have. I'm staying away from it all. When this thing blows over, I'll go back to good screwing—but not till them. For the time being, I'll work."

Recently an article in the *New York Times Sunday Magazine* dealt with the rising number of men in their 30's and 40's who have not wed—and may not. Their reluctance didn't stem from a riotous life style of easy sex with readily available young women. In fact, as these men get into their middle and upper 30's they seem to be backing off from sexual relationships altogether.

When people respond in extreme fashion to a particular situation, there is generally a deep underlying fear behind their actions. Perhaps we are seeing the flip side of that feeling of invulnerability that seemed to permeate the sixties. Now hypochondria, and extreme fear of becoming ill or diseased, is prevalent. Such a reaction often occurs among those people who have a strong sense of their bodies and who actively pursue physical fitness. Eating right and keeping fit are splendid goals, and they're perfectly justifiable. Excessive concern with developing the body, though, may indicate a subconscious fear of bodily decay. Are we trying to become so healthy and strong because underneath we feel weak and vulnerable?

Well, fear and apprehension over the consequences of sexual activity are nothing new. The pox (syphilis) and unwanted pregnancies posed severe problems for earlier generations, and "safe sex" has always had the ring of an oxymoron. But the threat of AIDS is now a real menace. People are confused about how you get it and how you can protect yourself against it—short of complete abstinence. The "experts" have provided little solace as they battle the same confusions as the public. Some alarmists have already suggested that such acts as "deep kissing" can transmit the AIDS virus while others argue that heterosexual intercourse and oral sex are safe practices. Whom are we to believe? Is it any wonder that people worry, especially when in the heat of passion?

What Are We Doing?

How are people responding? Have men and women come to feel that sex is just too complicated, that the object just isn't worth the price? Is there more caution in sexual behavior? Are choices more contemplative, selective and discriminating? As a society are we moving into a Socratic mold of being more examining of self and others? In order to arrive at some of the answers, we conducted a survey to add to the data from our clinical observations of everyday life and the findings of others—we wanted to get our own "feel" for the subject.

We sampled 374 volunteers, in a "survey of opportunity" i.e., gathering information from groups of individuals attending university classes, seminars, community centers, church groups and places of social interaction such as clubs and bars. Using a structured questionnaire, we were interested in examining attitudes, behaviors and practices regarding the impact—or non-impact of AIDS and STDs on their lives. We were not pursuing firm, fixed, statistical conclusions. What is the point, when tracking attitudes towards AIDS is like tracking a speeding train? The moment you determine its position it is already somewhere else. Medical bulletins can cause almost day-to-day changes in the way people view sexual activity. Our main purpose was to get a sense of how people think about AIDS. We wanted to see the range of responses, as well as get some indication of the specific precautions being practiced, like the use of condoms. The sample consisted of married and single men and women between 18 and 62. The average age was 35. (The complete questionnaire is reprinted in the appendix.)

The spontaneous comments of those who were willing to be interviewed in greater depth are most revealing about the confusion and variety of responses. Some felt that only a blood test can give you comfort and assurance:

> *Male, age 52:* "I guess at this age I've learned to be careful. When we first met and I knew I wanted to have an affair with her, I used my judgement in sizing up her history. I used my plain old intuition. I felt she was OK. But still I asked her about her experiences in the last few years. I was convinced she was clean. Still, I felt her sense of unease and mine. I told her it would be best for both to

feel really comfortable to go for blood tests—she and I together. Then we could start our relationship with honesty and feel free with each other. She agreed. We both went. All was fine and it's still great now.''

Female, age 42: ''I have a new lover and frankly it's been great. He's a very experienced, sexy guy. At first, I had the feeling that with his kind of sophistication he may have had some bisexual or homosexual experiences. He said ''no.'' I was still anxious. Before we actually made love, I asked him to have a blood test and said that I would too, though I told him he was my first lover and that I had only been with my husband—for over 20 years. At first he resisted. But then, since I didn't change my position, he gave in. We were both tested. I feel much freer now and don't insist he use protection. I trust him.''

Some look for a scapegoat to vent their anger and feelings of helplessness:

Male, age 62: ''To me AIDS means an anally inserted death sentence. The truth is I have no use for where it all began—I mean the homosexuals. If that's prejudice, then that's what I am. Me? I don't think about it too much. At this age I don't think there's much to worry about. But if in the past, occasionally I fooled around when I didn't think my wife would know, and it wasn't hurting anyone—now I'm careful. I just can't afford to take chances, with or without condoms.''

Some respondents answers are to avoid sexual intercourse:

Male, age 43: ''Sure I'm worried. You'd have to be crazy not to be. And I don't care if the woman is married or not— you don't know who she's been with last, who her husband was with last, who anyone was with. But I found my own solution. With any woman, married or not, I just pretend. I

mean, I go through the motions of making love. To be
specific, I don't penetrate. That's right. I make love up to
that point but won't go into her vagina. That's the way I
play it safe.''

Among those who chose avoidance are some members of the
homosexual population for whom the threat of AIDS has been
more virulent:

> *Male, age 34:* "I guess I have more to worry about than
> other people. I'm gay. I had a lot of lovers. I would pick
> them up at bars. I like younger men. With this scare I'm
> frankly terrified. In the last year I lost 28 friends—in death.
> Now I still go to my old bars, but just to talk, have some
> drinks, socialize. I don't bring anyone home with me—no
> matter how much I want to. My sex life is only in mastur-
> bation. That's ok. It's a lot better than dying.''

Some would like their partners to get a blood test, but for
various reasons don't press it:

> *Male, age 29:* "I'm in a recent affair with a very young
> woman. She's only 18. Though I know from asking her a
> long list of questions that she's had little experience—just
> a boyfriend she knew in high school—her first, and last,
> and only one. I still use a condom for both her protection
> and mine. She's never asked me to, but I wouldn't ever
> forgive myself if I brought something home to my wife.
> Besides feeling caught, I'd feel very bad about that. So,
> except for sometimes having thought that maybe I should
> have asked her to take a blood test, I just protect the both
> of us this way.''

Others worry but don't take concrete action:

> *Female, age 32:* "I guess you can say I'm reckless. He
> was coming around a lot where I work and I could feel this

tremendous pull toward him. I knew he had been married and I was thinking of leaving my marriage, so he seemed right for me. The first time we were together I thought about disease but didn't do much about it. I asked him about his sex history and he reassured me that he was ok. No, I didn't ask him to use anything like a condom. I guess I should have, but truth is, I hate those damn things. We don't use them at all. So far, so good.''

Many would like to pose questions to their partners but fear losing the relationship:

Female, age 36: ''When we first began our affair and I knew he had been single for many years, I was worried. I was very attracted to him but thought, what if I was really taking a big chance? I knew some of the guys he hung out with and they seemed OK but I didn't know his sex history or too much about his very private life. I knew only that I wanted to be with him and that if I asked him too much he'd resent it. He's kind of private and doesn't like to talk about himself all that much. Also, he was a little afraid of the fact that I was married. I didn't want to tip the scales. I kept quiet about disease and so did he. Maybe some day I'll talk about it, but not just now.''

Yet this respondent illustrates how difficult it is to know about your partner:

Female, age 48: ''I do have herpes, as a matter of fact. But I haven't slept with my husband for years now. With my new lover who is divorced a long time, I sometimes get a flare-up of my disease. He doesn't know I have it. When I get a flare-up, and I think it happens when I'm under stress, I don't tell him. I tell him I have a cold or sore throat, or give him some excuse. I don't want to lose him. At the same time, I don't sleep with him until the flare-up disappears. I think that's fair. At any rate, it has been ok until now and I'm hoping it will continue.''

Caught in the heat of passion some think about AIDS but then close their eyes and leap:

> *Male, age 45:* ''I met my lover at a professional conference. We were on the same panel together and had met for business reasons a few times before that. That night I asked her out for dinner. At that point we found that we really had a thing for each other. While I had never considered having an affair due to all the diseases around, I felt this was something special. Since I felt that this was not just a run-of-the-mill affair, but rather a spontaneous happening, and that her ideals and morals were similar to mine, I didn't feel it necessary to take protection, get blood tests or anything like that. I trusted her and she trusted me and it was never discussed between us. We accepted each other as it were. We still do.''

Others leap but rationalize it:

> *Male, age 54:* ''I should write a comedy about what goes on when two new lovers are in bed for the first time. It's more like a trial by judge and jury than a love affair. First thing, everyone lies. At least that's my thinking. Who in their right mind is going to say, 'Oh sure, I've slept around a lot and probably picked up all kinds of things, but don't worry I keep it all to myself.' I mean—it's crazy, the scene out there. How do you know what anyone has, including yourself? Point is, you don't. Me? I was open and honest. I told her I'd like to spend the night making love to her—our first time—and that I'd been around but considered myself sensible. When I asked her about herself, I got what I'd expected—she'd been with a few and is safe. Sure, but you can't stop living for fear of disease. Now can you?''

Male, age 41: "She's been married a couple of times and started sex early. I mean she's very, very savvy and must have good sense. You can't be hopping in and out of bed for the last 25 years of your life and not have smarts. Besides, she likes sex that much that she wouldn't go near anyone she would smell out as having any kind of disease. I think that with all her experience she's developed a sixth sense. Talk about disease? Any talk about that and I'd be sure to lose my erection. What's there to talk about anyway?"

Are married partners safer?:

Female, age 31: "I've been in this long-time relationship for about eleven years—off and on. He's a good guy but from a lower class than I and not a professional—so I wasn't sure. Then with this new AIDS thing, I found myself worried. I started concentrating more on married men. I figured they were safer, but then I thought, if he fooled around with me, what makes me think he didn't with others? But what really scared me was I started counting all the men I've been with since I started having sex when I was seventeen, and I counted 36. That blew my mind. I called my 11-year-long relationship guy and told him we should get married. We are this summer."

Female, age 38: "I've always like married men. I found they were better lovers and weren't so demanding on my time. I like my freedom. But now I want a health certificate, a bill of health from the Pope himself. I don't mean to be irreverent but that's how I feel. You can't be too careful. I mean, it's my life and I have to protect it—right?"

Marriage is getting to look better for a lot of people:

Male, age 29: "I'm having a hard time with this new AIDS scare. I like dancing and so I'm used to going to dances. Of course, I've always been able to pick up a lot of women—married and single. I've been playing it loose for a while—there are so many beautiful women out there—and didn't want to settle down. But now, I find the women will dance with me, have a drink, even let me take them home but then—the shutters come down and the sign says 'closed.' Frankly, going to bed has become difficult. If I didn't know better, I'd think I was losing my charm. I may just have to get married—or do something else just as drastic. That's what it boils down to.''

Female, age 38: "I've been with a married man for many years. I didn't care if he left his wife or not. We also both agreed that occasionally it was ok to be with others. That's all the tension in the air these days in the singles scene. All I would like now is my own husband, a house somewhere in the suburbs and the two to three kids. It's Americana all over again. Maybe that's the reason for it all—to get us back to a different style of life. It makes sense to me.''

Maybe older partners are the answer:

Male, age 47: "I always liked younger women. It's true what they say—an older man can get a younger woman. I did. But now, I go for the older ones. I figure a woman of 55, even with good looks, hasn't had as many men recently as one of 25. I'm not crazy about the idea, but what choice do you have these days.''

Are widows and widowers safer?:

Male, age 27: "This whole dating scene makes me nervous these days. In the past, women would ask you the usual kind of "warm-up" questions: what you did for a living, how your neighborhood was holding up, the usual getting-to-know-you stuff. Now, even when that still goes on, you know you're getting ready for the big one. I've been asked by many women—how long I've been having sex, with whom I've been dating, how many partners I've had, would I mind giving them my sex history, and so on. Sure I mind. It's like giving your doctor a whole medical history, and the truth is I can't be sure of any of it. I mean, what good is telling them how many I've been with. How do I know who was infected and who wasn't? I'm enough worried myself. The interrogation only makes it worse. Right now, I'm dating a widow. She's only 31 but her husband died of a heart attack after three years of marriage. I feel safest with her. Maybe because she's been through a lot with her husband, she doesn't bother me with this new scare. Besides—I like her.''

Then there is the ultimate fear when an affair is exposed:

Female, age 40: ''I caught my husband. That's right. We were in the middle of this argument and he told me he was having this affair. It was his way of getting back at me for doing something he thought I did. Well, besides wanting to kick him out the door that moment, I sent him to the doctor. That's right. I told him he had to get tested. When he told me that he had only been with one woman and for a short time, I told him I didn't care if it was with Mother Teresa herself. He had to go for the test—or be gone forever. In no way was he going to infect me. He just went for the test.''

Let's now look at responses to specific questions. Of our respondants, 78% say they are worried about AIDS in general, 36% are not personally worried about contracting AIDS, 90% are not worried at all about AIDS in their current relationships, and 67% say they are more cautious. Most have read articles or have listened to media presentation on AIDS within the previous month. How does concern about AIDS affect the number of sex partners?

Fifty-two percent said they now have about the same number of sex partners while 44% said fewer. Only 26% say they go to fewer social meeting places. Only 35% said they have more dates before engaging in sex. As far as condom use, 30% said they are using condoms more than before. In regard to innovative forms of sexual practices, 14% said they are doing that less while 72% reported the same; 14% more. As far as avoiding a relationship because of fear of AIDS, the vast majority (74%) said they had not. We have heard a lot about interrogations or prospective sexual partners over the last few years so we were curious about this topic. Surprisingly, half said they rarely or never ask about sexually transmitted diseases and the other half said they do ask some questions. Of perhaps greater interest is that 70% of these respondents say they are never asked, the remainder being sometimes or always asked.

Although these responses come from a limited sample and cannot necessarily be extended to the population at large, they are suggestive and make some interesting points as well as suggesting needing inquiries. First, if AIDS poses the public health threat that some say it does then it is alarming that so many people, and in this case fairly sophisticated and well-educated people who are knowledgeable about news reported in the media, are not taking the greatest precautions. (These findings are in line with a Gallup Poll which reported in late 1987 that only 55% surveyed said they had already taken or planned to take specific actions to avoid contact with AIDS).

Many people worry about what they hear but fewer act decisively or consistently. Some are worried but not about their relationships—what then are they worried about and how justified are they in their complacency about their relationships? If many are involved in numerous relationships, and AIDS, as some experts maintain, can be transmitted through second- and third-party contacts, the future portent is ominous. And the most troubling question is why intelligent people who are in touch with the latest information are apparently disregarding what they hear?

In light of these problems it seems to us that attitudes and behavior are clearly separate and often different from espoused beliefs and knowledge. For example, that many more people use condoms and that, as in our survey, they use them more than previously does not mean that those who use them do so all the time. If not, what does that say about concern? Recently there was a case reported of a young woman contracting AIDS through one sexual encounter. If the details of that case are reported accurately then not using protection once is as good as not using it at all.

To look at condom use in another way we devised a brief questionnaire that we administered to a few large groups of students and singles. The results were so consistent and one-sided that it is likely that they would hold up for the general population:

- 1. WHAT ARE THE WAYS IN WHICH A PERSON CAN GET AIDS.
- 2. HOW CAN A PERSON TAKE PRECAUTIONS AGAINST AIDS.
- 3. CAN A PERSON GET AIDS FROM HETEROSEX-UAL RELATIONS? IF SO, HOW?
- 4. IN THE LAST YEAR DID YOU EVER HAVE SEX-UAL INTERCOURSE WITHOUT USING A CON-DOM?
- 5. IF YOU DID HAVE SEXUAL INTERCOURSE WITHOUT A CONDOM HOW OFTEN DID THAT HAPPEN? (CIRCLE ONE)

  RARELY SOMETIMES FREQUENTLY ALWAYS

Of course the key questions are numbers 4 and 5. If a condom is not used all the time then how serious is the concern, considering what we know about the consequences of contracting AIDS? Yet the results are startling. Despite the fact that all the respondents believed a person could contract AIDS from heterosexual relations, over 90% of those queried said they had sexual relations in the last year without using a condom—some frequently, others rarely or occasionally. Most, if not all, of these respondents would show up on surveys as condom users, as indeed they are—*some of the time*. But if they don't use condoms *all of the time,* how are they protected against the possible threat of heterosexual AIDS? Where has the education gone wrong, or has it?

The topic of AIDS may seem dreary if not an outright turn-off compared to what is perceived as the fun and games of sexual affairs. But the fact is that it can't be avoided. The danger of contracting AIDS looms for anyone in a sexual relationship or about to get involved in one. Even being married does not necessarily make one safe. If we take the statistics on affairs seriously—that half or more of the married population has been or is involved in affairs—then the danger of contracting AIDS from a married partner is as great as that from the sexual relations of singles. Though AIDS is on everyone's mind, most people are not willing to give up sex—they desire sex, feel they need it, or they have to engage in sex to maintain a relationship—a decision on safe sex must be made.

The question is how much precaution to take? Many are clearly taking too few precautions. While there has been a sharp rise in the use of condoms, the rise may not be as dramatic as previously thought. The Guttmacher Institute in New York compared contraceptive use of 8,000 women between the ages of 18–44 in 1982 and again in 1987. In the light of AIDS, they expected a dramatic increase in the use of condoms in the 1987 survey. They didn't find it. While there was a significant increase in favorable *attitudes* toward the condom (from 61% in 1982 to 84% in 1987) few were actually using condoms; the pill was used far more frequently. The Institute went on: "Perhaps the greatest surprise is that there is no indication that levels of sexual activity have decreased, even among the youngest women. The proportion of never-married women age 18–44 who had ever had intercourse rose from 68 percent to 76 percent between 1982 and 1987, and there was little change in the proportion of women who said they had sex infrequently. These findings run counter to the assumption many have made that emphasis on urging teenagers to say no to non-marital intercourse out of concern about AIDS has caused large proportions of heterosexuals to abstain from non-marital sexual intercourse.''

While these findings are in themselves discouraging, they do not encompass the possibility that people have changed in their choice of partners and the number of partners, which the survey did not include. But still, people have clearly not backed off from sex. The question still remains, how in fact do people make decisions about the safety of partners, and how valid are those decisions?

Undoubtedly the decisions people make are often intuitive or impulsive. It is difficult to sort things out in the heat of passion. It is far better, before becoming involved, to consider the evidence and make a conscious decision to which one sticks. To that end, we will present the important issues and the different interpretations. Then you can decide on the proper course of behavior for you—or how much risk you are willing to take.

The Facts About AIDS Transmission

To be at risk for AIDS, the Human Immunodeficiency Virus (HIV) must get into the blood stream for distribution to target tissues. The AIDS virus is rather fragile and fairly susceptable outside the living cell. Many enviroinments, even prolonged drying in air, as well as many enzymes and fluids in the body will decrease its infectivity (i.e. its ability to enter cells and multiply). Therefore, the surest way to contract the AIDS virus is through direct exchange of injected blood or through the direct discharge of semen (which in an infected person has large concentrations of the virus) into another person's bloodstream. This explains why up until now AIDS has been most rampant among intravenuous drug users who exchange needles, and homosexuals who practice anal intercourse. In exchanging needles the blood of an infected person is injected directly into the blood of the uninfected person. In anal intercourse, because the penis does not fit comfortable into the anus, there is frequently rupturing of blood vessels. The semen of an infected person containing the AIDS virus can then efficiently enter the blood stream of the passive partner. Also, if there are lesions on the penis of the active partner and the passive partner is infected, there can be blood interchange so that the virus can enter the blood stream of the previously uninfected person. While these methods of AIDS transmission account for most of the AIDS cases in the United States and Western Europe, AIDS can be contracted by *anyone* whose bloodstream provides direct access to the AIDS virus. AIDS *is not* a disease of drug users or homosexuals per se. It is just that those groups have in the past engaged in specific practices that enhance transmission of the AIDS virus. In fact, since many homosexuals have altered some of their practices in the light of knowledge about AIDS transmission (not performing anal intercourse or using condoms), the incidence of new cases of infection with HIV has begun to fall dramatically. In April, 1989, *The New York Times* reported that a study of gay and bisexual men in the city found that "reducing the number of sexual partners or becoming monogomous did not significantly decrease the risk of contracting the AIDS virus. Only a halting of anal intercourse substantially reduced the likelihood of contracting the virus. . . ." The homosexual community thus has a clear opportunity to mitigate its risk vis-a-vis AIDS, and seems to be taking advantage of it. Unfortunately this has not been the case for IV drug users who continue to share needles—a practice which effectively transfers injected blood to previously non-infected individuals.

This discussion leads inevitably to the big question: Can AIDS be transmitted through heterosexual relations, i.e. vaginal intercourse and oral sex? Not only is this the big question for most of the population, but it has generated the most heated, confused and controversial debate. Yet for anyone engaged in sexual relations it can be a life and death issue. For a married person in a secret affair the possibility poses the added dilemma and responsibility of perhaps bringing AIDS home to an unknowing marital partner.

If vaginal sex and oral sex are not likely methods of AIDS

transmission then some simple precautions make the risk to heterosexual relations negligible. On the other hand, if AIDS can easily be transmitted in vaginal and oral sex, then what is the meaning of safe sex short of abstinence? This is no idle debate, given that people have already taken sides by voting with their behavior. Most surveys show that a large part of the population is either not taking precautions, is taking questionable precautions, or is not taking precautions consistently. For still others, precaution is a mental activity rather than a behavioral act.

In an effort to bring some clarity to the debate, we interviewed two of the leading experts on AIDS—Dr. Robert E. Gould and Dr. Harold W. Jaffe—who hold radically different views on the dangers of AIDS to heterosexuals. Dr. Gould is Professor of Psychiatry at New York Medical College and a practicing psychiatrist in New York City. He has been at the forefront of many social issues. In January, 1988 he wrote an article in *Cosmopolitan* magazine concluding, after examining the worldwide data, that there is little danger of AIDS through vaginal sex or oral sex. Dr. Jaffe, a specialist in infectious diseases, is the Deputy Director for Science in the AIDS program of the Centers For Disease Control in Atlanta, Georgia. Dr. Jaffe, who is one of the leading experts in the world on AIDS, believes there is a very real threat of AIDS through heterosexual relations. The controversy revolves around a number of key issues.

- 1. The reported cases of heterosexual AIDS are low. Why?

- 2. The stability of the virus and its ability to survive in the vagina and mouth.

- 3. Predictions around 1985 that AIDS would become epidemic in the heterosexual community by the 1980's. It has not. What does this mean?

- 4. The evidence that AIDS is a rampantly heterosexual

disease in Africa and elsewhere and that phenomenon will come here.

- 5. Reports of AIDS-infected prostitutes infecting their clients through vaginal intercourse and oral sex. Conversely the reports that prostitutes have gotten AIDS through vaginal intercourse and oral sex with infected clients.
- 6. Accuracy of reports. Are people who report getting AIDS through vaginal intercourse and oral sex lying?
- 7. Value of erring or overstating on the side of caution.
- 8. What is safe sex?
- 9. Politics and hidden agendas.

THE INTERVIEWS

*NOTE: These interviews were obtained one month apart in February and March 1989. Dr. Gould was interviewed first and then Dr. Jaffe's responses were obtained.

QUESTION: What is the actual incidence of reported heterosexual AIDS?

Dr. Gould: The latest figures from the Centers for Disease Control as of January 9, 1989 report 582 men and 1,776 women who claim to have contracted AIDS through heterosexual relations. This represents the entire United States population from the first reported cases in 1981 and would be a relatively small number even if the figures were correct. The figures are actually lower, considering that many of these are partners of IV drug users who have shared a needle with their partners on occasion even though they are not themselves drug addicts. Others in this group are bisexual and some have practiced anal intercourse with an infected partner. The CDC figures do not distinguish between anal and vaginal intercourse and the anal route is a ready conduit; the vaginal is not.

DR. JAFFE'S RESPONSE: The number of non-IV drug abusing persons with AIDS in this country is relatively low because most heterosexuals are not in high risk groups and are not having sex with high risk partners. But the risk of acquiring HIV heterosexually varies. In Iowa there is a lower risk than in New York City because there are fewer people with HIV infection in Iowa. Are you putting yourself at risk by going to singles bars? Yes. But also, many are taking precautions.

QUESTION: Why are many people lying?

DR. GOULD: Some do not think of it as lying. It's a matter of not being aware that the women, many of whom are the sexual partners of men who are drug addicts who are infecting their female partners, are saying that they are not drug takers. They are not lying in that they are not addicts, but if they have had one or two sessions of sharing a needle with their men, that's all they have to do to get the disease.

QUESTION: So you are saying that it is commonplace for somebody who is living with a drug addict to, sometime in that relationship, even if it is once or twice, shoot up.

DR. GOULD: That's right. It is psychologically very important for many men to share a needle. In some ways it symbolizes sexual intercourse and it's an important thing. Just as with pot smokers there is a group pull—the importance of passing around one joint so that everyone participates. Even if you had more joints for everyone it was fun to pass it around—it was a ritual and it is a ritual to share a needle and it is hard to see a woman who belongs to a man either married or common law who is told by the man, "hey honey, I just want you to share this needle with me one time—it can't hurt you and it means a hell of a lot to me—if you love me you are going to have to do this with me." Very few women are going to say no to that but they very well might say no to an interviewer who says are you a drug taker, do you share needles? No I don't. And they may be telling the truth because they only did it once or twice.

DR. JAFFE'S RESPONSE: That may be true and it may be distorting some of the studies. But if you look at the partners of IV drug users the rate of infection is 50%. If you study partners of hemophiliacs and others who got infected from transmissions you find much lower rates—ten to twenty-five percent. So the difference may represent drug sharing by the partners of addicts. But still, if you eliminate it and don't deal with that and just look at partners of bisexual men or transfusion recipients you do find infected partners—so lying is not the entire story.

QUESTION: What about anal sex?

DR. GOULD: By the same token there is lying by women who have had anal intercourse and have developed the disease that way. For many women anal sex is a taboo subject and they are embarassed to talk about it: this may especially be so for women who have submitted reluctantly to anal intercourse. Almost none of the studies have ever asked women who have contracted AIDS through so called heterosexual intercourse, do you have anal intercourse? Only one AIDS study conducted in San Francisco of women which concentrated on women married to bisexual men who developed AIDS found that sixty percent of them admitted to having anal intercourse. I submit that it is most likely that they got it that way rather than through vaginal intercouse which I think is very difficult. Now by definition they got it through heterosexual intercourse, because anal intercourse between a man and a woman is heterosexual intercourse—but it is not broken down as to whether these woman have had anal intercourse or vaginal intercourse. So when you add together the two groups of women—those who have had anal intercourse with bisexual men who are infected with AIDS, and those who have shared a needle with men who are infected, the number 1,776 women is brought down to a much lower figure.

QUESTION: What do you think that number would be?

DR. GOULD: I can't tell you exactly what the number is but it could be only a fraction of the 1,776 the CDC reported. There may well be cases that defy the odds or are unexplainable because there are oddball situations where anything can happen—as with any other disease. Certainly if you have open vaginal lesions that can do it—theoretically.

DR. JAFFE'S RESPONSE: In the end you never know for sure about lying because you are relying on people to tell the truth. You're not going to give them truth serum. So what you are looking for are consistent patterns. There are enough studies that are consistent that you can't just dismiss them. We keep coming up with the ten percent figure among different groups who we believe were infected heterosexually and did not perform dangerous practices and are not lying. The figure will vary depending on the group. In the case of IV drug users there will be more contamination in the reporting since some partners may shoot up occasionally with a shared needle. Among the partners of hemopheliacs who are HIV positive it is less of a problem determining the source since they have no other exposure but heterosexual relations.

QUESTION: Is it possible that at some point AIDS will spread more epidemically into the heterosexual community?

DR. GOULD: From 1984, 1985 through 1987 they were saying that. The Surgeon General C. Everett Koop and the Secretary of Health and Education Edward Bennett and other experts like Otis Bowen all said there would be a rampant spread in the heterosexual world. In fact Bowen likened AIDS to the Black Plague that would take over the whole world. It didn't happen and now none of them is saying that.

DR. JAFFE'S RESPONSE: I did not make those predictions. We at the Centers for Disease Control have been very consistent and we have added to what we have to say. There has been a tremendous swing in public perception but this is not because we have put out different sources of information. People get confusing information from the media which comes from different sources.

QUESTION: Why do you think it hasn't spread into the hetero-sexual world?

DR. GOULD: Because of the nature of the disease and the way it is transmitted. I have long said that you need to have a direct innoculation of the virus into the blood stream in order to produce AIDS, and it takes a whopping dose. It is a fragile virus that dies easily in the air. It is supposed to die within 10–20 seconds. Any neutralizing agent that dilutes it will kill it. So that saliva has been shown to kill the virus in a test tube. The vaginal secretions dilute, neutralize and kill the virus and nobody talks about that. They confuse the severity of the disease which is enormous—it is deadly, fatal—with contagion of the disease. It is very hard to contract the AIDS virus except through these two main ways that directly put the virus into the bloodstream: (1) through contaminated needles where you are taking blood from one vein of the person who has it into another person—and one needle stick will do it; (2) and anal intercourse which is enormously effective as a conduit because the mucous mem-branes are very thin and they are superficial. They bleed easily—the superficial veins, the hemorrhoidal veins. Look at all the people who have hemhorroids and who have had no trauma to the area. The penis will certainly disrupt the mucous membranes and the superficial blood vessels and if you make the anus large enough through fisting or artificial ways of enlarging the anus, you've already damaged the vessels and the mucous mem-branes. So it is an extraordinarily effective way to spread the virus into the blood stream.

DR. JAFFE'S RESPONSE: At the microscopic level I don't think that anyone knows for sure how HIV is transmitted. All we can say is that the virus is found in vaginal secretions and semen. If there are lesions or abrasions present that would facilitate transmission. If a couple practices rectal sex, that would further increase the risk. But lesions have been over-played. It has been shown that cells in the cervix can be directly infected—how the male gets infected is less clear.

QUESTION: The AIDS epidemic in Africa is reported to be a heterosexual epidemic. Doesn't this pose a serious challenge to your views?

DR. GOULD: There are countries like Uganda where the Prime Minister says that there is no homosexuality and it is common in a number of countries for officials to say there is no homosexuality. Now this is nonsense. My work for six years with African nurses at Metropolitan Hospital who are trained to do sex education and family planning in their local communities in Africa taught me otherwise. They told me that homosexuality is not acknowledged in many of their communities and not talked about, but they know it exists and if these people will not talk about it in their own countries they are certainly not going to talk about it to western researchers and tell them about homosexual activity.

In addition to that, in African clinics a single unsterilized needled is often used for many patients and, if anything, the needle is washed in cold water. These clinics do not have enough money for heating and sterilizing so by using one needle for transfusions and other injections, they are going to spread AIDS. A couple will go back and have intercourse and have no idea that they got AIDS from a needle. By the same token, blood transfusions are done without the blood being tested and without the needles being sterilized; so if they do a blood transfusion from a person with AIDS to another person without AIDS, that person will get AIDS just as surely as if you have a drug addict with AIDS who shared a contaminated needle with another person. The immune system of many Africans is already compromised by the fact that they are impoverished, weak, and their nutrition under par. Any small infection will further decrease the immune system and if an AIDS virus is present, they are more likely to get it than someone whose nutritional state is intact.

There are other factors that make the situation in Africa not relevant to the AIDS problem in the United States. About one third of African men who have AIDS have venereal disease, which affects the penis causing oozing, pus and ulcerating lesions. A smaller number have open lesions due to skin infections such as *yaws*. This does not stop them from having intercourse, so that if they have sexual contact with anyone with AIDS it can go right into the blood stream. I didn't mention that, on the female side, there is the factor of infibrillation, where in many instances the vaginas are sewed up and clitorectomies are performed where the clitoris is cut off and this already compromises the genital system. In intercourse, a woman whose vagina has been sewed up may have considerable tearing and bleeding, which greatly enhances the possibility of AIDS transmission. Therefore, you see the conditions in Africa are dramatically different and not very instructive for understanding AIDS transmission in this country.

DR. JAFFE'S RESPONSE: In every country in Africa where AIDS has been studied, heterosexual transmission has emerged as a major factor. It is true that transfusions as a risk factor for AIDS are much more important there than here and there is more bisexuality and homosexuality than people admit to, but every study indicates heterosexual transmission in Africa is greater than in the United States. It is spreading more rapidly among heterosexuals in Africa because of several factors including the high frequency of genital ulcer disease. For those reasons it may never reach the same proportions among heterosexuals in the United States.

QUESTION: There has been a lot of talk about prostitutes getting and transmitting AIDS through heterosexual relations. In fact there was a television program last year about the threat of AIDS to our troops in various places in the world through prostitutes. How great a threat are prostitutes?

DR. GOULD: Prostitutes have been considered very high risk because promiscuous sexual behavior has been considered high risk behavior for AIDS. The fact is that prostitutes who are not IV drug users are no more at risk than women in the general population. Experts are perplexed that prostitutes are not more heavily infected than they are. The problem is that there were studies done in New Jersey—in Newark and Paterson—and they found that 65–75% of the prostitutes had AIDS. But they neglected to emphasize that these prostitutes were taken off the methadone program and every one of them was an IV drug abuser. Studies done in Las Vegas of 138 prostitutes who were not drug users found not one infected with the AIDS virus. Studies done in France and England of prostitutes who were not IV drug users also showed not one was infected with AIDS.

QUESTION: So why have prostitutes been so often implicated?

DR. GOULD: What made prostitutes seem like higher risk is that men who contracted AIDS either through IV drug use or through homosexual activity lied and said they were out with prostitutes—that they were drunk one night and picked up a hooker and got AIDS. Now the men who said this were studied by Joyce Wallace. They were men who were married and so it was much more comfortable for them to say they saw a hooker one night and got AIDS than to admit that they actually got AIDS through sexual intercourse with other men.

QUESTION: There is a real problem then in getting accurate reports?

DR. GOULD: Right. And especially in the Army, where, in some studies, men claimed they had contracted AIDS through sex with prostitutes. In fact, in Germany, when these particular individuals were studied and their contacts studied carefully, it turned out that every single one of them—these United States Army Personnel—were either drug users or had had homosexual contacts. Either of those admissions would put these men in jeopardy of court martial. But if they happened to have gone to a prostitute one night, they wouldn't even face a petty fine penalty for it. So it is not reasonable to expect people in the armed services to tell the truth and yet some studies were done by an army doctor who believed them. These reports are extraordinarily flawed.

DR. JAFFE'S RESPONSE: It is not true that not one prostitute has been infected from normal heterosexual relations. We just completed a seven city study under the direction of Sociologist Bill Darrow of the Centers for Disease Control. The findings have been reported at a number of scientific meetings and will soon be published in a journal. While it's true that the Number One risk factor is IV drug use, clearly there are some prostitutes who were infected from heterosexual intercourse. Now a lot of them have boy friends who are IV drug users but they say that they are not and they don't have tracks—but you can't know for sure.

QUESTION: You say there are no confirmed cases of AIDS transmission via oral sex. Yet in January 1989 the *New England Journal of Medicine* reported a "confirmed case of AIDS transmission from female to male through fellatio." I heard that reported on the network news and very promptly the next day searched out the article. I was a little alarmed since I know that most sex surveys cite oral sex as the most preferred form of sexual activity. What is your reaction to that report?

DR. GOULD: Well, it is hard to believe. Again, there is always the oddball case, the one in ten million that can happen in the craziest way and no one can explain it. Maybe that's the one case. But even if that were so we are talking about one case when in eight years oral sex occurs in sixty to eighty percent of the population which must include sixty to eighty percent of those with the AIDS virus and it has never shown up in another person—and this one is the case? It is either a fantastic oddity or it isn't true. After all, this 60-year-old man is a diabetic who probably uses needles. He saw a prostitute for three years and was supposedly impotent. So I don't know exactly what the fellatio consisted of. He thinks he had a genital ulcer in the past but doesn't recall having one when he had fellatio performed on him. If he had a genital ulcer I find that interesting. What was that due to? This report was a letter to the editor by two physicians. It is hard to imagine that a full sexual history was obtained or that they necessarily knew how to do a sexual history. If this is not duplicated anywhere else can you take this report seriously when oral sex has occurred as frequently as it does?

DR. JAFFE'S RESPONSE: I don't know how true that case is, but there are enough case reports of people getting AIDS from oral sex that I'm inclined to believe that it happens—but it's very unusual. It is not a common method of transmission.

QUESTION: On March 11, 1989 there was a disturbing report in the *New York Times* about a 23-year-old woman (Alison Gertz) who purportedly got AIDS from a single sexual encounter with a male acquaintance seven years earlier. He has since died from AIDS. She says she did not use drugs, did not have any blood transfusions and implies from the newspaper report not to have had anal sex in that one night encounter (although this, as with many other reports, was not clearly ascertained). She also describes herself as "not at all promiscuous sexually." Her AIDS was just diagnosed this past summer, approximately six years after the sexual encounter. How do you explain this kind of occurrence and what implications does it have for others?

DR. GOULD: Remember, I never said it can't happen. There are flukes. Even if this case is true, the mere fact of it being featured in the *New York Times* indicates how rare this occurrence is.

DR. JAFFE'S RESPONSE: We believe it can happen that way, if the male is infected. It is difficult to predict who will be vulnerable.

QUESTION: Even if you are basically right you still acknowledge that not everyone is necessarily lying. There can be flukes, even if they are rare. Not everyone can be sure that they don't have small lesions on the penis or wall of the vagina. Therefore, what is wrong with erring on the side of extreme caution or even recommending abstinence? After all, the consequence is death.

DR. GOULD: I say that life is full of chances for being unexpectedly killed in an airplane crash, an automobile accident and the like. But people don't stop flying, they don't stop driving. If every third case of AIDS occurred through heterosexual intercourse you would stop having heterosexual intercourse, but if it's one in a million then it seems to me that to give up sexual enjoyment, to be scared stiff when there is no reason to be makes no sense. Having children, being pregnant is a danger to life. There are women who die in childbirth and yet very few women will not have children for that reason because it happens so rarely. And I am suggesting that normal vaginal intercourse is safer than any of the accidental possibilities I have mentioned. The statistics would bear me out—even those compiled by the Centers for Disease Control.

DR. JAFFE'S RESPONSE: It's difficult to convey that the risk you are talking about actually represents a tremendous range of risk. If you are talking about a middle class person who has a few sex partners a year the risk is not great. It is less of a risk in some areas of the country compared to others. If you're talking about a person in the South Bronx who may have had sex with a hundred partners last year, you are talking about a substantial risk. For an individual who has sex with an infected person there is a high risk.

If a person says "I don't want to take any chance ever" then what you are really saying is that you can't have sex. I think it is much more realistic to tell people that if they want to decrease the risk that means having sex with fewer people, getting to know them better before starting sexual intercourse, and using condoms. Yes. Getting to know them better is not completely valid and that's why you have to add condom use. When a couple gets into a steady relationship at what point do they decide they will not use condoms any more? Is it at a point when they decide they are going to be tested for HIV infection? Or is it at a point when they decide that they just trust each other—that they know enough about each other? I don't know how you make that recommendation. Obviously it happens.

QUESTION: Yet some people would say, what is so terrible about giving up sex? Are we so pleasure oriented that even in the face of an epidemic of the AIDS proportions and the possibility of death that we still insist on our sensual pleasures?

DR. GOULD: Well, I've been a psychiatrist for thirty-five years and I have worked a lot with couples who have sexual problems and I have done a good deal of sex therapy with people who have sexual difficulties and I can tell you that people's lives are severely compromised when they can't enjoy sex. So the actual amount of time one spends having sexual intercourse may be very little in the course of a week, but if it doesn't work it is enormously important. If it does work it is also enormously important.

We went through a Victorian period in this country and in the world where sex was considered dirty, wrong; there was a lot of guilt, and indeed people suffered needlessly in their quality of life because they couldn't enjoy sex. We then went through a period in the sixties where as a reaction to that there was a hedonistic flavor to sex, a widespread abandonment of moral restrictions and even of the notion that sex had to be linked with love. In a real way I think this looseness turned out not to be so terribly wonderful either. People had a great deal of sex with no feeling and no compassion and empathy for the other person. In any event, it did seem to set a new standard of sexual freedom, the notion that sex is natural and one had the right to enjoy it.

DR. JAFFE'S RESPONSE: From the public health point of view we have to be on the side of caution. AIDS is not something we understand fully and we can't be sure of its future course. That's different than a private citizen or expert giving an opinion or advising an individual. Also, it is very difficult to get people to take precautions in something as basic as sex. It may require a whole generation before we can get significant changes. Maybe at some time in the future people will consider it very strange for someone to have sex without condoms.

QUESTION: Now your own medical and psychiatric profession has been down on you for what on the face of it seems to be a reasoned point of view with persuasive evidence. Are there any other issues and agendas here than AIDS *per se*?

DR. GOULD: Well AIDS *per se* can't be shunted off to the side. It has become a big profession and there are groups that have vested interests in AIDS being an even bigger problem and more widespread than in fact it is. There are fundraisers and the people who want grants to study AIDS. If the disease were preceived as limited to homosexuals and drug addicts these are two outgroups that would not attract generous funding for research. But if it were seen as a major health crisis threatening the heterosexual middle class white community then funding will be increased enormously.

Furthermore, conservative social and political forces have a vested interst in using the AIDS threat as a cover for enforcing or bringing back chastity, monogomy and strict control over social and sexual behavior. And simultaneously there is pressure from the homosexual community which still suffers from widespread discrimination in every area. If AIDS were perceived as a homosexual disease—which I have taken great pains to say it is not—a lot of hard fought ground would be lost. So you have a number of different groups that stand to gain by keeping AIDS in the public mind as a heterosexual problem.

DR. JAFFE'S RESPONSE: That's a hypothesis which is difficult to document. How can you prove it?

The message to heterosexuals has been ambiguous. While they are told AIDS is a big problem for everyone, most of the problem is concentrated in specific population groups. The biggest and growing risk is in the inner cities in the Northeast among IV drug users and their partners. If you have thirty million dollars to allocate for AIDS, that's where you would want to spend most of your money.

DR. GOULD: I certainly agree that the biggest problem is among IV drug users. That's where most of the new cases are coming from."

Summing Up the Interviews

The preponderance of now available evidence suggests that normal heterosexual relations, which include vaginal intercourse and oral sex (both fellatio and cunnilingus), are not primary or volatile ways of transmitting AIDS. If that were the case AIDS would be epidemic in the population. Present statistics indicate AIDS is not currently epidemic in the heterosexual population of the United States and a number of studies have shown that, under scrutiny, many of those claiming to have gotten AIDS heterosexually in normal intercourse did not. Many were bisexual and others engaged in anal sex or shared needles. The actual number of authentic heterosexual AIDS cases are, therefore, probably fewer than the number reported. How many fewer is hard to say precisely.

Some cases are fuzzy or suspect. Is it possible that some people have contracted AIDS in heterosexual relations but are unaware of it because they do not suspect they have AIDS, as there can be a long incubation period of up to eight years and possibly even longer? The average incubation figure is four years, meaning that many people get the AIDS symptoms sooner and others later. This is certainly the case with the high-risk categories—homosexuals and I.V. drug users. If it has shown up within these groups, why not with heterosexuals? Such questions pose important points of inquiry. There are reported high levels of sexual activity in the single community where there are many possibilities for unknowing sexual contact with a high-risk person. One woman we interviewed revealed the complications in telling her story. She was having sex with a man who she considered "safe." They did not have sex immediately. Each felt the other was a sensible person who practiced safe sex. Later, the woman inadvertently discovered that the man had had a brief relationship with another woman whom she knew. The man thought that woman was safe. She just separated from a husband of 18 years and had been faithful during all that time (let's accept that this was true). Yet, unknown to this man but known to the woman we interviewed, the other woman separated from her husband after learning that he was bisexual and had been having homosexual relations for a number of years. After ending the brief relationship, the man had no thought or concern about his "safe affair" with a woman previously monogamous for 18 years. He felt safe in his next encounter, yet we know he had possibly been exposed sexually to a person who had a long-term sexual relationship with a bisexual man. If we imagine ramifications of similar kinds with all sorts of unknown and unsafe contacts which are then passed along down the line, heterosexually transmitted AIDS should show up in much greater numbers than the current statistics reveal. This had been predicted a few years ago. Thus far it has not happened.

Nevertheless, despite all the analyses and evidence that question the probable heterosexual transmission of AIDS, *no one denies that a risk is present*. We can't be 100% certain that all the reported cases of heterosexual AIDS are flukes or lies— no doubt many are. Also, if lesions or sores on the penis or in the vagina make a person more susceptible, how can one be certain that he/she doesn't have such a condition? Can women be certain about the condition of the walls of their vaginas when they are about to make love? Similarly, can men be certain that the skin on their penises is completely intact before or during lovemaking? Dr. Gould is accurate in his observation that people do things all the time despite risks—childbirth, driving, flying, and so on. But the fact is that some, as few as they may be, choose not to expose themselves to those risks; e.g. they don't fly. Also, as in flying, driving and the like, we know precisely what the risks are, based on fairly reliable statistics.

The situation with AIDS is more uncertain and no one can predict positively what course the disease will take in the future. So no matter how small the risk of heterosexual AIDS appears at the present time, it exists and requires decision making. What will you do? You have to decide, based on evaluating the evidence, how much risk you are willing to take given the consequences—possibly death. Consider also that our present understanding of the AIDS virus is very primitive. What if a new strain were to emerge that could be easily transmitted by almost any means. Remember, AIDS was around for quite a while before authorities formed their present theory as to how it was transmitted and what was safe and what wasn't—many lives could have been saved if we were told immediately that anal sex was a primary method of transmission. If a new strain develops then you can throw all the current discussions out; it could make current theories on spreading the disease obsolete. On the other side, one can present a whole list of frightening "what ifs"— what if the sky should fall, what if the earth would fall out of its orbit, what if, if and if? (Recently a meteorite came close to earth and reportedly will return in the future.) This can also be the food for paralysis in life. So one has to make decisions.

The fact is that people of all ages, educational levels, socio-economic levels, ethnic groups, and marital status continue to engage in sex. And as one of our respondents said, can you really be one hundred percent sure about your partner, whether single or married? Surely, in most single situations new partners are not going to spill out their previous histories of unsafe practices and questionable partners. So people, in effect, have voted with their behavior regardless of their fears and concerns. Many people who violently oppose Dr. Gould's positions are themselves engaging in sexual relations that can't be one hundred percent safe. People often think that beliefs and emotional intensity protect their behavior. As stated before, studies show that most people are not taking precautions or are not taking them consistently.

For instance, Carl S. Avery, in an article in *Self* magazine dated July, 1988 reported on a survey of 500 heterosexual women between the ages of 20 and 45. The article concluded: "While some women are backing up attitudes with action, many more have good intentions about taking precautions but are less than optimal in following through." Although 85% were "concerned" about getting AIDS, "a whopping 31% haven't changed their actions at all. Of greater concern was that women dating more men were the least concerned. Some 88% thought condoms to be effective against AIDS, *but* only 37% bought or carried them, while 53% counted on the man to take care of it. And 25% of the singles said they would still sleep with a man even if he refused to use condoms.

The article also reported a 1983 *Playboy* survey of 20,000 females that found that 61% had tried anal sex; a *Self* magazine survey in 1984 estimated the figure to be 51%. It was also pointed out that some experts think the extent of bisexuality is vastly underestimated. Given these factors, what is the validity of getting to know your partner? How many, especially in a new encounter, will really own up to dangerous practices? Interestingly, seven out of ten married women said they would insist their spouse be tested if they found out about an affair.

So we urge you to make a conscious decision about your sexual behavior and AIDS. Of the arguments we've just presented, which do you accept, reject? More importantly, what are you doing about your beliefs? For some the answer is total abstinence. Many experts and religious people support this. Others take a different view. Where do you fit in? The arguments can't tell you that; only you can make the decision. Once you make a conscious decision, STICK TO IT. If you strongly believe there is little risk to you after carefully considering all the evidence, then continue what you are doing but stay tuned for new information. All the evidence is not in and the book is not closed. If you decide that you will use condoms, make sure you use them ALL THE TIME. Remember that most people we interviewed, even those who use condoms most of the time, don't use them at all times. If you believe that condoms will protect you, then not using them even once is a contradiction. If you contract AIDS, it is of little solace to say "but I only didn't use it once."

Of course what is most needed is an effective treatment cure and an effective immunization or inoculation to end this scourge. With cure and prevention the arguments will recede into the background. Unfortunately we are not willing as a society to make the necessary investment, even though we are possibly confronted with one of the greatest public health crises ever. It is ironic that we will pay athletes millions of dollars (even some fairly mediocre players command huge salaries) yet fund raisers for AIDS research often have to go begging with cup in hand.

Perhaps, in addition to the traditional grants, we need a program modeled after the McArthur Foundation Awards. Give a hundred brilliant scientists, young and seasoned, outright tax-free grants of a million dollars to do nothing for two years but think about and work on a cure and prevention for AIDS.

The Big Question

The question of heterosexual AIDS is *the* issue for people involved in affairs or sexual activity outside of a long-term monogomous relationship. There was a hiatus of a year or two in which it appeared that the sexual revolution was over and the ghost of the Don was laid to rest. Affairs and easy sex dropped off the fashion charts. People were afraid or stubbornly cautious. That period seems to be coming to an end.

In November, 1988, *Harper's Bazaar* boldly announced that sex was back in an article entitled "Sex Is Alive and Well." Dr. Jacqueline Forrest of the Gutmacher Institute was cited in the article as indicating that the number of single women having regular intercourse increased over the past few years. How is this possible? Are people bored with AIDS already? No, they are not crazy or especially reckless. The fact is that almost no one we interviewed personally knew anyone who got AIDS through normal heterosexual relations. None of the therapists we interviewed could cite one case that they could authenticate as heterosexual AIDS. This was despite the fact that most have large numbers of single patients, many of whom continue to have frequent and, in many instances, indiscriminate sexual relationships where condoms are not used. The documented cases, as authentic as they may appear to be, are relatively rare. We need to know more about this.

Coping With the Experts

Adding to the confusion is the debate among the experts. At one extreme are those like Masters and Johnson who suggest that

AIDS poses a great threat to heterosexual relations and that it can be transmitted through such common practices as kissing (although they present no evidence to support this). At the other end of the spectrum is psychiatrist Dr. Robert Gould, who holds, as we've seen, that transmission of AIDS through vaginal or oral sex is highly improbable and at best extremely rare.

Most experts, however, believe it is better to err on the side of safety in this situation. One popular view is that researchers who qualify the dangers of heterosexual AIDS should just keep their mouths shut and tell people the worst in order to scare them into taking the most extreme precautions. But aside from confusing and frightening the public, this tactic has little to show for itself in the way of getting people to actually change their behavior. As it has been pointed out, even those who profess to using condoms more now do not do so consistently.

The lesson here is that the public is not näive. There are continuing scare stories about actual or impending epidemics of AIDS among heterosexuals who are not I.V. drug users. This is not to say that an epidemic will not occur in the future. But for now, most people have no evidence of this in their personal experience. It's like hearing a report that "all the food is poisoned with chemicals and additives." It's difficult to integrate such sweeping and far-reaching statements into our everyday experience. Many people simply ignore them lest they become paralyzed and unable to act rationally at all. Similarly, most people say that they worry about heterosexual AIDS, but don't take serious or consistent action.

By presenting these positive and negative arguments and as much information on the gray, unclear areas as possible, we hope to give you a way to assess where the real, documented dangers are. When the real dangers are isolated and concentrated on, people can see their authenticity and begin formulating real responses to them.

Would the great Don Juan have anything like 1,003 affairs in Spain today? That's hard to say. He scorned all the threats of his own day, and he might very well give short shrift to ones of our time. One wonders what the Don or any of his conquests could really have gotten out of his sexual marathon. Treating intercourse as a form of gymnastics is not so much of a turn-on today—and it's not only the threat of AIDS that prompted the change. We are not about to give up the search for sexual fulfillment—no plague is likely to make us do that—but by the same token we may be losing our taste for finding that fulfillment in a pell-mell dash to any bedroom door.

Chapter Eight

THERAPISTS VIEW AFFAIRS

66**I**just found out my husband is having an affair. I'm devastated,'' Jennifer blurted out to the therapist even before he was able to complete his first question about why she was seeking therapy.

Bob came to therapy in a high state of anxiety. He thought he was involved only in a parallel play affair with an attractive and sexually exciting lawyer who worked in his office. Over the last year, however, he found things getting more serious. His mistress, Kendra, was pressuring him to leave his wife and two children and marry her before her biological clock passed the eleventh hour. Bob didn't want to disrupt his family life, although he felt he loved Kendra more than his wife. He just wished the whole problem would go away, so he could return to his cozy, uncomplicated parallel play.

These situations are not unlike many in which an affair drives someone to counseling or therapy. But how will the therapist view the affair? Not all therapists are alike. It is commonplace to select a therapist based on his or her theoretical persuasion and school of psychology—psychoanalysis, gestalt, self-psychology, behavioral, or cognitive, among others. Yet therapists, regardless of the overall theory to which they subscribe, differ on the issue of affairs. Some think affairs are quite normal. Some even endorse affairs. Some believe that affairs can enhance marriages; others believe they are usually destructive. Some therapists are moralistic about affairs, while others are not.

Will the therapist even focus on the affair in therapy? Despite Jennifer's fixation on her husband's affair and Bob's heightened anxiety and need to make a decision, some therapists would want to talk about other issues going back to childhood and early relationships with parents before dealing with the affair. For example, in a strict psychoanalytic approach the affair would just be one problem among others, and there would be no effort to focus on it in any special way. On the other hand, for a behavioral therapist like Barry Lubetkin the presenting problem would be given direct attention. As Dr. Lubetkin colorfully expressed his position in cases like Bob's, "I wouldn't ask about relationships with his parents unless he was having an affair with his mother."

If you are in therapy or planning to seek help, and an affair is one of your central concerns, then you should know something about how your therapist views affairs. We interviewed six leading therapists from different schools of therapy concerning their approaches to the issue of affairs. Their responses amply illustrate the great diversity of views and treatment strategies you are likely to encounter, and the following discussion is by no means all-inclusive.

Therapists Credentials

Dr. Albert Ellis, President of the Institute for Rational-Emotive Therapy, he is the founder of RET and the grandfather of Cognitive-Behavior Therapy.

His major publications include *The Practice of Rational-Emotive Therapy,* (New York: Springer Pub.), 1977, *A New Guide to Rational Living,* (New Jersey: Wehman Bros.) and *How to Stubbornly Refuse To Make Yourself Miserable About Anything—Yes, Anything* (New Jersey: Lyle Stuart), 1988.

Dr. Gerald Epstein, Psychiatrist, is on the staff of Mt. Sinai

Medical Center, New York City, where he is an Assistant Clinical Professor.

His major publications include *Healing Visualizations: Creating Health Through Imagery* (New York: Bantam Books), 1989; *Waking Dream Therapy: Dream Process as Imagination* (New York: Human Sciences Press), 1981; *Studies in Non-Deterministic Psychology* (New York: Human Sciences Press), 1980.

Dr. Shirley Zussman is a sex and marital therapist in private practice. She is past president of the American Association of Sex Educators, Counselors and Therapists (AASECT) and currently Co-Director of the Association for Male Sexual Dysfunction. Dr. Zussman writes a column on Sex and Health for Glamour Magazine.

Dr. Barry Lubetkin is Founder and Clinical Director— Institute for Behavior Therapy (NYC); President, American Board of Behavioral Psychology; Clinical Supervisor, Hofstra University.

Publications: *Bailing Out—What To Do When Your Relationship Is Over* with Elena Oumano, Ph.D. (New Jersey: Prentice-Hall), (In Press).

Dr. Marjorie Taggart White is Founder and Director of the Seminar in Self Psychology for Practicing Psychotherapists (1971-current); Advisory Board Faculty and Fellow of the American Institute for Psychotherapy and Psychoanalysis (AIPP); Publications: *The Theory and Practice of Self Psychology* with Marcella Bakur Weiner (New York: Brunner/Mazel, Inc.), 1986; *Self Constancy: The Elusive Concept,* Lax, R. F., Back S., Burland, J. A. Eds.; *Self and Object Constancy* (New York: Guilford Press), 1986.

Dr. Seymour Coopersmith is past President of the National Psychological Association for Psychoanalysis (NPAP), Past President of the Council of Psychoanalytic Psychotherapists. Publications: Object-Instinctual and Development Aspects of Perversion, *Psychoanalytic Review,* Vol. 68, #3, 1981; The Terminating Patient in *The Psychotherapy Patient* (New York: The Haworth Press), 1984.

How Prevalent Are Affairs?

First, we were curious about the incidence of affairs among the patients of the therapists we interviewed. The literature reports a high incidence among married people, usually more men than women. Although Shere Hite recently found that 70% of the married women she interviewed had affairs, our therapists surprisingly indicated quite a range among their patients. Jerry Epstein, who takes a strong and hard stand on affairs, reports that almost all of his patients have affairs. Seymour Coopersmith finds affairs to be common among his patients. His single patients do not consider the marital status of prospective partners important. The critical factor is whether they want to be with the other person. Albert Ellis, who has written entensively on sexuality and even wrote a guide to having an affair, finds affairs not that frequent among his patients. Others find a moderate incidence of affairs among their patients. Dr. Ellis said: "I'd say less than 25% easily of the married people I see are having an affair, including most who are having a poor marriage. On the other hand, I hear many instances of past affairs. So I hear a lot about affairs."

Dr. Lubetkin saw it this way: "Well, probably a lot less common than Hite reported recently. I would say maybe one out of every three couples, or three people that I have interviewed, have admitted to having an affair. But I always ask as part of my individual intake evaluation, "Have you had an affair?" This may be information they are unwilling to share in front of the spouse but it would be very important for me to know in order to determine the direction that I want to go in therapy."

Normal Behavior or Pathological Behavior?

Do therapists regard affairs as reflecting emotional conflicts and pathology, or do they view them as normal parts of living? Back in the 1950s, therapists generally took a negative view of affairs and tended to see them as pathology (any deviation from a normal condition). The therapists we interviewed generally did not share this view. Although they recognized instances in which an affair, like any other behavior, could be tied to an emotional problem, they did not see most affairs per se as pathological.

Lubetkin summed up this view: "I don't think that an affair in and of itself defines a neurotic problem." He went on to add that affairs could also be positive. "In fact, sometimes I think that having an affair is a sign of strength and solid mental health, particularly if one is responding to a difficult situation in the married relationship that one feels it is impossible to solve at the particular time." Lubetkin went on to acknowledge that affairs may indeed reflect deep-rooted problems, but he stated that for the last few years that destructive type of affair is in the distinct minority. Generally, the people he sees "are having affairs from a positive point of view."

According to Ellis, some people do have affairs for neurotic or disturbed reasons, but he sees many affairs that are not. "People just get very attracted to or fall in love with others after they are married, and they either have the permission of their mates to have an affair, which is not that common, or they are pretty sure that the affair will not disrupt their married relationship. In certain cases, some people don't care any longer for their marital relationships, but they stay married technically because of the children, finances, or some other reasons. Very frequently, people have affairs for non-neurotic reasons."

White, looking on the positive side, sees many situations in which an affair performs a useful safety valve role that can actually help preserve a basically good marriage. "Maybe I'm a little too liberal here, but let's say that a couple has been having a long-standing sexual problem, for instance, the man for some reason is not very interested in sex. Maybe it would be a better idea if she finds a man she is very attracted to and gives herself a chance to fulfill this need rather than, as many do, turn angry, leave the husband and get a divorce, and then find herself winding up all alone." Rather than putting labels on people, Dr. White prefers to look at the whole picture, "I'm particularly

interested in the quality of the person's self experience and how
he or she feels about him or herself as a total person.''

Similarly, Zussman also prefers to concentrate on the individual situation, feeling it unwise to make generalized judgments. ''There are many reasons why people have affairs. You
have first to understand why they are having the affair. Affairs
can have very different kinds of meaning. Some are one-night
stands or instances where a chance meeting, say on a plane,
results in a one-time affair. Thus, just using the generic term
'affairs,' I could not say if they are neurotic or not.''

For Coopersmith, if affairs were part of a pattern or ongoing
lifestyle of an individual, he would see them as part of the
personality or characterological makeup: ''It would be looked at
as symptomology of the underlying conflict.''

Epstein, coming from a more spiritual and religious orien-
tation, was more definite about affairs representing a central
conflict that needs to be resolved. Although he is not insistent
upon labeling an affair as *ipso facto* pathological, he views it as
ultimately destructive to the individual and the family. ''I see an
extramarital affair primarily as an extraordinarily negative influence in a family staying together and in keeping a family in trust
and mutual respect for each other.'' Not surprisingly, Epstein
focuses attention on the affair in his therapeutic work with
patients. In line with his ethical, open, and direct approach to
patients, he presents his view in the first few therapeutic sessions. He tells them that their general mental balance requires a
resolution to the affair—not necessarily to break it up but to
work to a decision about whether to go with the marriage or the
affair.

The other therapists were more inclined to focus on the
affair in therapy only if the patient brought it up as a central
problem. But there still were differences, especially in the methods of relating to an affair in therapy when it did become an
issue.

At the other end of the spectrum are the more directional
therapists like Zussman. She would ''very definitely'' encourage
a patient to talk about an affair. ''I think it needs a lot of

attention. I think that even though the person may put it in a little compartment some place in his or her life and try to keep it separated, compartmentalized, it doesn't always work. It spills over into the other issues and other experiences with a mate— and I think often because of its very secret nature, very frequently the patient needs an opportunity to talk about it and to deal with it and to decide what he or she wants to do about it.''

Most therapists, then, except for those holding particularly conservative or openly religious or spiritual viewpoints, do not regard having an affair as, in itself, especially pathological. In some cases, it may indeed indicate a deep-seated problem that needs attention; in other cases, it can signify a positive, activist approach to coping with an otherwise impossible situation. To therapists, the importance of an affair is often determined by you, the patient. If the affair is of overriding concern to you, most therapists will treat it in conjunction with therapy as a whole—according it no more concern than any other problem you may be seeking to overcome.

Therapists with a strong directional bent, however, may want to concentrate on a patient's affair, feeling that it is of immediate concern for the day-to-day behavior of the patient, coloring as it does the whole of the patient's relationships with his/her spouse and family.

Thus, if you are looking for therapy or counselling because you are involved in an affair, you should first try to assess how important the affair is to you. If you need help in coping with it right away, you may want to look towards a directionally-oriented therapist. On the other hand, if you feel that your affair(s) are not central to, but rather symptomatic of, why you want help, you may be inclined to opt for a more psychoanalytic method of therapy—one that will consider the affair as only one among a pattern of behavioral responses and will then devote its attention to investigating this pattern.

When Do Affairs Hurt? When Do They Help?

We were especially interested in our therapists' views on when affairs have positive effects and when they have detrimental ones. We felt that this could help guide those who are genuinely interested in assessing their own affairs. Some of the therapists were quick to endorse the possible positive benefits of an affair. Frequently, sexual incompatibility in marriage is the reason given.

Ellis said: "No question, it can (have positive effects). For example, take a case where the husband and wife love each other, like each other, and get along well together but are rarely sexually compatible . . . they haven't had sex for years or there is very little sex right now. One of the reasons why they are able to stay married without too much hassle is that they are quietly, or with the tacit consent of the other, having affairs on the side." Dr. White goes further in stressing the needs of the individual in a relationship. "Well, I'm thinking of a type of man who may need the reassurance of being able to attract a number of different women. . . . Typically these men have been very unloved by their mothers. . . . Well, it's compulsive, but people are stuck with their compulsions until they are able to get rid of them. . . . I would see it as a working solution—perhaps it's the only way he can let himself stay in a ongoing relationship if he has an alternative woman."

Lubetkin gives the example of a man "who never would have considered having an affair until his wife developed a debilitating illness. He then found himself driven to develop a liaison with somebody else who gave him warmth, physical contact, and the sex that he longed for but which his wife was unable to provide. As a consequence of getting the nurturing from the affair I think that he became a much better care-giver to his wife."

Zussman sees a positive benefit from an affair primarily when it forces an examination of the marriage. She even holds that affairs are sometimes undertaken with the desire to be caught so that a confrontation can take place. "I think then it sometimes can have a positive effect in that it becomes something that the two of them need to confront and look at and examine and understand, and sometimes from that comes better communication and a decision to work at the marriage. . . ." In this regard, even though Epstein is opposed to affairs for solving problems, he has seen on occasion a positive benefit of an affair in getting a married couple to face their problems. He insists, however, that this positive benefit can only occur at the beginning of the affair: "maybe six months—after that it's chronic." If the affair goes on it will, in his opinion, have only detrimental affects on the individual and family.

In citing the negative effects of affairs, all the therapists described instances in which an affair inflicted pain of various sorts: the pain of the marriage breaking up because of a discovered affair, an infatuation that took an affair beyond parallel play, the use of an affair to avoid dealing with problems in the marriage, and the use of an affair to express anger at the mate.

For Zussman the most detrimental effect of an affair lies in its erosion of trust in the marital relationship. Sometimes the damage can't be repaired. "It can be very destructive in some instances where the partner who has been deceived can't deal with it. . . ."

Dr. White added: "Well, unfortunately, both men and women who have had very unhappy childhoods may have a kind of vengeful attitude toward their mates, particularly if there are money difficulties, differences in how to bring up the children, or other problems. Here you get a kind of civil war going on. One or both partners may take a great deal of satisfaction in flirting openly at a party or actually having an affair. This kind of vengeance gives them a certain kind of excitement to life, a certain kind of power."

For Dr. Lubetkin, it was the irretrievable nature of the situation that was mostly damaging: "I am thinking of one woman who was married to a fellow who was very giving, warm, and loving. She began to have an affair to fulfill some needs that she felt were not being fulfilled in the relationship. It turned out that the needs were for a more take-charge, narcissistic, mysterious type of man, a type she finds erotically pleasing and which her husband simply can't play. The husband found out about the affair and now, of course, wants out. She feels a tremendous amount of regret. As a consequence of having the destructive affair, she has now become more willing to deal with where it comes from and so on, but the damage is already done."

Dr. Epstein saw an affair as damaging to the whole family. "I remember one man who was carrying out an affair . . . but meanwhile he had a wife and two children who were suffering enormously at home because of his absences and his change of behavior—he acted in unusual ways at home. . . . He was getting into arguments with his wife more readily, and he wasn't able to give the proper attention to his children because he wouldn't be home when they were going to sleep, and other things. So the whole family ultimately had to go into treatment because they were suffering so much. In the long run, I think everyone in an affair is eventually going to suffer." Coopersmith also sees the greatest potential for destructiveness in an affair in its effect on the family: "Marriage is such an interwoven process that when one person has an affair it's likely to be far-reaching in terms of children. Of course, it depends on the family's reaction to the affair. It generally does have an impact on children but it also depends on whether it brings rancor into the home—arguments and fights. If the husband and wife are not intimately involved and one or the other was having an affair, it might be handled much more casually—it wouldn't make that much difference to the children."

Should Therapists Ever Recommend or End Affairs?

Because most therapists, to varying degrees, acknowledge that affairs can have positive value, we wondered if they ever encouraged patients to have an affair. Dr. Epstein definitely ruled this out. Dr. Coopersmith felt that encouraging an affair would be inconsistent with the role of the psychoanalyst. While this was not common practice for the others, they could think of situations in which they would suggest the possibility of an affair.

Dr. Ellis said: "Only rarely. If for example, one of them is not into sex . . . and this lack threatens to break up the marriage, which the frustrated partner doesn't want to do . . . I might explore the advantages of having an affair. It might in some instances save the marriage.''

Dr. White saw another possibility: ''Well, I think in tragic situations, let's say where a mate cannot have sex any longer maybe because of a disease or an accident, where there is a lot of tenderness in connection with the caring, then I think I probably would recommend an affair. I think it would be a question of how the person might feel about letting the ill partner know. But I think that it might make the relationship much less hard, much less depriving for the partner who still needs and wants sex.'' Dr. White also cited relationships in which there was little sexual activity, with one partner feeling very deprived. However, she would primarily encourage the patient to try first to change the situation in the marriage.

For Dr. Lubetkin, encouraging an affair may be a way of helping a patient out of a bad marriage. ''There have been times when it was clear that a person was extremely dissatisfied with the relationship and yet he or she was not emotionally capable of getting out and was feeling increasingly trapped and conflicted. For individuals like that, I have on occasion encouraged them to explore the possibility of developing a liaison with someone else. Suggesting an affair is a way the therapist can help provide a bridge—to help such people find someone who will be there for them when they leave the marriage. It may be just a temporary bridge but one that they need in order to act.''

The other side of the coin asks the question whether or not therapists should ever tell their patients to end an affair, and, if so, under what circumstances? Dr. Epstein believes that all affairs should be terminated or the marriage ended if the person is to achieve stability in his or her life. Others are more reluctant to actively encourage the termination of an affair if it is filling a need of the patient, even if that need is somewhat pathological. Dr. White is particularly sensitive about masochistic affairs and will discourage them. ''This is very self-abusive and masochistic, and it's too high a price to pay for revenge.''

Others, too, would discourage neurotic and self-destructive affairs. Dr. Lubetkin gives an example: ''Like a woman who needs mysterious, emotionally distant, very narcissistic, somewhat sadistic type men to turn her on. Even though it is erotically satisfying, it is not going to be ultimately emotionally satisfying because this type of man will leave and drop her and she will be devastated.''

Dr. Ellis, too, would discourage neurotically motivated affairs that will ultimately create difficulties which far outweigh the gratifications they are designed to provide. Such neurotic behavior, according to Ellis, stems from one or another of three main *musts*. "One: *I* must do well and be approved by significant others. So even after such people are married they feel that they have to do well, that they have to be loved etc., and they need affairs to achieve this. Two: *You* must do well by me. You must be kind and considerate to be my mate. Such people then can have affairs out of hostility to the mate who falls short. Finally, three: *Life* must give me everything I want just because I want it with no great barriers to overcome. Even though these people may be jeopardizing their marriages, they feel they have a right to extra sex and love on the side.''

In short, having an affair was not a recommended method for dealing with marital or personal problems as far as our therapists were concerned. In extreme cases, it might be considered, but as a therapeutic strategy it involves too great a potential for pain and too great a chance to avoid the real work of self-discovery on the part of the patient.

Likewise, actively seeking to end a patient's affair is a rare practice among these therapists. Most agreed that therapists should move to end an affair only when it is clearly destructive or inimical to the patient.

When The Affair Becomes Known—What Then?

In Chapter 6, we talked about the pitfalls and benefits of breaking up a marriage and turning an affair into a new marriage. We, therefore, were curious about the experiences of our therapists in situations that went beyond parallel play.

First, we wanted to know about the frequency of affairs

breaking up a marriage. The therapists unanimously agreed that affairs do not usually lead to the break-up of a marriage, even when they are discovered by the mate. Ellis' comment typifies this observation: "Over the years I have known scores and scores of affairs that didn't break up the marriage. And a lot of those I have known, for example, involve the male who is married and has children in the suburbs and is having an affair with a woman, sometimes his secretary, in the city. Now he does not normally leave his wife for this relationship." Lubetkin concurs: "On at least a couple of dozen occasions throughout my career I have had couples admit to each other in joint therapy that they were having an affair. That was the appropriate thing to do—marital therapy would not move on effectively unless such an admission was made. Very, very few times, however, have I seen the marriage dissolve in these circumstances."

While Zussman has cases in which an affair has led to the break up of a marriage, she says that is not typical. When marriages break up, they do so for other reasons, and the affair is just the symptom of the underlying problems. More commonly she cites the punitive use of the affair, especially after it has ended. "I have seen more of a kind of ongoing punitive attitude about the affair—the deceived partners stay in the marriage but somehow always bring the affair up or refer to it." Zussman also reminds us that an affair does not always upset the other spouse. "You know there are many affairs that suit the other person. We sort of accept the idea that the partner is going to be upset by it. I find that where one partner—a man, say—has a considerable problem with lack of desire and there is a lot of pressure on him to be more sexual, he might say, 'Look I can't deal with this.' Then, to be satisfied, the wife might go out and find someone else, almost with his permission. I have a case now where it's not an affair but a series of affairs, and the marriage still has many positive features. They are both interested in the children and in maintaining family life and there's considerable amount of sexual avoidance between them, but apparently the faithful partner is able to accept that because he has a lot of difficulty in dealing with his own sexuality in the relationship and is, therefore, willing to tolerate the affairs as one solution. Although at considerable cost to his self esteem they are both motivated to work this out.''

According to Coopersmith, there is very often conscious or unconscious approval or encouragement of an affair. He has many cases to support this view. Consequently he feels that an affair is serving a purpose in the relationship and, therefore, not likely to break up the marriage.

With respect to this question of the impact of an affair on a marriage, we would like to cite some figures from a study by Dr. Frederick Humphrey, a Marriage and Family therapist and a professor at the University of Connecticut. Dr. Humphrey recently surveyed 179 Marriage and Family therapists on their last case involving an extramarital affair. In 87 instances the husband was having the affair, in 64 cases the wife was having the affair, and in 28 cases both spouses were having an affair.

Shock was the greatest first response for women (45%) learning about their husbands' affairs and less so for husbands (19%) learning about their wives' affairs. Anger was the greatest as an initial response for men (38%) although 35% of the wives also responded initially with anger. However, despite what is portrayed in the media of men and women packing their bags right after learning about a spouse's affair, very few did so according to this survey—1.7% of wives and 3.8% of husbands. Although these are relatively small percentages, nevertheless there were twice as many men as woman who left—a point of interest for risky business.

How did spouses find out about an affair? Most affairs were revealed through direct disclosures—46% told their spouses. But 26% of the husbands' affairs and 23% of the wives' affairs were revealed through clues. Another 11% of the husbands' and 17.5% of the wives' affairs were revealed through suspicions (no doubt related to risky business). Very seldom were affairs revealed through friends (4%) or the extramarital partner. But, of course, for those whose affairs are revealed in this manner the consequences and pain may not be so small.

The Long-Term Secret Affair—Possible? Desirable?

Indeed, some people have argued that the spouse always knows, and when it is not obvious it is denial or what is sometimes called "selective inattention." Sometimes a knowing spouse will not reveal his or her knowledge for fear of breaking up the marriage or inability to confront or deal with sensitive issues.

However, many of our therapists believe that an affair can be secret. They acknowledge that often they are getting their information from one of the partners, so they can't be 100% sure that the spouse didn't know. But some have had the opportunity to meet with husband and wife and, in some cases, have noted that an affair was secret, even affairs that went on for many years.

Dr. Ellis relates: "Well, I'll tell you a very interesting case which I have cited to a good many people. This man and woman were having an affair with each other. They were both married to other people and the four of them got together every Sunday to play bridge for two or three hours—they were very friendly. Then one of the husbands and one of the wives took an apartment in Manhattan (they lived in the suburbs). They got together in the apartment twice a week for ten years and the other two never found out about it. They finally decided that their children were old enough (the couple were 30 when they started and now were 40) and they told the other two and went off and moved to another state and got married. It was shocking to the other two but presumably for ten years they didn't know about it. So it's possible. But that's a rare case."

Zussman cites cases of lengthy affairs—in one case, ten years—that were secret. For her, the problem of secrecy is often the dilemma the therapist faces when she is doing couple therapy and knows that one party is having an affair. While Zussman may encourage the person in the affair to reveal it openly, "not everybody is going to do that or want to do that and then where do you go with that?" Now not only is the affair secret in the marriage, but the therapist has a secret as well. Some therapists, she reports, will not continue the therapy unless the affair is revealed to the spouse. While Zussman is struggling with this moral dilemma, she is not sure that terminating therapy is the answer.

Escalating An Affair Into Marriage: Bliss or Disaster?

Nevertheless, affairs do often come to light. And sometimes the partners in the affair decide to escalate the relationship into marriage. As we've already mentioned in earlier chapters, some authorities say that people tend to make the same mistakes over and over again. According to this view there is a tendency to make the same unhappy choices with the second or even the third mate as with the first. When an affair turns into a marriage, then, are these relationships the same, better, or worse than the previous marriage? Surprisingly, all our therapists disagreed with the popular notion that the same mistakes are repeated (Freud called this the "repetition compulsion"). In fact, our therapists almost uniformly felt that in their experience when the affair became a marriage, the new relationship worked out very positively.

Perhaps the fact that the people involved here had had the benefit of a therapist's support and guidance had led more frequently to constructive decisions. In other words, those who decided to go with the affair did so for sound reasons. Lubetkin's comments characterize this view: "I'm impressed with how they do work out. I think people find in a second relationship something that they really need, that they didn't even know to look for in a first relationship. My point is that people mature, people's needs change over time, and frequently a new person can fulfill that."

Ellis supported this view as well. "There's no question that many do (learn and profit from relationships and make better decisions).

White resonates a similar view. "Oh yes, I'm convinced that the new person offered my patient a lot of what he or she wanted and wasn't getting from the other relationship." Zussman agreed: "We also know that sometimes the second relationship is better. I'm not one to always see a repetition of neurotic conflicts.''

Escalated affairs would seem to have a generally good prognosis, according to our group of therapists. The question, though, is whether the partner going into the new marriage has learned from the affair and broken marriage. It would seem natural, as suggested here, that people in an affair who decide to go into therapy *would* be the ones who would examine their behavior and learn from their experiences. The repetition compulsion ones are generally not the ones who seek help; they don't, by and large, know they're in a repetitive pattern and need help to break out.

Is Continued Parallel Play a Viable Option? Is Monogamy?

Can an affair be a legitimate ongoing lifestyle? Do our therapists think that in the life of an affair a decision needs to be made for ending it and staying in the marriage, or vice versa? While our therapists recognize that life long affairs exist, they generally do not see those as desirable lifestyles.

First, Zussman feels that if the marriage is just being tolerated, affairs will ultimately not be the answer and a long-term affair generally runs into trouble because eventually one or the other wants more or less.

On the other hand, Coopersmith feels that for some people the long-term affair is the only kind of relationship that can work. He cites a 25-year affair in which a man lives with his wife who he does not want to leave. At the same time, he can't wait to see his mistress. They don't want to resolve the conflict: the resolution makes them too anxious. They want to split their sexuality, their ego structure and their sense of themselves because it gives them a greater sense of security.

Ellis also feels that some long-term affairs can work. He mentions different possibilities: ''Sometimes one who is deprived of a mate would just as soon really live without a mate— see somebody twice a week and have a relationship rather than a marriage. If nobody is getting into trouble of any kind, and everything is going well, then they would have much less reason to do anything about it than if it is resulting in serious difficulty.''

He cites one long-term relationship that he feels worked out reasonably well: "A woman who was widowed started having an affair with her dentist; for ten years or so nothing happened—he was married but he was not inclined to move away from his family. He finally retired and that ended the affair and nobody ever found out about it. . . . Certainly, in some sense, it helped the widow. Now, maybe it didn't in a different sense, in that she didn't go out and get her own man. Some people settle for less. But *she* thought it helped her, and the man had an extra affair on the side and got along with his wife and children, so that's one where nothing happened. But I'm not saying that's typical. Nobody really knows what's typical. Yes, I can cite this one, but we don't know about lots where pretty dreadful things happened as a result."

Lubetkin reminds us of the difficulties and the toll of conducting a long-term affair: "First let me say that I believe it always has costs—emotional costs. It doesn't come free. Human beings are not built to be that deceptive for that long a period of time. I think it is an exhausting effort to keep that information away from a spouse. . . . I think the people who are planning on having that kind of long-term affair need to be prepared for long-term consequences—depression, anxieties, what have you."

This led to a discussion on views about monogamy. We asked our therapists how they felt about monogamy or, put another way, we asked them whether they thought it was possible for one person to fill all of the emotional and physical needs of another person.

Lubetkin was the most explicit in questioning the validity of one relationship over a lifetime. While he believes in monogamy, he gives it a new twist. "What I am saying is that I believe that ultimately it makes more sense for human beings to move into new monogamous relationships as their needs change. Though what I believe might be better for the human race certainly might not be appropriate for most people. Serial monogamous relationships would disrupt families, and so on."

Ellis sees people caught in a bind. They want monogamy (one at a time) but they also want variety. Societies that allow this, he observes, generally are chauvinistic and allow it only for men.

For White, the modern way of life almost demands multiple relationships—people on the go for professional reasons and the increased exposure to sexually stimulating circumstances. Moreover, she doesn't feel it is possible, except in rare circumstances, for two people to satisfy all of each other's needs. She points out that we accept multiple relationships in famous people: "Well if Sartre and De Beauvoir can do it, why can't everybody?"

For Epstein it is not so much that monogamy is sacred, but rather that it is the system that is accepted in our society and, therefore, the only one that can work. For him it is the rules, structure, and supports in a society that count: "There have been cultures in the world where polygamy held sway and the cultures did very well. If the cultural drift here is toward monogamy, that is the stability and organization of the family system as we understand it here, and to keep it intact you have to have a monogamous system. . . . If there is a polygamous culture in which you are permitted to have many wives then there are rules established that allow these wives to live together, to know each other, and to join in having a shared communal relationship with the man." Coopersmith de-emphasizes the personal views of the therapist. "Whose morality are we talking about? The moral issue is basically the breaking of the contract." He sees the role of the analyst as understanding the patient and the meaning of the patients behavior. To accomplish this the analyst must transcend personal judgments and accept the patient. To this he adds a very human note: "As I've gotten older, I've gotten more tolerant."

The Crucial Factor: Is It Sex or Something Else?

How important is sex in an affair? Is it the most important and driving force behind the affair or are other things, such as

communication and intimacy, as important or, in some instances, more important? Do these factors differ for men and
women? We pushed the discussion even further by asking if a
non-sexual relationship can even be called an affair. For Coopersmith, an affair by its very definition is sexual. But Coopersmith introduces a new twist to affairs by placing the fantasy
affair on a par with an actual affair. "The partner who is not
having an affair but is fantasizing about an affair presents
interesting issues for treatment that are sometimes very similar
to an affair. A woman may say that she doesn't want to be with
her husband sexually and when he confronts her and says 'Is
there another man?,' she says 'no.' But when you talk to her the
answer is 'yes,' there is someone about whom she dreams,
fantasizes and eroticizes about all the time. When that happens
it creates very similar problems. . . ."

Ellis held that there were all kinds of affairs. Although most
of them begin for sexual reasons, other things can come to play
a more important role. He gives one vivid example. "They both
were attracted to each other emotionally and sexually when they
began, but after a while they were having very little sex, just as
many marriages involve very little sex. But they like to go out
with each other. You see, I have one woman right now who is a
widow about 60 and she finds great difficulty getting a man that
she wants. She is still looking for one but in the meantime she
has this married lover. This married lover, as far as we know, is
asexual—he just takes her out, and she likes that. She would
rather have him as a real lover . . . but she enjoys companion-
ship. Yes, she has had it (sex) with him a couple of times, but
very rarely."

White feels that sex is extremely important in a relationship. When good sex is missing, she feels that there is nothing
that can really compensate. Then an affair or a number of affairs
becomes likely. But then, she adds, there are other kinds of
affairs. "There are people, very different people, often creative
people who are much more interested in sharing feelings, emotions, interesting music, art, literature and so on with another

person and for whom sex is secondary. In this case, it would be possible to have this kind of relationship without any sex."

Lubetkin observes that sex is the crucial factor in the affair: "Sex makes it special, it provides the out from whatever pain they are experiencing." While communication is important, Lubetkin reminds us that affairs do not have a lock on good communication. "There are affairs where there is very poor communication, you know, and it's purely a sexual response. There are affairs where they both don't talk very much at all and don't really share very much at all."

For Epstein, sex is always the crucial factor. If intimacy or communication are the main motives, he feels those things can be had without having a sexual relationship.

Zussman sees sex as an important motivating force for some people, but she sees other motives as well: ". . . the sex could really be exciting and a kind of letting go which one does not allow oneself to do in an ongoing relationship or where all other factors of life and its daily problems affect the way in which one enters into the sexual relationship."

Other motives she cites are proving oneself, recapturing youth and vigor, and warding off depression—this is much more common than is recognized; then there is the narcissistic person who needs constant reassurance that stops coming from the partner.

While all our therapists acknowledge the important of sex in an affair, on reflection most of them feel that it is generally more important for men than women. But there are exceptions.

Lubetkin says: "Men and women usually both talk about the need to feel understood more, and the affair seems to fulfill that, but I think for men it seems to be a more sexual experience than for women. I know many women who can have an affair with a man and really go for weeks and weeks without sleeping with that person and still feel very satisfied in the affair relationship. That is not the case with most men that I have seen."

White reminds us of the power motive of many men: "Well, I think the image of the desirable, active man who is irresistible to many women, dies hard. Maybe in a sense it gives them a feeling of some power in a relationship."

Ellis said: "For the vast majority of women, just as in marriage, the woman has the affair for emotional reasons, because she loves the man and not because she is attracted to him. She is attracted to him physically and, therefore, loves him, but not because she is interested in sex. . . . Married women rarely go out and just have affairs for sex even if they are unsatisfied at home. They look for a man they can love, while men frequently have affairs for sex. Coopersmith concurs. He notes the vast social changes that have taken place in recent decades. Whereas previously affairs were more the male province, now "women will have affairs if they so choose." However, he does see a pattern of difference between men and women: "When women have an affair it is generally because they are dissatisfied with their current relationship, whereas men will more often do it just for sex."

Zussman questions some of the stereotype: "I think it is inaccurate to say that all that men want from affairs is sex. Many men just want to talk and have someone who just listens to them. . . . I see men very often who talk about what they get from the outside relationship—a kind of separate space, a situation where, at least for a time, there is no measure, no demand.

"I think women want the sexual part of it more often than is recognized. I mean that women are often dissatisfied with their sexual partners, and they enjoy the excitement and the variety, and the feeling of being desired. Men are perceived as having affairs for sexual dissatisfaction—because the wife is not sexually responsive or, as Martha Stein said in her book, that wives will not engage in certain activities like oral sex and a lot of other things. But that's changing because women are much more involved, much freer to be involved in those things than they used to be. . . .

"Then some women only want a space where the man just admires them. I was thinking about a patient I had who was having an affair. She said that one of her problems in growing up was that she never felt special. That's the feeling she gets in an affair—being very special, that work doesn't exist for him (the lover) during the time that he is seeing her. It was this kind of satisfaction of the need to be special which had never been fulfilled, and I think that probably operates for a lot of people, especially in the initial phases of an affair.

The Seven-Year Itch: Are There Dangerous Times?

In light of these opinions on what was most important in an affair, we wondered when affairs were more likely to occur. Do they tend to occur after a certain number of years of marriage or at any particular age? Are there particular crises that tend to spark affairs? In other words, are there sensitive periods for affairs to occur?

Zussman finds no special pattern: "I've seen them in middle-aged women whom I would never expect to see having an affair, and also soon after marriage."

Lubetkin echoes this view: "I've seen affairs at all points. I've seen them before the marriage begins, and they continue right into the marriage, where the lover is invited to the wedding. I've also seen them start after 30 years of loyalty."

White, on the other hand, sees many sensitive periods for affairs and cites two of them: ". . . in the early years of raising children the woman may be really overwhelmed with the whole child-raising situation. Particularly these days, when the woman works, too, and still has to arrange for care to be taken of the children, the home, and so on, she may find that there's not much time or energy left to devote to the husband.

Then there can also be a time when the children are grown up and maybe the woman is still in her early 40s and would like to try a career and her husband might be at the point where he is well established and would like to play more. Here again there might be a divergence of interests and goals and, at that point, he might find a girlfriend feeling that, well it doesn't look as though what I had hoped would be a time for getting closer is going to eventuate, so I'll look around for myself."

Ellis find affairs less common in the first few years of

marriage: ". . . in my experience the people who start the affair have been married for several years and, therefore, familiarity has set in and lack of sex excitement, so they more easily get attached to somebody else."

How Has AIDS Changed Attitudes on Affairs?

We asked our therapists about the newest and most threatening issue in affairs—AIDS. First, we asked them how the AIDS crisis had affected the sexual behavior of their patients in general, both married and single. Then we wanted to know how AIDS has affected affairs and thinking about affairs. All agreed that AIDS was an issue that their patients thought about, talked about, and worried about. But they differed in the degree to which they thought their patients took serious precautions and actions.

Ellis finds a dramatic change in his patients, especially the married and gay ones. "Some of them are completely abstinent, some are completely monogamous, which they wouldn't prefer . . . but . . . they have a partner who they know doesn't have AIDS so they stick to that partner. The single people, too, are much less prone to go off and get into bed quickly—and are having fewer premarital affairs than before. And the married people are also more cautious."

Ellis advises his clients to find out about their partner's sexual histories over the last 10 years. He recommends "dry sex" before they know each other and urges them to have an AIDS test before they go ahead with "unsafe sexual intercourse and other sex practices."

Coopersmith observes that few of his patients have changed their practices despite the AIDS crisis. He does note, however, that AIDS anxiety sometimes relates to unconscious aspects of the meaning of sexuality, particularly feelings of vulnerability. He describes a strange case of a young woman who, despite her fear of AIDS, had her sexual contacts almost exclusively with bisexual men. "But what she was afraid of was the man who was vital and the man she couldn't control, because under those circumstances she felt more vulnerable and without psychological defenses. This parallels the AIDS syndrome where the biological defenses are impaired. She was trying to avoid vulnerability but was in fact closer to the AIDS potential by being with bisexual men.''

Zussman is surprised to find much less precautions being taken than she feels are warranted. Only half of her male patients use condoms. While this is a greater number than before the pre-AIDS crisis, she feels it is not enough. ''Women particularly are buying condoms, carrying them, and suggesting that men use them—that is one of the differences. But people are still going to bed early in the relationship.'' Zussman adds that married people are much more cautious about sex outside the marital relationship and much less tolerant of a partner's affair in the age of AIDS.

She observes that the younger patients—men and women— are less cautious than the older singles. ''I think there is some anxiety and concern, but it is very interesting that panic, it seems to me, has faded a little bit. . . .'' But she philosophically notes: ''What if the information doesn't do a damn bit of good. Yes, you can get to know a man, but nice guys have sex too.''

Note that this statement of Zussman's seems to contradict the Gallup Poll finding that we discussed in Chapter 7. There, you will remember, Gallup found the most concern about contracting AIDS in the 18-29 age group (27% very concerned). The ''very concerned'' drops off as age increases—30-49, 20%; 50-64, 13%; and 65 and over, 17%. Such discrepancies only point up how volatile the public's attitude towards AIDS and sex is. People's fears can alter quickly depending on the news of the day or in light of a personal encounter with the disease (e.g., someone they know tests positive for the virus).

White finds the men to be more cautious than the women, particularly with women who they know ''play around.'' For single women, she finds that their quest is still for relationships: ''it doesn't really come up as a big issue. I mean lots of single women will talk about their relationships or the lack of them and meeting men, but you find that the talk hasn't shifted that much to AIDS. My impression is that they think about it afterwards. But that may be a little too late."

Epstein finds many of his young patients starting exclusive long-term relationships as a defense against AIDS: "Long-term relationships are beginning to emerge between couples now in their 20s in which they go for months and months with each other exclusively and do not get engaged or married—they portray a feeling of loving the other person but of not being *in* love with him/her and they never take the step to cement the relationship. What it comes to is the relationship is made this way so as to have safe sex."

Lubetkin sees a reduction in relaxed casual contacts, but he sees other offshoots of the AIDS crisis as well: "It has also helped some men and women to be more open, honest and reflective about sex. It has also helped chauvinistic men to be less chauvinistic by helping them use condoms, whereas in the past they never would, leaving the responsibility for birth control protection entirely to the women."

He has also seen some negative effects. Some men and women who tend to be obsessive have now become what he considers overly obsessive in finding out the histories of their partners. "I also believe that it has provided, interestingly enough, the shy, socially reticent patient with another excuse, another justification, for not getting out there and taking social and emotional risks. . . . It is a socially acceptable way of justifying their social reticence."

Affairs: What Should the Therapist's Goal Be?

What do these therapists consider their goal when dealing with an affair in therapy? Most emphasize understanding. Ellis in particular seeks a rational basis for decision making. "My goal would be first to get rid of the neurosis and then to see what they want to do. Unless it's something very foolhardy, I don't tell people what to do or not do. If you are going to be shot for having an affair that's another thing. Also, you do risk jealousy of your mate. Once in a while you get into real trouble. If so, I would bring that out to them. But mainly my goal is to get them to have affairs for rather sensible reasons, if they are going to have them at all, and not for driven, compulsive, and disturbed reasons."

Ellis suggests a self-assessment technique to some of his patients. ". . . write down all the advantages of having an affair and weight them from 1 to 10. Then you will see. You never get a perfect answer, though, because you never know what will happen in advance."

Epstein works on clarifying for the patient what he or she wants. But he emphasizes a speedy decision. "I would point out my understanding of the difficulties engendered by having the affair. . . . Are they coming to therapy because they want to end the affair or in order to continue the affair and not feel the pain and the conflict? What do they want? The way I start my work is to always ask the person what he wants. I never ask for a history; I just ask what he wants to get from this work. He has to make a statement about that. Let's say he says he wants to reduce the pain and conflict of the affair. Then I would take up with him the connection between the two. The affair and pain and conflict go together, and then I would explain simply why they go together and why this is something he has to confront. To have an affair and not have any disturbance because of it is asking for an impossible situation."

Zussman strives to help the patient understand why he or she is in the affair, what needs the affair is meeting and whether other solutions may be better: "Among the people I deal with I sometimes find that the reason for maintaining the marriage is an economic one. They have everything they want materially, but underneath they are very unhappy and very dissatisfied and feel very empty, which is a common reason for looking for something else in one's life. That emptiness is often not satisfied by the affair, and the end of the affair only intensifies the feeling of emptiness, which is often a feeling of low self-esteem and low self-worth. Repeating the pattern just intensifies the feeling."

For Coopersmith "the whole notion of having an affair has profound implications unconsciously for the other person's wife or husband. We are often dealing with unconscious aspects of relationships that have been unresolved. These relate to early oedipal issues which reflect the attempt to be the winner over the same-sexed parent.'' Ultimately he feels that this is the area that needs to be explored.

How Should One Choose a Therapist?

Finally, in light of the fact that all of our therapists are distinguished and represent different points of view in psychotherapy and somewhat different attitudes toward affairs—in some instances some crucial differences—we wondered how they would advise someone who is in pain over an affair to seek help. What guidelines should such people use in selecting a therapist?

Most acknowledged that selecting a therapist because you are in pain over an affair poses the same problem as selecting a therapist in general. The client needs to ask questions in order to determine if the therapist will offer what he or she wants. Lubetkin summarized this view and then went on to express some more personal points, emphasizing the patient's right to know about the therapist: "I think people ought to shop around for a therapist. They ought to ask searching questions—what is your bias? Do you have any moral compunctions about affairs? It is like choosing a jury. You have to ask questions up front. Can this person be a fair and impartial observer and really help you understand what is going to be in your best interests and not reflect his or her particular bias? So I say you have to be up front, ask questions. I've had patients ask me whether I've had an affair, and I think that's an entirely appropriate question to ask. I think that the therapist has a choice as to whether to answer that. Generally I don't, but I think it is a legitimate question to ask. I think that you also have to find out how the therapist works to alleviate anxiety and depression. Is he/she going to zoom right in on a presenting problem and pinpoint it, or will the therapist neglect it and attend to other issues—like historical issues or other psychodynamic ones—that may really be quite irrelevant to helping you get out of this quandary you are in. So I would want to know if they have dealt with this kind of thing before; have they resolved this kind of thing for other patients, and so on.''

Finally, why do people in affairs come to therapy? Most often, they come to save the marriage and to deal with psychological pain. Surprisingly, as Dr. Humphrey's survey shows, it is most often the spouse who was *not* having the affair who is most interested in saving the marriage. The one having the affair most frequently comes to therapy to deal with uncomfortable feelings. Another significant number come to explore general unhappiness, possibly resulting from a stalemated situation.

Therapy, then, serves different needs depending upon the participants. Self-awareness of those needs can be an important guide for choosing a suitable therapist with whom to explore your affair and its meaning in your particular life situation.

Chapter Nine

REJECTED PARTNERS

King Mark (with great feeling): This to me? This, Tristan, This to me? . . .
Tristan: Oh King, I cannot tell you, and what you ask must remain forever unanswered.

When an affair stands revealed, no matter how satisfying or justifiable it's been, the moment is a moment of pain—for everybody. For all the glorious love music in Wagner's *Tristan and Isolde,* the moment that breaks one's heart is when the betrayed King Mark confronts his beloved nephew Tristan and asks why. The moment is doubly poignant, Mark's incomprehension and pain and the lovers' realization that they can never explain. At the moment of truth, all the glib rationalizations that lovers use to justify their affairs along the way suddenly turn tawdry and self-serving. "How could you," is a question with many answers but none that really satisfy.

Despite the fact that both the rejected and the offending partner in a triangle situation feel hurt, their pain is not identical. The offending party more often than not feels *guilt,* a sense of not having lived up to a promise made, of having, no matter how extenuating the circumstances, done wrong. One has lied, one has deceived, one has hidden. In the cold light of day, (which Tristan and Isolde detest for good reason) all those stolen hours and exciting larks can look rather shabby.

Painful, yes; hopeless, no. Guilt comes with its own built-

177

in repair system. When one feels one has offended, one can admit the presumed fault, redress, insofar as possible, the wrong, atone for the misdeed in one way or another, and by bearing punishment (imposed or self-inflicted), work one's way to redemption and forgiveness—if not in others' eyes then at least in one's own. Guilt can be destructive, but it can also offer a path for overcoming a perceived wrong and picking up one's life to begin anew—presumably a sadder but wiser person. In short, guilt can be empowering as well as enervating, and straying parties in an affair are often able to use their guilt to regroup their lives and get on with something better. After all, it was by their own acts that they got themselves into a situation where they feel guilt, and it is by other acts that they can extricate themselves from that same situation.

The rejected partner in an affair is in a much more vulnerable and ambiguous situation. Initially, it would appear that the aggrieved partner should feel superior, even self-righteous. After all, he/she didn't do anything wrong. The rejected partner is a victim, not a perpetrator. Victims, however, do not cut very dashing figures. After shock and anger, the rejected partner is most likely to feel *shame,* a failure to live up to one's ideal of self. Rejected partners feel dismay because, just as *their* acts didn't get them into trouble, they don't see how any act of theirs can restore the self-esteem that betrayal took from them. They are hurt and they have nowhere to turn. There is vengeance, maybe, but that's more melodrama than life. Besides, it doesn't get to the root of the matter, the sense that one has been deemed unworthy. If Tristan and Isolde, caught up as they are in a tragic love affair, are celebrated in myth and music, King Mark, the one they betray, plays only a secondary role, moving, poignant, admirable even, but not central, not tragic.

Rejected Partners; Anatomy of a Bad Time

There are certain reactions that the aggrieved party goes through when the spouse's affair breaks that are fairly universal. These responses stem from the development of our emotions during infancy. By examining one case study in detail, we can track some of these responses in detail, trace them to their origins, and see in what ways they can be used to help repair the person's psychological damage.

> She was coming home late, saying that in her business it was usual—that you had to stay late to talk to buyers and sometimes to go to dinner with them. She said it was part of being in the garment business and everyone knew it. I believed her. We'd been together for three years before marriage and we'd been married for two. I thought I knew her. Then her cousin—not mine but *her* cousin—told me she was having an affair. It was a cousin I felt particularly close to; the family saw him as kind of spacey and didn't treat him right. I did, and we became close. He said he felt it was his moral duty to tell me.
>
> I was surprised, really. At first I couldn't believe it. But I guess inside I thought I was not good enough for her. I questioned what kind of man could I be not to satisfy her, either sexually or in some other way.

This is Evan, a 31-year-old man in a therapy session talking about the discovery of his wife's affair and his reactions to it. We'll listen to what he says and examine the range of emotions he went through as he tells us about them.

As Evan reported, his first emotion was surprise. What does surprise mean? Theorists Dr. Robert Plutchik and Henry Kellerman hold that surprise is a positive emotion in that it alerts you to need for change. "Surprise" first appears in early infancy—generally during the first six months. At this age, the infant is learning to respond to particular persons and objects. Surprise occurs when the infant is presented with persons or situations which are new, strange, or unfamiliar. "Surprise is a transient state, typically brought about by a sudden, unexpected event that serves the purpose of clearing away an ongoing emotion, thus readying the individual to respond to change. That is, surprise momentarily dominates consciousness. Thus, it interrupts ongoing emotion or emotion-cognition processes and, in effect, clears the channels of the nervous system for processing the information relevant to the eliciting event.''

The news that one's spouse is having an affair is almost always a surprise, even when one knows it, one doesn't know it—doesn't want to know it—and hopes maybe it will all turn out to be a bad dream. The shock—the surprise—certainly did clear Evan's nervous system in preparation for dealing with the event.

> Then the surprise settled in, and I became really angry. I was angry because I felt I had married a 'slut.' That was the only word I could think of—and also because of the great difficulties she was bringing into my life.
>
> You see, I was in dental school, which was tough, and now there was this thing with all its problems. I'd have to move out, change things around, and deal with my feelings, all at the same time. I also had to rethink the whole situation. I mean, what was really happening with her was that she was in love with her boss. The talk about her staying late with buyers was a lie; she was with him. My anger was at her not being honest. She should have been open with me then the two of us could have worked to find some solution. I don't know what, but something. This way it was just sprung on me, and I had no control over anything.

So Evan went from shock and surprise to anger. Anger is a blaming response. We are angry at some*one* or some*thing*. It is "extrapunitive," that is, directed outwards toward some target (earlier theories held that anger directed inwards defined depression, but now most theories hold that depression is usually associated with loss rather than inward-directed anger).

Anger first appears very early in infancy. Seen as necessary to the human experience, anger is regarded as a motivator. As author Robert Plutchik says: ''. . . anger attempts to deal directly with restraints and barriers, resulting in a new form of the experience of self as agent. In the anger experience, the infant can become conscious of its own distinctness from the

frustrating object, in part, through the latter's opposition."
Evan's anger served some of these same functions. Through his
anger he became aware of his own self, and he became aware
that he was capable of direct action (he told her he was leaving
and took action in that direction). He also experienced—quite
strongly—his "own distinctness from the frustrating object."

Anger can also do more. Anger ". . . stimulated by the
feeling of being physically or psychologically restrained, mobi-
lizes energy, providing a feeling of power and confidence." For
Evan, the feeling of anger was probably healthy since he was
able to get in touch with his own sense of self and from that to
gain the power and confidence to act. It is generally not helpful
to label an emotion "positive" or "negative." It can be one or
the other depending on the person and the circumstances. The
value of an emotion like anger is that it provides us with stimulus
and energy so that we may respond to a changing and threatening situation.

> Also, for a while I was dealing strictly with my lost self-
> esteem. I blamed myself for being such a nerd as to fall for
> that "working late" stuff. Than I got really depressed. I
> really loved her but I couldn't reconcile loving her and her
> being a slut. It drove me crazy.
>
> To help my depression, I thought I'd start dating. But
> that had its problems, too. For one, even though I was only
> 29 at the time, I hadn't dated for some time. For another, I
> felt that women would consider me, a formerly married
> men, as "used" or second-hand material. They'd know I
> had already made one mistake so there must be something
> wrong with me. And I was suspicious of women. I doubted
> that I could find a down-to-earth woman who would con-
> sider me and not her career, the most important thing in
> her life. I was sure my wife had played up to her boss to
> get ahead on the job.

The most problematical time for the rejected partner comes
after the anger has cooled and depression sets in with its feeling
of loss, its lack of self-esteem, its sense of having failed in

something of great importance. Part of Evan's depression—and not the least part—was the sense of shame, shame that people would know that he had been duped, shame that he could be such a naive and unrealistic romantic, shame that other women would see him as damaged goods and inadequate.

Shame, too, is an early emotional response, appearing in rudimentary forms in the first year of life. It comes into being as the infant tries to discriminate between "strangers" and those familiar to him/her. Shame then creates a heightened awareness of the self. It is first experienced by infants when they try to interact with people they don't know and find that these strangers do not respond in familiar ways. Shame, the vulnerability of the self, is experienced acutely.

Psychologist Dr. Carl Goldberg sees shame as a fury of "passive suicide." He also sees it as being necessary to the human race, an adaptive drive that compelled people to wear clothes (going naked induced shame and self-castigation), and this compulsion to be clothed enabled the human race to spread to inhospitable climates where clothing was vital for survival. He acknowledges that shame is or can be an "excruciating experience" for the individual, for through it, "we question our own perceptual reality, as compared, for example, with guilt, where we question another's." Goldberg sees shame as a total castigation of self, but he plots it on a negative-positive continuum. The negative (pathological) aspect of shame, if not coped with, can lead to despair and inability to act, while the positive aspect of the emotion lies in its ability to lead us to self-reflection and change for the better. By overcoming shame, we foster the "development of competencies and skills to increase self-esteem and decrease shame experiences." As mentioned at the beginning of the chapter, however, the road to overcoming shame is not an easy one. Self-reflection is never a simple process, and rebuilding self-esteem after rejection requires maturity, judgment, and a good deal of courage.

Along with shame, the rejected partner feels a sense of loss. There's loss of self-esteem, of course, and, more immediate perhaps, the actual loss of the partner. In both cases, there is a tendency to blame one-self—if only one had been good enough, rich enough, exciting enough to be *the* only chosen one. All our childhood nightmares (and many of our beloved fairy tales) come into play here, for what child has not at one time or another wondered if he/she were really one of the family? You know the feeling. You suppose that you're adopted (and no one will tell) or that you were deposited on your family's doorstep some wet, rainy night and they took you in out of pity. Your real parents are lost to you forever, and they wouldn't have abandoned you if *you* had been really worthwhile!

Where the rejected has suffered an actual loss in early life, such as the loss of a parent through death or divorce, betrayal by a spouse is even more keenly felt. Old wounds, only partially healed by time, reopen. This further blow to one's self-esteem seems only to confirm an earlier fear that one is in fact not worthy. In such a situation, rebuilding one's ego and sense of self can be a long and trying process, far exceeding what an outside observer might expect would suffice to deal with the problem.

Finally, the rejected partner feels most powerfully the loss of what mankind has been seeking since its inception—love. If love is as necessary as oxygen to an infant, it is not less so to the adult. Young, middle-aged, or old, we all need to feel cared for sometimes, somewhere by some*body*. If we are fortunate enough to have had this somebody early on, we will develop enough self-love to tide us over, as it were, those times in our lives when we don't have another providing it to us. When love is torn away from us, as in a betrayed marriage, the sense of outrage and loss is devastating—the more so because we can't help but feel that he/she has been taken from us by someone we feel is more worthy—or why the betrayal?

Some theorists tell us that men and women have different types of anxieties with respect to love. Women are presumed to be anxious about losing their lovers; men suffer anxiety that love, springing suddenly into their lives, might just as well spring right out again, and for the same unknown reasons. Shakespeare's *Romeo and Juliet* gives us a good literary example of the two approaches: Juliet fears losing her lover Romeo while Romeo fears that love itself might disappear. For both, love creates a validation of the self. Bergmann states in *The Anatomy of Loving*. "Love makes men feel masculine and women feminine." It's no wonder then that Evan, upon discovering the betrayal, felt a loss of gender identity—his very manhood was at stake. Women, too, in the same situation have comparable doubts and heap masochistic self-reproaches on themselves: "If only I were more . . ." Often this is a repetition of an earlier loss, with the added pain of having re-found what was earlier lost—and then losing it again. The despair here can become quite deep, with the hope vanishing forever that somewhere there is someone who can safely be trusted. To overcome this sense of despair is no easy task. We must then be lenient in judgment if some of the strategies rejected partners use to overcome their sense of shame seem rather shallow and self-serving. They *are* literally self-serving.

> Well, I promised myself that I would never again date or marry a Dinosaur. That's a word a friend of mine made up for women with beautiful bodies (like my wife) and with little brains. He called them dinosaurs because they're also slated to become extinct. And so the woman I met about a year later—my present wife—is not so beautiful but she's caring and wants a family. I think it's going to be O.K. At least we're honest with each other. I don't think what happened could happen again. Right?

Was it Dr. Johnson who said something about remarriage after divorce representing the triumph of optimism over experience? Well, isn't that really the behavioral pattern that governs nearly every aspect of our lives?

Rejected Partners: Re-Examining Some Earlier Examples

Throughout this book, you have met many players in marital round-robins. Let's concentrate now on the partners *not* having affairs in some of the studies we've discussed and try to under-

stand them from the pictures we have of them from their
spouses. No matter how unsuitable, inadequate, or downright
awful they were when presented to us, we must see that they
had their stories, too. Their reactions form an integral part of
the extramarital process. Such an examination will give us a
better, more binocular view of those situations, which were
never meant to be seen as merely one-dimensional in the first
place.

In the section on "Mirroring" (Chapter 2), we met Denise's
husband Vic, her critic par excellence, the "honest, bad mirror"
that Denise rejected for her lover Sam. Vic, so easily outraged,
was now the one being rejected. What would he feel? He would
be flabbergasted. He would think, "How could a woman with so
many shortcomings dare to think that some other man was
preferable to me!" His pathological narcissism would likely boil
over into what psychoanalyst Heinz Kohut called rage stimulated by "disintegration anxiety" and described as "the deepest
anxiety man can experience." Though deeply suffering, Vic
would not be in touch with the profound anxiety he was experiencing but only the fury. It's unlikely that he would go past
shock and rage to shame and self-reflection, psychological repair.

He would think his wife was "a fool to be taken in by this
twit who was sure to fuck her and leave her." He might decide
to get back at her by screwing every woman he could—not even
caring about the problem of AIDS in this post-flower generation
world. (This would be in keeping with his self-destructive behavior and would repeat the early lack of care he had received from
parenting figures). He might even go so far as to doubt that
Richard, their child, was truly his. ("There was always something about that kid that turned me off," he might say, "and if I
find out there's a chance he's not mine, out he goes.") Through
these rationalizations Vic would be demonstrating his destructive hostility, which he would use to fend off the assault on his
selfhood and masculinity.

In short, the two partners, Vic and Denise, entwined in a
web of similar psychological problems, find very different solu-

tions. She, the product of faulty mirroring in childhood, seeks to correct the lack with her lover; he, likewise a product of unresponsive parents, seeks a solution not in the normal development of self-confident assertiveness but in the acting out of hostile-destructive impulses. His injury, deep and painful as any real lesion, will linger. So will his rage.

How different would our "mirroring junkie" Brenda (also Chapter 2) be? Let's catch Brenda at the moment of revelation that her husband is entangled in an affair. She looks in the mirror and throws the bottle of Shalimar that Ed had given her as an anniversary present at it, shattering both to bits. "Don't I smell good enough that he's got to give me a bottle of perfume! Anyway, I like Oscar de La Renta better—always did. But he never could remember the name." As for sex, well, she had real medical problems. And if Ed had only had the mother wit to tell her with feeling how beautiful he found her, she very well might have been able to be more physically responsive.

For Brenda, and those like her, continuous mirroring is essential. Feeling less loved by her parents than her brother was (and having some ambivalent feelings about men in general as a result), she turned to love as a kind of opiate. As with many women who are clinging and demanding, Brenda's needs for a man were not especially sexual. Instead of being caressed sexually and brought to orgasm, Brenda wanted attention, admiration, constant encouragement. Touching and caressing were for her too demanding, too reciprocal in nature. Women like this, and men, too, for that matter, are the ones who do the demanding in a relationship. As long as they continue to seek the mirroring they failed to obtain in childhood, they will overwhelm their partners with demands. In fact, with each repeated failure they may become even more insistent in their demands for attention and encouragement, thus making inevitable the rejection and betrayal they most fear. So while suffering from feelings of betrayal (and hating them), at the same time Brenda needs these feelings to re-create and play out her life themes. This is a vicious circular bind of entrapment.

We also met Joey, Gloria's husband, in the "mirroring"

chapter. He was always rageful, and there is little doubt that he would continue to be so after finding out about her affair. His rationale probably would be that he must use force, as Gloria (or any woman) is insensitive to his needs. It was her fault that she didn't understand him better; why did he always have to spell everything out to her? Shouldn't she know what he wanted without his always having to tell her?

Joey had been an only child, left alone for much of the time with a baby-sitter who ignored him and watched TV—and occasionally had a boyfriend over with whom she sometimes made love. Joey was ignored and aroused at the same time. When he complained to his parents, the baby-sitter lied and said he was making up stories about her. His parents believed her and he got punished. This was indicative of his relationship with his parents, and, as the years went by, his internal rage grew and his violent temper became more and more a part of him. Also, as an adult he drank too much. As with all people suffering from addiction (alcohol, drugs), he used the addictive substance as a replacement for part of himself that was missing. In Joey's case, the lack came from the failure to experience an idealized figure in early childhood. An idealized figure calms the young child's fears and offers him/her a sense of almost omnipotent strength. The child internalizes this sense of strength, and can draw on it as an adult in times of crisis for self-soothing and calming. Where the early experience does not take place, the later self-structure is missing. Not infrequently, the lack is made up by using an addictive substance, which, if only momentarily, calms the underlying devastation the psyche feels. One learns to depend on the substance for one knows that certainly one cannot depend on oneself. Can the vicious circle that Joey finds himself trapped in ever be broken? Perhaps. With work and with age, Joey may find himself mellowing, growing more able to administer to his own needs with less of a sense of rage at the insensitivity of others. Without self-reflecting therapy, though, he will likely continue to seek out women like Gloria; keep his rage intact; use alcohol to hide his pain, frustration, and humiliation; and never find the missing part of himself.

Rejected Partners: Reactions Aren't Predictable

Logic isn't the greatest predictor in the world of how an aggrieved partner in a marriage will react to the spouse's infidelity. We have seen by now how tied into our personal history our emotional reactions are. For instance, feelings of hurt, rejection, anger, guilt, and shame can be as intense in a bad marriage as in one previously thought to be good. Reassurances can fall on deaf ears. "But Madelaine, you hated Bill and were dying to get out of the marriage. You said so yourself. Why are you falling apart now, just because you found he was screwing some bimbo at the office? It doesn't make sense."

Sense or not, all Madelaine can now concentrate on is her rage that Bill had been "fooling around" for the last six months with his attractive secretary. It galls her terribly to think that he enjoyed sex more with his lover than with her. The fact that she herself had "fooled around" a couple of times over the last year didn't enter into the picture. Nor did the fact that Bill frequently suffered from impotence, a major problem in the marriage and one for which Madelaine showed little sympathy. "God," she'd say, "you've got some kind of sexual disorder now in your 30s. What'll you be like in your 60s?"

Despite all this, Madelaine was hurt and enraged at Bill's infidelity. It rankled her to think that Bill was sexually inadequate with her but quite active with his secretary. Madelaine's territoriality had been intruded upon. Good, bad, or indifferent, Bill was *hers*. At the point where feelings are riding high, the emotional self says loud and clear, "My mind's made up; don't confuse me with the facts."

Henry's initial reaction to his wife's affair is another example of feelings that seem out of sync with the facts of the situation. He was totally devastated when Renee abruptly left him. It hurt especially that he was the one who had encouraged her to pursue her career in fashion design. He felt she was too talented to simply remain idle (which she could easily have done as Henry was quite affluent from his West Coast real estate business). So when she returned from a business trip and stormed into their beachfront house announcing that she was going to live with her lover who had been with her on the trip, Henry was stunned and went into an emotional tailspin.

At first, he felt far more self-blame than outrage at the betrayal, which is not uncommon for the aggrieved partner in rejection situations. Even though he had a prenuptial agreement with Renee, Henry had to make an effort to restrain himself from giving her much more than the settlement called for.

Two months later, however, the emotional turmoil, guilt and shame had largely worn off. He began to feel elation and a sense of real freedom as the truth about his relationship with Renee began to dawn on him. He saw that it had been essentially barren and loveless; the only thing that held it together for as long as it lasted was his generosity—expensive gifts and the like. "For the last two years," he said, "we didn't have sex. I can't believe it—I'm a guy that loves to fuck." When asked how it was that the relationship was so bad for so long without his doing anything about it, he shook his head and said it now surprised him, too. "I guess I just denied it. I got all tied up in my business, and I just didn't see how bad things were."

By the time of this interview, Henry had totally transformed himself. "I'm like a new man," he said. "I have some great relationships with women. I get laid a lot, have a lot of fun, keep up with my business—and feel better about my self all around. I really owe a debt of gratitude to Renee for walking out."

Fortunately for Henry, his feelings caught up with his reality. Often there's a kind of inertia about feelings. You know what you're supposed to feel about a certain situation and you go on telling yourself that's the way you *do* feel. Henry had decided that he was married and he was in love with his wife, and then he went on about his other business and put his feelings about the marriage on auto pilot. In such a situation, you need a strong emotional shock to jar you out of your complacency and put you back in touch with your real feelings. That's just what Renee's sudden bolting did for Henry. At first he felt just what he thought he ought to have felt, deprivation, shame at having failed to keep Renee, shock. Then, as he got more in touch with his inner self, the mood changed to one of relief and elation. At least for the moment that's what he felt, but emotions change like quicksilver. That's why it's crucial to consciously examine your feelings and attitudes often. Your inner life could be tied into a reality that hasn't been true for years.

Angela exhibits a different mix of emotions. Six years after her husband walked out on her to live with his lover, she still feels the hurt of abandonment as though it were yesterday. Her husband had been carrying on an affair with the other woman for a year, and Angela could not let go of her anger at this deception and betrayal. She admitted that their relationship had not been good, but as she said:

> I come from a very traditional family where people get married and stay married. If he had come to me right away when he started up with her, I could have accepted that and we might have been able to work things out. I don't expect perfection. But he put me through some very bad years while he was enjoying his new wife. That's hard, really hard.

After their separation, Angela not only had to struggle through hard financial times and battles to get minimal support for their young son, but she had a tough balancing act juggling child care and the necessity to establish a new career for herself. Now, at the age of 39, she is quite independent and more secure, but the bitterness remains.

Angela's story reminds us that circumstances exert a powerful influence on our feelings at times of crisis. For example, financial security and independence can make a world of difference in an aggrieved partner's feelings of anger and betrayal. Would Angela be less bitter and more positive now if she had had Henry's financial means and independence when her marriage broke up? Would Henry be as elated two months after his breakup if he were scratching around for a living with no opportunity for the travel and good times he enjoyed after Renee left? It's had to tell just what their reactions might have been had their positions been reversed, but one major point to keep in mind is that rejected partners' reactions will be tempered by the situation in which they find themselves.

As Henry's case illustrates, there are times when good things can happen to get a person back on the track again. This was certainly true for Shirley, who felt her life destroyed when her husband finally admitted having the affair she had suspected him of for three months. She was relieved that the truth was out, but she was deeply wounded. Part of her was "disgusted," and wanted out of the marriage with Don. Another part, though, was confused and frightened. She didn't know what would happen, and she especially feared being alone.

She dealt with these jumbled feelings by throwing herself into her fashion design business. Although this was probably overcompensation for her underlying anxiety, it turned out positively. She was quite talented and, much to her surprise, met with great success. The good feelings engendered by these successes provided some much-needed confirmation of her self-worth. Also, she met new men who were attracted to her, which reaffirmed her femininity—previously she had pushed such approaches aside or hadn't even noticed them. Although she didn't enter into an affair with anyone, she felt more secure within herself. Eventually, she did work out many of the problems with Don, and she felt more in control of herself and less vulnerable while doing it. She also came to feel that her new relationship with Don was on a much more equal footing and, hence, much firmer than before.

If Shirley had not had a career to give her the kind of success she needed at the time of her rejection, her development after she found out about the affair might have been entirely different. She might have been, like Angela, still angry and hurt after many years passed.

Rejected Partners: Humiliation Or Liberation?

While the rejected partner often registers intense emotions like shock, anger, shame, fear, disgust, grief, and the like, some

partners may experience just the opposite. Some may feel relief
and others may be only too happy to extend acceptance, either
overt or covert. Fred's wife, Barbara, ("Parallel Play," Chapter
5), was one such case. She was married to Fred for 38 years but
was never passionately in love with him. Indeed, she was hardly
passionate about anyone or anything. A woman who loved
stability, she married "when it was time" a man she knew to be
kind and of similar background, but with enough interests of his
own to give her what she termed "peace of mind and time for
my own needs." A quiet person, she had few friends and few
hobbies, but she seemed to manage well enough with the resources she had. She cooked, cleaned the house, took proper
care of the children when they were small (and even the grand-
children later when she was asked), read her books, and kept to
herself.

An exploration of her psyche might reveal a woman who
learned early to avoid deep commitments of any kind, perhaps
because she came to fear losing them or feared over-attaching
herself to anyone or anything. People capable of feeling ecstasy
can also feel intense pain. Conversely, a low-level commitment
of joy can also cushion a person against deep disappointments
and deep personal hurts. If you settle for little, there's not that
much that can be taken away from you. Minimal gain to be sure,
but a minimal risk.

At some level, Barbara knew about Fred's affair with Paula,
an affair that continued for five years. In her heart of hearts,
though, she felt not so much anxiety as relief. No longer would
she have to feign sexual fulfillment, no longer feel the obligation
towards communication, friendship, sharing of feelings and
ideas, and all the rest of the togetherness paraphernalia. In a
way, both Fred and Barbara were in parallel play situations. He
with an outside lover, she within her internal life. They both
colluded in this, each wanting to keep their marriage intact while
pursuing his/her own needs at the same time. Their unspoken
pact was converted into a lifestyle, and rejection, as a concept,
just didn't come up. No one was rejected and everything was

accepted. Neat, but not likely to become a widely adopted solution to the serious underlying problems in relationships.

In the same vein, it might be well to mention here what the well-known researchers Joseph Zubin and John Money characterize in *Contemporary Sexual Behavior* as the two types of extra-marital affair: the conventional and the consensual. The former, they say, involves deception and remains unknown to the spouse or is discovered only later. The consensual type involves the case where the affair is known to both spouses in the marriage, and where consent is given by both partners. Such arrangements can be very tolerant, allowing each partner the freedom to engage in extramarital experiences at will. In this instance, deception is not needed and does not exist, the pact between the partners obviating any necessity for subterfuge. Such arrangements, where they are possible, do away with some of the thorniest problems we've been wrestling with in this book. As Zubin and Money point out: "Deception has previously been a characteristic feature of adultery, and the effects of adultery have turned more on the success or failure of the deception than on the omission or commission of the adulterous act itself. Adultery is often accepted when it is practiced with discretion and when no one is the wiser, and yet it is the deception that provides a large part of the sting when it is discovered."

A further variant on this adultery tolerance idea is known as "swinging" or mate-swapping. This is a form of consensual adultery where both partners participate and participate as a dyad. "Co-marital relations" is the more formal term for this behavior, and is preferred by some who engage in the practice. They believe the term "swinging" connotes only "recreational sex" with little or no emotional involvement, which they feel does not accurately describe what they do. Still another form of consensual adultery, much rarer than ones already mentioned, is group marriage. In this form, all the parties consider themselves married to each other. Since this form of marriage is not legally recognized in the United States, although it is practiced in some areas, it constitutes an ambiguous category.

While consensual adultery of one sort of another does exist for subgroups of people, most people who are involved in extramarital affairs fall into the conventional category. Deception goes with the territory—and may be its most corrosive ingredient. What if we replaced deception with honesty? Is that a viable option—what are some of the things it would entail? Let's look at this "honesty option" in depth.

Rejected Partners: Is Honesty the Best Policy?

So far we've explored quite a range of emotional reactions experienced by the rejected partner in an extramarital affair. The question is could all this have been avoided if the partners had been open and honest with each other all along? Could there have been a mutual sharing, a re-creation of the basic trust essential to a good marriage, a binding up of the hurts and the narcissistic injuries of long ago, and a new contract for the future? How can one be "true to one's self" and dishonest with another?

In "Risky Business" (Chapter 4), Oscar raised those questions when he told his wife Tina about the affair. If you recall, she demanded an immediate divorce. Oscar, stunned, wanted a reconciliation. After 22 years of marriage, he did not want to change partners. For him, the excursions into infidelity were mere side trips; his home was the mighty fortress. Tina, feeling herself to be a reasonable woman, agreed to hold off on a divorce. Instead, she suggested—demanded really—that Oscar have himself tested for AIDS—every six months for a period of two years. During that time she and he would have no sexual contact at all. As she explained to her therapist during one session:

> It's bad enough he exposed himself. Don't think I'm going to let him drag me into disease at this stage of my life. I'll have to be completely sure he's ok before I let him touch me again—if I ever do.

What was Oscar to do? Sheepish and ashamed, he agreed. But he was baffled. He had tried to be totally honest, thinking this was a good thing, and it had backfired miserably. Again and again he bemoaned exposing himself to his wife:

> She just couldn't take it, I guess. I thought that maybe if I told her, she would see how frustrated I'd been with her busy schedule and how much I really wanted to cut down on affairs and be with her. Instead, just the opposite happened. I created a jail.
>
> Now I can't have her. Each time she looks at me, I feel she looks in disgust—and it hurts. And I can't go back to having affairs; I'm terrified she'll find out. I tried reasoning with her, explaining that the women I've known weren't the types to get AIDS. But she won't listen. In her mind they were as "dirty" as I was, and nothing I can say can change that. Why, oh why, did I ever tell her!

There are many reasons lying behind the impulse to be "honest"—and some of them are more honest than others. First, honesty is taught to us as a moral good. One is either honest, and in good order with society, or one is dishonest, and out of favor with all the other decent, honest people. Yet, think of the times you have not been totally honest, perhaps with a complete stranger, perhaps with someone very close to you. Taxed with, "Tell me the truth. What do you think of these new curtains I just bought?," would you really answer, "They're god-awful and they clash with everything in the room." Chances are you'd fudge a bit and hope your friend wouldn't notice.

We're all used to "white lies" that are told more to protect someone's feelings than to gain a personal advantage. "Tell me the truth" often means "Agree with me." When you want to demur, you offer "constructive" criticism: "I love the way you look in green, but I'd wear the beige outfit for your interview." The completely honest thing to say might be: "Frankly, you look dreadful in green, like death warmed over. Whatever made you think of wearing that to a job interview?" Honest, but a good way to lose friends and alienate people.

In certain other cases, the impulse to honesty itself becomes questionable. Sometimes, for instance, a person is merely
rendering an opinion because that is what is expected. Our
society does not put a high premium on quietude, reflection, or
contemplation. Rather than internalize and experience, we are
urged to "let it all hang out," "get it off your chest," "tell it
like it is," and so on. We use honesty as catharsis, as a way of
escaping inner scrutiny and self-examination. Basically an external society, we concentrate little on our interior selves, and we
often deny ourselves the opportunity to develop internally by
too quickly sharing or verbalizing our experiences. Our "rush
to communicate" more often seems to stem more from a need
to relieve our own anxieties than from a desire for real sharing,
which can lead to mutual growth. This is not to urge you to keep
things to yourself for the purpose of deception. Rather, we
suggest that the impulsive sharing of experience, veiled as
"openness" and "honesty," can be deceptive in its own way.

There are other perils, too, in telling the truth about an
affair to the rejected partner. For example Bob's experience, (a
case study in "Beyond Parallel Play," Chapter 6). As Bob
related it:

> I not only went crazy when Amy told me about her affair,
> I was totally obsessed by it. I had to know all the details.
> At first I thought I'd have him followed. Like in the movies,
> I'd hire a private eye and find out what this guy's life was
> like. I already had his name. I didn't know what I'd do with
> the information, but it seemed important to me then. I gave
> up that idea; it sounded a little foolish even at the time, and
> it also would be expensive. I did the next best thing. I spent
> hour after hour getting all the details from her. I wanted to
> know everything—and she told me.
>
> I had to know about the lovemaking especially (I had
> met him so I already knew what he looked like), and I
> wanted every excruciating detail. I even called his house
> and hung up when he answered, just to hear his voice. I
> wouldn't let up on her. I wanted to know what his erection

was like—whether they made love more than once at a meeting—what positions they used—whether they bathed or showered together—how her orgasms with him compared to those with me. You can hardly believe it, but I was a crazy man. And the more she told me, the more I had to know.

Finally, she screamed at me that she felt she was in some kind of torture chamber and that this would have to stop or she'd lose her mind. It was then that I realized that I couldn't go on living with her. It was then that I saw I was ready for someone else. As long as I was with Amy, it would be like being with her lover. I couldn't take that.

It took years of treatment to get Bob to the point where he could be comfortable with himself and a life without Amy. One lesson we can receive from this experience, however, is that the revelation of an affair can sometimes trigger curious reactions in the rejected partner. This might involve voyeurism and—on occasion—an accompanying, an underlying homosexual component. If the unoffending partner has not overtly acknowledged this homosexual component, its sudden appearance can create much anxiety. Bob's fixation with the details of the couple's lovemaking was also a focusing by him on the male experience, and it contained a possible homosexual component that was simply too much for him to handle.

Thus the compulsion to know each detail of the relationship, and the anxiety that this very compulsion engendered, made life a nightmare for Bob and a hell for Amy. Unwittingly, Amy contributed to the situation with her feeling that if she could "make a clean breast of it all, the craziness would stop, and we could go on with our normal lives." Good intentions, but they were futile in this difficult situation. The more honest and forthcoming she was, the worse the relationship became.

Rejected Partners: Children of the Storm

No discussion of extramarital affairs would be complete without touching on their impact on children. While the offending part-

ner may not intend to reject them—quite the reverse—the psyche of young children is at once more vulnerable and less elastic
than that of adults. Children often identify with the rejected or
"deserted" parent, and have little patience with the parent who
sought solace outside the family. Likewise, the outcome of the
liaison—whether it is life-renewing or devastating for the involved partner—is totally uninteresting to the child, especially
the young child. What is of interest, what really matters in the
triangle, over which the child has no control, is that the child
perceives one parent as being "unfair" to the other parent,
usually the one involved in the affair. As both parents grapple
with the situation, they move the triangle to center stage in the
family's deliberations, and the child perceives very keenly that
he/she is no longer the center of attention. Young children
particularly are vulnerable to fears of desertion. They ask:
"What will happen to Daddy/Mommy? What will happen to
ME?" Children do not see the lover as Venus or Apollo but as a
stranger coming between Mommy and Daddy and threatening
the whole structure of the only world they know.

Children's feelings towards an extramarital affair are similar to those expressed by adults when remembering a childhood
experience of walking in on the "primal scene." Ignorant of
what the act of love entails, their recollection is that of "Daddy
choking Mommy while Mommy was making strange noises."
They recall an immediate fear that one parent was being hurt,
and a secondary apprehension, perhaps on a subconscious level,
that the act they had just witnessed was a very private one—one
from which they were excluded. Such anxieties may well underlie a young child's inability to resolve the classic oedipal complex and cause the later adult much grief. An affair that interrupts the family's life at the oedipal stage of a child's
development may well have very serious consequences.

We do owe Freud an undying debt of gratitude for exploring
the whole area of infantile sexuality. Newer ways of looking at
this phenomenon, though, see it somewhat differently. Adher-
ents to the concept of self-psychology hold that working out the
complex need not be the terrifying, self-destructive drama por-

trayed in *Oedipus Rex*. Rather, they feel it can be a joyous process, if the parents are psychologically healthy enough to welcome the advent of their child's natural heterosexual desires, along with the competition this entails with the same-sex parent.

In an unresolved oedipal complex, the child's longings for the opposite sex parent and envy of the same sex parent have not been accepted by parents and child alike. The child is left with terrifying oedipal longing and oedipal rage, reflecting the unresponsive nature of the parents' reaction to the child's needs at this crucial time. The child, at this period of his/her life, needs to be at center stage of the family's attention of one or both parents. At this time, the child feels excluded, unable to deal with his/her own longings, and unable to turn anywhere for help. The unattended child at this state tends to "fragment" as White and Weiner say in *The Theory and Practice of Self Psychology*. For instance, the child of five, normally ready for the development of a new assertive-affectionate self, experiences under these circumstances a disintegration of self in response to the unhelpful environment. This can lead in later years to adult feelings of lust and hostility with respect to love and sex.

It is not only the young child but also the older child—the teenager or young adult—who also faces difficulties in dealing with an extramarital triangle. The reactions here will vary, though, depending on how the young person has developed and what role he/she plays in the family.

I kept feeling my mother's unhappiness all the time I was growing up, and I identified with her. As a girl, I felt that maybe that was the way things were supposed to be. She seemed to be crying most of the time. Somehow I sensed, even when young, that it was related to my father. I blamed him for that.

It was only when I was in my teens, and Dad and I became close, that I understood. His affair was out in the open, and they were getting a divorce. He wanted it, and only then did he tell me that my mother had been depressed most of her life, and it wasn't he who had created her depression. He said it got so bad after my brother was born—she had terrible post-partum depressions even the doctors couldn't relieve—that he felt he had to act to save himself.

He went into an affair but couldn't tell anyone because they would think he was cruel and selfish what with a sick wife and all. I came to see that he did have a right to save himself if he could. It's not that I don't sympathize with my mother, but he had to choose something to keep him going. My mother is a good deal older now, but she hasn't changed much. Come to think of it, neither has my father. He's remarried. Me? I guess I understand it all now, but it was tough back then.

Other adults who have lived through parental affairs are less understanding. Here is a memory described by an 81-year-old man that goes back in time 71 years.

My father was having this affair. Everyone knew it.

I adored my father and tried not to think about it. Then one day my mother threw him out of the house and told him to go live with his whore. He did. My mother said she didn't know or care where he was, but I found out by asking some of his friends. And then I went to visit him after not seeing him for weeks. He wouldn't let me come in. His friend told me he couldn't see me or my sister, who was two years older than I.

I was crushed. I thought I had lost him forever. Also, I felt it was my fault, though I didn't know why. Now I see that that's just the way that children often see things, but at the time what does a 10-year-old know? I cried all the way back home and was in shock for weeks and weeks. Some time later he did get in touch with me, but I never forgave him. How could I?

The point to remember here is that if an affair can be said to have beneficial effects for anyone, the children involved in a marital tangle will not be able to recognize them. For the affected children, an affair is an intrusion and a threatening one. Unable to appreciate any of its benefits, they generally cling to the known, fight against change, and see more harm than good in the whole business.

Although it may be all but impossible to do, married partners caught in an extramarital triangle must make heroic efforts to spend time with their children. They must reassure them over and over that they are loved and will not be abandoned. Much of the problem when an affair is finally out in the open stems from the fact that so many demands are being made on the participants all at once. There are spouses and children, families and careers, friends and neighbors, all clamoring for attention, for solace, for reassurance. This at a time when one's own personal hopes, fears, guilt, and rage are in maximum turmoil. Considering the stresses involved, it's no wonder that the participants act a little crazy at times. Even so, care must be taken not to put too great a burden on small shoulders unequal to the task. If this requires heroic efforts on the part of the adults involved, well, so be it; heroism may be out of fashion, but isn't it the small heroisms of life that make civilization and love possible?

An affair discovered by a spouse can certainly trigger ferocious emotions that do not serve anyone—least of all children. This is not to say that all affairs have only a negative impact on children. Sometimes, the effects of an affair on children can be positive. For example, Mary was depressed about her marriage. She and John had grown distant over the eight years they had been together, and, when she returned each day from her teaching job, she felt completely drained. She had nothing left over for her seven-year-old daughter, who suffered from her mother's psychological absence.

When Mary began an affair with an assistant principal at her school, everything changed. The "demanding" job that had taken everything out of her suddenly became energizing. She felt a renewed sense of being alive, an eagerness to meet the present and the future. These feelings spilled over into her relationship with her little girl. Mary was more cheerful, more

involved. She was more "there" for her daughter even though
she got home later on the two days when she would go to her
lover's apartment after school.

Jessica's case is similar. She had been getting increasingly
frustrated because of her husband's depression. For one year,
he came home from work and flopped down in front of the TV.
There was hardly any communication between them, and they
had had sex only two or three times during that period, each
time initiated by Jessica. She felt herself becoming more and
more immobilized.

At the same time, she felt sympathetic towards her husband, who attributed his depression to traumatic stress resulting
from his service in Vietnam. After treatment by six psychotherapists, however, he showed no signs of improvement, and Jessica despaired about her future and the future of her two sons,
aged seven and ten.

To maintain her own sanity and boost her spirits with some
adult contact, she registered for a course at a nearby college. It
was a special program for adults returning to college so there
were a number of people in it around her age (36). Soon she
became friendly with Howard, a banking executive who had
taken early retirement. In a short time, she began an affair with
Howard and had her first sexual experience with someone other
than her husband.

The affair colored her whole life. Although things didn't
change much at home, she became more tolerant of the deficits
and also found more inner resources to share with the children.
She didn't feel she had to get away from the house anymore
because she had Howard. She decided to get out of the marriage
and make a better life for herself and the two boys. This
hopefulness enabled her to focus her energies better at home
and school, and the children benefited.

Sometimes, we tend to over-romanticize the "intact" family, imagining it as a TV sitcom with delightful Mummy; daffy,
wise old Daddy; pert, wisecracking kids; adorable pets; all in a
cozy split-level in southern California. Well, what about the
unhappy marriage? The ones where the partners are constantly

looking for escapes from the home? Think about all the shopping trips, the workouts at the gym, the "important business meetings," the club functions, all the hundreds of things people will do rather than go home and fight—or suffer what seems to be terminal boredom. All of this takes time and attention away from children. Thus, an affair, by restoring a stalemated partner to him/herself, can in fact restore much of that person to the family. Prior to their affairs, both Mary and Jessica were always trying to get away from the home. Afterwards, they both were more content and more alive when they were home.

It's not possible to give a categorical answer to what effect an affair could have on the family and on the children. Casual one-nighters on a business trip would not have the impact of a committed affair that is intended ultimately to replace the marriage. An affair that is set up deliberately to provoke a confrontation has its own agenda. A parallel play situation may go on for years without adversely affecting the participants' children or families at all. When an affair blows up into a storm, it can wreck families and harm children. But not all affairs end in turmoil.

Rejected Partners: Picking Up the Pieces

The rejected partner is, well, rejected. No getting around that. The rejected partner most often also suffers the further indignity of having been lied to and deceived. Repairing the psychological damage of shame and humiliation is a major task. Rebuilding courage so one can trust again is a monumental task. And then there are the myriad practical problems to cope with which must be solved. Divorce, so common now in our society, is one answer, but it has a significant cost. Women, particularly women with small children who divorce their spouses and do not remarry, run a great financial risk. Much poverty in this country is concentrated in single-parent households headed by women. For men, divorce offers a brighter picture, but certainly no panacea.

While the first impulse upon learning of a spouse's infidelity may be to smash the marriage to bits, taking time to cool down is very much advised. If there ever was a time for thinking and self-reflection, it's now. It's vital to determine if the infidelity was psychodynamically or situationally driven. Was it a momentary lapse, an unpremeditated roll in the hay? Or are there deep psychological conflicts between the married partners that will drive one or another again and again to seek solace elsewhere? The rejected partner is often at a disadvantage here in that he/she must undertake this serious self-examination generally alone. The straying partner has or at any rate had, a lover, and that often provides strength for the ordeal of self-examination to follow. The betrayed spouse is on his/her own. Help is available, though, and as distasteful as it may be to some, it's not a bad idea to take advantage of it, even if it's only to learn how others have suffered in the same way and were able to put their lives together again.

What is certain is that a change in one's life is at hand. It may be a step up, down, or sideways, but a step will be made. For the rejected partner, it may seem as if all is over, but that's not likely. Many beginnings come in the guise of an end, and learning something new often feels at first like losing something old. In the next chapter, we will discuss how you can analyze your own situation and feelings vis-a-vis affairs using a self-awareness guide we've developed.

Chapter Ten

AFFAIRS: YES OR NO? A SELF-AWARENESS GUIDE

As demonstrated in the movie, "Fatal Attraction," affairs, like wars, are easier to begin than to end. They are also harder to assess because of the self-absorbing intensity of the affair itself. So compelling is an ongoing extramarital affair that people often lose sight of why they began it in the first place, what it is doing to them now, and whether or not it is ultimately in their own best interests.

Evaluate? Yes. But in What Terms?

How then can we begin even to *think* about affairs, let alone *evaluate* them? An affair, after all, is not a new stock issue complete with prospectus of potential gains, possible losses, and neatly compiled hedging strategies. Even so, as we have shown throughout this book, there is much about affairs that can be grasped by the rational mind and so much in our own behaviors that can benefit from careful thought and judgement. For instance, as discussed in chapter 7, AIDS has had a definite impact—hard as yet to delineate fully—on our attitudes towards, and behavior in, sexual relations or what direction they will take. People try to be much more cautious about casual relationships—one-night stands, pickups, etc. Affairs are most likely to involve people who know each other—friends, co-workers, members of the same social club, and the like. Rationally, we see that we have to change our sexual practices and choose our partners with more selectivity, and from recent data, some seem to be doing that.

By the same token, we should take the further step of realizing that close-to-home extramarital affairs are the ones that entail the greatest risks of being discovered and present the greatest potential for a traumatic reaction when they are. A quickie with a stranger at a business meeting in another town can elicit an immediate furious response from an aggrieved spouse who discovers the affair, but a lingering affair with a spouse's friend or associate may trigger the complete destruction of the marital relationship. Thus, if we can use good judgement in evaluating the danger to our marriage and ourselves, and moderate our behavior to allow for it, we should be able to use our reason to analyze and cope with other aspects of our affairs.

All well and good, but what kinds of considerations do we use to examine our individual wants and needs and so create a basis for analyzing behavior? Am I happy? Too general. Am I worried? Too obvious. No, you need to examine your feelings and behavior in a number of areas already covered in this book. Now that you've been exposed to a wide range of experiences in affairs, you're aware of what issues are crucial to uncovering your present state of mind and your sensibility toward affairs. You may not arrive at a decision that is "beyond reasonable doubt," but you will, as in a civil law suit, discover where the "preponderance of the evidence" lies. You will have a keener sense of yourself through which to begin making such decisions as: Is this affair good for me or not? Is it more likely to cause pain or pleasure? In which direction will the balance tilt? (These questions can also be posed for evaluating a potential affair.)

The Process

Few people feel fulfilled and content with themselves and their lives for long stretches of time. No matter how much we have, we always seem to want more. Moreover, just maintaining the "cohesive self" we mentioned in Chapter 1 is an ongoing process, likely to take a lifetime. Before you begin evaluating your attitudes towards affairs and marriage, you should take a moment to consider how you feel about yourself.

What we recommend is that you begin to assess your feelings, as honestly as you can, using the following techniques of brainstorming and probing. Afterwards, we will provide more specific guidelines. The process is much like free associating in a psychotherapy session, but it is more directed. Perhaps it most resembles how writers—some of them anyway—attempt to generate ideas and approaches to a subject on which they intend to write an article. They simply write the topic they're interested in at the top of a blank page and then write down, in no necessary order, any thought, idea, or phrase, that the topic brings to mind. When a number of random thoughts have accumulated this way, the writer goes on to probe the topic by asking himself or herself questions that bring the freely associated ideas into sharper focus. For instance, you might write down at the top of the paper the topic: "The Cohesive Self." Then jot down every notion that comes into your head which you feel would represent a cohesive self—an integrated, whole, "together" personality, capable of functioning on a high level. (It might be useful to reread chapters 2 and 3). What characteristics would you expect such a personality to exhibit? How would you recognize such a person? What would you look for? Remember, just jot down your thoughts quickly—a word or phrase will do, no need for extended sentences or paragraphs. The brevity is important because you want to capture all your associations. Writing down your thoughts is important because mentally daydreaming about the topic will not produce the mental concentration necessary. Day dreams are evanescent; you won't remember your thoughts ten minutes after the exercise unless you write them down and analyze them.

The next step is for you to view yourself in light of what you have just said about the model cohesive personality. You examine the subject by probing, asking yourself questions. Your aim here is to build up, as it were, a profile of yourself with respect to what you see as a desirable, integrated self. Cover all the areas you feel are really important. Be sure to include positives as well as negatives. You might use such questions as:

• How many characteristics of a cohesive self do I share? (competence on the job? No undue stress? Close friends? Good relationship with spouse, lover, children? Have goals to attain? Moments of elation and fulfillment?)

• Where is the greatest discrepancy between myself and a functioning cohesive-self personality? (No goals? No hope of attaining goals I want? Unable to function in work roles? Lack of warm relationships? Caught in an unsatisfying relationship— marriage, affair? Suffering frustration and anger? Stressful feelings all the time? Depression? Lack of self-esteem? Fall apart easily? Overly sensitive?)

• Does my present situation seem generally supportive or is it now—or likely to become—"stalemated"? (Communications with spouse, family? Sense of being blocked? Where? By whom? Lack of stimulation? Lack of recognition? Indifference? Open hostility? Excitement and fulfillment? Where? With whom?)

• What at present is most satisfying (Job? Marriage? Children? Affair? Friends? Special activities—sports, cultural, professional, or social events?)

• What at present is most frustrating?

• Is self-fulfillment possible or impossible in my present circumstances? If yes, how? If no, what avenues are there to pursue my self-realization?

• When you have free associated and probed a topic in this manner, you will have, at the least, verbalized some of your thoughts and feelings on the subject. In light of these responses, you can weigh different courses of action and what their probable impact will be on you.

If, for instance, your probe of the concept of "cohesive self" brought you to the realization that you feel a very real sense of being in a stalemated situation, you can begin taking steps to deal with the problem consciously and rationally. You may work to open new lines of communication with your spouse to unblock the stalemate in the marriage. For all you know, your spouse may be having the same feelings of frustration and resentment. It's possible that together you can find ways to recover a sense of fulfillment and enjoyment in your marriage. This is obviously preferable to stumbling out of subconscious resentment into an affair that may prove to be quite beside the point—your own development—and quite harmful to boot.

Likewise, if you are involved in an extramarital affair—or have been—using this technique to evaluate your experience can help clarify what it was you were really looking for and whether or not you really came close to achieving it.

Probing the Dynamics

In Chapters 2 and 3, we examined two common needs—mirroring and idealization—that often play a crucial role in relations with others. Here, we suggest that you use our process of free associating and probing to uncover your feelings about how these needs relate to you.

Head a paper "Mirroring" and free associate about how necessary you feel it is to be assured of the acceptance and affirmation of others. Do you feel your self-esteem is independent of the regard of others? Do you look for mirroring in the ones you love? Do you provide mirroring for ones you love? (You may want to refer to Chapter 2 to refresh your memory on mirroring.) Most specifically, do you constantly need to be admired? Can you feel good about yourself even if others fail to show their appreciation of you? Can you applaud yourself for a job well done—a way of looking—a way of feeling—a state of being? Can you also applaud others freely and generously with-

out feeling something is being taken away from you? Can you be
your own self-soother and offer the same to others?

Now ask yourself questions about the ideas you jotted
down. Some questions that should be included are:

• Did I have good mirroring as a child? (Incidents with
parents? friends? others? A general sense of well-being? People
acting positively toward me?) Did my parents show appreciation
of me? Did they value me for who I was and not what I could
do? Did my parents see me as a unique person and not only as
an extension of themselves? Did my teachers at school afford
me positive self-regard? Were my friends caring toward me? Did
I mirror friends and lovers as I was growing up? Has my positive
appreciation of myself become part of my philosophy of life?
Do I experience any joys of living?

• Was my early mirroring experience generally negative?
(Little or no reinforcement? Constant criticism? Always under
stress to do better? Feelings of neglect? Sense that one cannot
satisfy expectations of others no matter how hard one tries?)

• Can I find a pattern of unmet mirroring needs in my
present-day relationships—especially with spouse or lover?
(Constant need for partner's reassurance?) Do I find myself
feeling unsure until he/she tells me they care, helps me select an
item, accompanies me on trips, tells me the "right way to feel,
says that without me life would not be worth living?" Do I find
myself doing anything to please? Am I not able to say "No"
when I'd like to? Do I go along with what others want to do
rather than assert my own needs? Am I always taking care of
others to the neglect of myself? Am I afraid to voice an unpop-
ular opinion for fear of criticism? Am I "super-nice" too much
of the time? Do I have self-worth only when receiving attention
of others? Do I indulge in denigrating or bullying my partner
because of my own lack of self-esteem? Do I become insanely
jealous when my partner pays any attention to someone of the
opposite sex? Do I become angry at my partner when I'm feeling
unsure of myself? Am I critical of my partner and become picky
when I'm feeling shaky? Do I need-need-need?

- Do I need my partner to appear virtually perfect on all occasions?
- Can I say my marriage definitely lacks good mirroring, which I know I need?
- Could I make my needs known to my spouse? (Would he/she understand? Be able to deal with it? Would it go over like a lead balloon?)
- Are my spouse's mirroring needs more than I can handle? (Necessity for me always to reassure? To be perfect? No room for me to explore my needs?)
- Could I say that I had (am having) an extramarital affair largely because of mirroring problems in my marriage? (How do I know?)
- Is my extramarital affair now supplying the mirroring needs I felt I lacked? Or is it tending to repeat the same problems as in marriage?
- If it is, perhaps it is time to end the affair and look more closely at myself, e.g., am I too needy or do I choose lovers who fall into the pattern of not supplying me with what I need?
- Is there anything I can do to overcome what I feel are unmet mirroring needs from my early childhood and so put my relationships on a better footing? (Know enough about concept of mirroring and how it pertains to me? Study more? Therapy? Find more responsive friends and partners?)

Now do the same for the concept of idealization. (Again, you may want to review Chapter 3 before proceeding.) Some of the probes you would want to use will include:

- Do I feel that my early idealization needs were met? (Again, incidents from early childhood? Sharp memory of idealized person? Sense of security and strength as a child?)
- Do I feel strongly that my early childhood idealization needs were unmet? (Lack of strong adult figure in childhood? Feelings of neglect, of abandonment? Pervasive sense of powerlessness? Lack of a strong value system? Loss of a beloved adult in early childhood because of death or other reason? Overwhelming need for a strong person to give me a sense of security now?)

• Is my relation with my spouse largely determined by my ideals? (Do I insist that he/she be someone I can look up to? Am I crushed if my spouse turns out to be less than perfect in a situation? Have I gone from one relationship to another, always disappointed with how ordinary and unexciting my partner turns out to be?)

• Are there any truly idealizable people in my life now? Have my ideals gone sour?

• Can I take on the task myself of repairing what I feel was my broken idealization from childhood? (How? With whom? Next steps?)

As you become more adept at posing questions to yourself that reflect your specific situation, you will be better able to appreciate the value of this kind of exercise. You'll understand that low-key, non-stressful free associating gives you a wealth of material—pertinent directly to yourself—that you can gently probe to bring to light many of your unspoken feelings. When you have enunciated these feelings, you can use that self-knowledge to examine your behavior in your marriage or in an affair to weigh if you are acting in your own best interests—and in the best interests of those you love.

Setting Risks Against Gains. Odd how astute financial managers will take great pains to cull out the potential risks and gains of a proposed investment strategy while at the same time putting their marriages, careers, reputations at risk in an ill-conceived affair without a second thought. We should take at least as good care of our emotional selves as we take of our investment portfolios.

Well, you might think, it's the nature of extramarital affairs to foster extreme behavior. Yes and no. True, going into a sexual relationship with someone other than your spouse can be a spur-of-the-moment, let's-go-for-it sort of thing. Yet, as an affair goes on, there must be some way you can tell whether it's good for you or not. As we have seen, some are and some are not. The risks you pretty much know beforehand, and they're obvious throughout each day of the affair (see chapter 4).

Affair Vs Marriage; How Do They Really Rate?

While basking in the delights of an affair, all many people can think of are the pluses of the affair and, if you are married, the minuses of the marriage. Understandable, yet this "skewing of the data" may be just a temporary blinding of reality, necessary to you perhaps to regain some self-confidence, self-esteem, and to feel loved. Sometimes we just don't want to look at the whole picture because that could mean putting a crimp in our games or could suggest giving something up. So we choose not to see. But when it comes to affairs, and especially "risky business," blindness can mean going over the edge. If, instead of narrowing our view, we apply a wide angle lens, how would the two relationships—the marriage and the affair—stack up? If you were to really do an assessment, how would the two relationships rate?

With this in mind, it may be useful for you to have some guidelines or frame of reference for examining specific areas of your affair and marriage. Dr. Albert Ellis's idea of weighting the pros and cons of an affair is a good approach. We have modified this somewhat by specifying the areas to be weighted or rated. While we are not presenting you with a list of "do's" or "don'ts", we are putting forth some guidelines that can be helpful in better understanding your "state of affairs." We have chosen some key factors for you to honestly examine. Your "score" can act as a sensitivity barometer which can provide you with cues for possible reassessment of action.

Study the following "SELF-ASSESSMENT CHECK LIST". In the column titled "Importance To You," rate each of the items. For example, if sex is moderately important to you then check the box under the number three next to 'sex". If communication is extremely important to you then check the box under the number 4 next to "communication." Similarly, rate all of the items under "Importance to You." This will give you a frame of reference for evaluating and comparing your marriage and your affair. In order for this assessment to be tailor-made for you, we have left space for you to fill in other categories that might be personally important or meaningful to you. Rate those items as well.

Now you are ready to compare your affair and your marriage. For each of the categories or items, including the ones you have added, place checks in the appropriate boxes under "Marriage Ratings" and "Affair Ratings." For example, if sex is fair in your marriage then check the box under number 2 next to "sex." If sex is excellent in your affair then check the box

CATEGORY	IMPORTANCE TO YOU					MARRIAGE RATINGS					AFFAIR RATINGS			
	EXTREMELY	MODERATELY	SOMEWHAT	NOT AT ALL		EXCELLENT	GOOD	FAIR	POOR		EXCELLENT	GOOD	FAIR	POOR
	4	3	2	1		4	3	2	1		4	3	2	1
1. SEX														
2. FRIENDSHIP														
3. COMMUNICATION														
4. FUN TO BE WITH														
5. DEPENDABILITY														
6. CARING														
7. ATTITUDE TOWARD CHILDREN														
8. ATTRACTIVENESS														
9. PHYSICAL APPEAL														
10. PERSONAL HABITS														
11. FINANCIAL SUPPORT														
12. COMPATIBILITY OF INTERESTS														
13. COMPATIBILITY OF LIFE OUTLOOK														
(YOUR ADDITIONS)														
14.														
15.														
16.														

under number 4 in rating the affair on sex. If friendship in the marriage is poor you would check the box under 1; if it is excellent in the affair check the box under number 4. In this manner continue to treat all of the items. After you have completed these ratings you will not only be able to compare the affair and the marriage, but you will also be able to assess whether the similarities and differences are in relatively important or unimportant areas.

As we have pointed out elsewhere (Chapter 9), "The Rejected Partner," perceptions and feelings do not always correspond to objective reality. For example, you may assume that an affair is fantastic and much better in all respects than your marriage. On closer examination, however, when the concrete areas are rated, it may turn out that only one or two areas are really different and not that greatly different. If so, you might then want to look at the whole picture and gain a better understanding of why your feeling about reality is so different from the objective reality. Are there, for example, other agendas that you are not facing or dealing with?

Let's look at a specific case to see how the self-assessment technique can work for you. Jennie rated sex 2 (fair) for her marriage and 3 (good) in her affair. This is not a huge difference. At the same time she rated sex 3 (moderately important). Communication in the marriage and the affair were rated the same (3-good). On dependability the marriage rated higher (4 vs 2). On many other ratings, the marriage and affair are not dramatically different. Yet if you asked Jenny, she would tell you that her marriage is boring and the affair a turn-on. She has no plans to give up the affair. Since this affair may not be giving Jenny as much as she feels (although those feelings may be very important), she might want to evaluate the risks of the affair and their real consequences if the affair were exposed. She might also want to take a look at the possibilities of improving her marriage since it has many positives. Is she perhaps not working on the marriage in order to justify the affair?

Now the situation with Glenda is quite different. She rates sex in the affair 4 (excellent) and sex in her marriage 1 (poor).

She also rates sex 4 in importance (extremely). The gap in communication is also great. Other areas of importances to Glenda show big pluses for the affair. In the light of these perceptions her attachment to the affair is understandable and risks may not be as threatening. However, in the light of these wide discrepancies it might be wise for Glenda to seek help in understanding why she is staying in what she sees as a very unsatisfying marriage, especially when she has experienced a more gratifying relationship.

Sometimes the overall assessments are not as important as one area that takes priority. For Adrienne her two daughters, aged 13 and 14, were her most important concern. Although sex, communication, friendship and other areas on the checklist were clearly better in her affair than in her marriage, her single lover had little interest in or tolerance for children. When she realized that (even though the other areas were rated extremely important) she decided to end the affair. John would never be the caring step-parent for her children that she would demand. The risk, therefore, of disrupting her home life and the well-being of her children was just too much risk for her.

More to Look at

Now that you have rated your marriage and your affair, you should be more sensitized to what is objectively gratifying and what is not. Still, there are other questions and issues that need to be explored for more complete awareness.

1. *Discretion.* In "Risky Business" (Chapter 4), we have seen many examples of carelessness (Carl and Gloria) and flamboyant grandiosity (Ed and Phyllis). Discretion had been discarded and lives pulled apart. What had gone wrong? Discretion requires a great deal of planning, tact and the ability to foresee. While no one can be a genie with a lamp predicting the future, some safeguards appear natural. The ability to be discreet requires that you plan all actions as carefully and methodically as possible. Indiscretion—leaving things to chance, acting upon im-

pulse, choosing the wrong confidants—is one of the danger signs.

Many qualities are subsumed under the word "discretion." For example, are you self-disciplined? Are you an organized person? Can you prepare an agenda and then act upon it? Conversely, is your life and style haphazard whereby you act much on impulse? Discretion requires that your antenna be raised to its maximum and that your sensitivities stay at a high level of awareness. You have to be in control. You also need to be aware of all the persons involved, not only yourself and your lover. How can you best protect your spouse (if such is your conscious intention) and your children and/or extended family? When Johnny left photos of the women he had been with exposed for others to see, would his children also be subject to this sight? While he may have been able to get away with one set of prints with an: "It's someone I work with, taken during a conference," etc., how do you explain the two sets of prints? And so—discretion becomes a critical issue in the affair. Its opposite can boomerang for all involved. How do you rate yourself?

EXTREMELY INDISCREET	VERY INDISCREET	MODERATELY INDISCREET
5	4	3

SOMEWHAT DISCREET	NOT INDISCREET AT ALL
2	1

Are you happy with this rating? If not, what are you going to do about it. How and when??

2. *Jealousy*. Jealousy can be the burning flame which destroys. Like Medea, whose rage and jealousy led her to destroy her own children, it can be ravenous. The jealous man or woman is out of control and sees devils under all tables and chairs. A glance at another person, a whisper, a thought unspoken are all evidence of the betrayal to follow. Suspicious to the extreme, the

jealous one never rests, gathering clues, seen and unseen, forever. The sense of possessiveness in these people is a driving force.

Are you a jealous person? Do you feel that you must "own" somebody totally and that unless you can monitor all or most of their actions, you will be left behind, duped, made a fool of and ultimately betrayed for someone else? Do you interpret a lover's actions with the opposite sex as possibilities for their union? Is every moment away from you filled with your images of "he/she with someone else?" Has jealousy always been a part of your way of being? How would you measure yourself?

EXTREMELY JEALOUS	VERY JEALOUS	MODERATELY JEALOUS
5	4	3

SOMEWHAT JEALOUS	NOT AT ALL JEALOUS
2	1

How did you rate yourself? Were you surprised at your rating? Did it heighten your self-awareness? What action will you take now?

3. *Money.* Mark, the "fuckaholic" we met in "Parallel Play" (Chapter 5), travelled a good deal. This travelling was very much part of his business and involved him in using his own monies much of the time. This may or may not have had to be accounted for in his family system but one thing is certain, monies have to be managed and accounted for in one way or another. Birthdays, holidays and vacations involve a laying out of funds—both for the man and the woman. In some families, this is no problem. In others, it becomes a major catastrophe. This sometimes explodes into: "And what does this bill mean? I never bought anything in that store. How could they have made such a mistake?" In other situations, it may mean simply—being short. "I don't know what happens to our finances lately but as much

as we earn, there's always a shortage. Maybe we should go over our budget again. Something is out of whack." Indeed.

In deciding how money fits into your scheme, you need to be aware of your finances, your family system and all persons involved in your financial dealings. Can you afford the expenditures of an affair (or would-be affair)? Are you willing to spend? Think of your attachments to money, your attachments to the affair and see if there is a congruence of fit. Is there? If not, what can you do about it?

4. *Record-Keeping*. In "Parallel Play" we have also met people who manage two lives—one within the marriage and one outside it. This requires a great deal of balancing. For one, simple memory, as obvious as this seems, is an essential component. You have to remember who is in bed with you at the moment. Calling out "John" when it is "Henry" there beside you can be disastrous, to say the least. A form of accurate record-keeping needs to take place. You have to keep track of what you said, what he/she said, the places you met, the places where you said you'd meet, whose birthday is at which time, and so on. A poor memory is no vehicle for an affair or intended affair. Parallel play almost always means having two memories riding side-by-side; the actions you said would take place and those which actually did take place—and never that twain shall meet.

While we assume, incorrectly so, that failing memory is an attribute of aging, some people have poor memories at every age. One young woman said to us: "I've always been unable to remember. The day I begin to remember, I'll start worrying that I'm getting old." Memory also involves attention to detail, necessary to recall at a moment's prompting. Not only immediate happenings need to be remembered but related events as well. For example, which child of your lover is away at college, who is returning home, who became ill during the last holiday, etc. Essential to get straight is which resort you both went to and which name you used. The list and complexities are endless. You need to maneuver and maneuver fast. Thinking on your feet has to become second nature. You have to be facile—and then some. Are you?

How do you rate yourself? How are you going to improve your record-keeping and balancing "the books?"

5. *Sexual Protection Quotient (S.P.Q.).* While there is a debate as to the likelihood of AIDS being a threat to heterosexual persons who are not drug abusers, still the threat exists, as does the possibility of a sexually transmitted disease. In order for you to protect yourself as much as possible—for again, it is not only you who need protection but those others involved with you as well—you need to be extremely careful. Remember the outrage of Tina ("Risky Business") when Oscar revealed his affair to her? Her fury was not only at the affair *per se* but at the fact, she said, that he had exposed her to the possibility of disease. She felt unprotected and victimized in an action over which she had no say and yet from which she might have to suffer extremely serious consequences.

In the heat of passion, you may fleetingly feel that your lover will be aware of the dangers lurking in the possibility of acquiring a disease but—shouldn't you have control in the situation too? Some women have left it entirely up to the man to use a condom. Some men have complied and used them and some have not. As we have shown, almost no one uses condoms all the time. As noted psychologist Albert Ellis stated very bluntly: "It's hard to talk logic to an erect penis." The woman who "doesn't want to know" is leaving herself open to possible danger. In these times, you would have to become familiar with this item in your drugstore. You need to develop a whole new understanding of condoms. This would include where to buy them, the different varieties and—ultimately—how to use them. For the woman, learn how to put them on the male. Practice with a cucumber or a dildo. It can be an erotic activity and part of foreplay. But note: you must be adept for it to work. Men find this type of play very erotic when it is done comfortably and skillfully. Having this option gives you a big edge of control.

The male too would need to be direct and acquaint himself

with the sexual history of his partner if she is new to him (although we have pointed out this is hardly foolproof, even with the most detailed knowledge). Later on, as people get to know each other, all of the above falls into a routine, but, at the beginning, some guidelines for protective behaviors need to be established. Some comments we have heard on this topic are: (Male) "I didn't expect this to happen this weekend. I only came here to rest and mellow out. I don't have any condoms but I really want you." (Note: Always carry them.)

Are you protective or unprotective about yourself in the sexual arena? What is your S.P.Q.?

EXTREMELY PROTECTED	VERY PROTECTED	MODERATELY PROTECTED
5	4	3

SOMEWHAT PROTECTED	NOT AT ALL PROTECTED
2	1

What are your beliefs and feelings about the possibility of sexually transmitted diseases? Does your protection/unprotection behavior match your beliefs? If not, what action are you going to take?

6. *Addictive Behaviors.* Addictive behaviors indicate a great deal of dependency. Dependency need not only revolve around alcohol and drug abuse. Dependency may also be tied to everyday behaviors which go unnoticed, except to those upon whom they have an impact. A new affair, and sometimes a longer-term affair, can be exhilarating, intoxicating and sublime. You feel wonderful, your friends comment about the new radiance they see in you and even your spouse may notice it and, if not suspicious, dismiss it as some piece of luck in your business, your age, or some biological change unknown to science, But glowing or not, you may have become dependent/addictive—to the affair. If/when this happens, you may indulge in behaviors

similar to our mirror junkies ("Mirroring") or those super-idealizers ("idealization") we have met before.

If you (female) feel: "If he doesn't call me today and tell me how much he loves me, I'll die," you're in the danger zone. If you (male) feel: "If she doesn't come over and make dinner for me tonight, knowing everyone is gone for the week, then she really doesn't care," you're moving towards the warning light sign. While a relationship needs closeness, this type of intensity burns with a short, quick fuse. The "I want you" has crossed the border into the "I need you." A "want" is a relaxed state. You feel a gentle pull such as "I'm in the mood for pizza, seeing a funny movie, visiting Aunt Marie," or "taking some refresher courses." It's an option you give to yourself. If you act on it and all goes well, fine. If you choose not to act on it or if the situation does not permit it, that's O.K. too. Life goes on. Not so with "I need." This leaves no options. It is a demand that must be heeded—or else! It is the child who, instead of crying: "I want my bottle" (but can be placated with something or someone else), is the driven one who screams "I need . . . my teddy-bear, my Mommy, Suzy to play with me," etc. The driven quality and the fear behind the drive are apparent. When the affair reaches the "I need" level, you are in the danger zone. Your needs have taken you over.

Are you addictive/dependent in your behaviors? Do you usually drink, smoke or love with a super-intensity? Would cutting down or withdrawing from any of these activities leave you without a sense of self? How do you rate yourself in a relationship or affair?

EXTREMELY ADDICTIVE	VERY ADDICTIVE	MODERATELY ADDICTIVE
5	4	3

SOMEWHAT ADDICTIVE	NOT AT ALL ADDICTIVE
2	1

Are you satisfied with your score? If you scored high on addictive can you see this leading you to possible damage? What are you going to do about it?

7. *Vacation Time*. When you are in an affair, a first impulse is to get more involved. When pleasure is on the upswing and pain on the downswing, why not go with the pleasure? Sounds reasonable. This means you may throw yourself into the affair with a high-powered intensity. You may feel this helps to get rid of some of your everyday anxiety. Compulsive busyness is often a way of not letting yourself feel the pain and complexity in a situation. You're too busy doing—instead of thinking rationally and calmly sifting things out. This may just be the time for a vacation! Similar to "dependency" your emotional attachments may need to be put "on hold" for a while. Distance yourself from the situation—and your lover and other important persons in your life, if only temporarily. Getting away from it all can give you perspective. It may act as a retreat from the drivenness of your everyday experience. Use the time away for your own benefit.

On vacation you can evaluate, contemplate and, most of all, integrate all that is going on. Refreshing your mind-body-spirit connections can offer you exciting rewards for new attachments of self-to-self. Let go. The outside world will wait for you. Re-connect to your inner self. A true retreat allows you to move away from your known emotional attachments and refocus. Distancing from others brings you closer to your self. Can you detach yourself? What is your ability for distancing?

8. *Guilt*. Although an affair can bring you personal ecstasy, if you're lucky enough, it is nevertheless condemned by society. Men, it is said, "do it naturally." Yet it is, even for them, not a brownie point but some basic flaw in their character covered over with, "It's just his style," or, "It has nothing to do with family life. He's a good family man. . . ." The woman fares much worse. Even in this age of liberation, the married woman in an affair can be treated as a leper, particularly if there are

children involved and friends or relatives feel neglect has occurred. Once accused as an "affair person," the woman is
labeled "adultress," "temptress," "siren," or the like. (Interestingly enough, there is no accepted female equivalent of the
male "womanizer." When women are so bold as to "manize,"
the terms used to describe them are much more vulgar and
disapproving than the relatively wimpy "womanize." You may
have come a long way, Baby, but you have a long way to go.)

The woman in an affair then may face social ostracism,
even the loss of her children. At best, she will be the occasion
of some harsh epithets from society, and, perhaps, some envy
turned into voyeurism on the part of her friends who "want to
know it all" but who are condemning nevertheless.

If you are someone who easily feels guilt over an act others
deplore rather than the kind of person who affirms his/her own
behavior despite what others may think, you should take this
into careful consideration. The affair, although quite commonplace in our society, is still taboo to the public at large. You
could suffer much pain and anguish from this situation. If, in
your lifestyle, you have played pretty much close to the rules
you may have done so to defend against feeling guilt. How do
you rate yourself with respect to feeling guilt? What is your guilt
potential? If you are in an affair (or are thinking about one), how
guilty do you (would you) feel?

EXTREMELY GUILTY	VERY GUILTY	MODERATELY GUILTY
5	4	3

SOMEWHAT GUILTY	NOT AT ALL GUILTY
2	1

Toting Up. The eight items we have chosen here are in no way
all-inclusive. They do, however, seem to be crucial to affairs.
Having given your responses to these areas, have you learned
something more about yourself? Are you more aware of your
feelings and habits of mind with respect to yourself and your

immediate situation? Self-awareness is the goal of many philos-
ophies, most therapy, and all of this book. We hope that the
exercises in this chapter have helped you in this endeavor. It is
not so much the result that is important here as the process. The
questing, questioning, self-evaluating mind is the one that most
nearly gains self-knowledge. There is no final answer, of course,
only a steady unfolding—over a lifetime.

For all our emphasis on knowing, however, we would not
want you to think that this is nothing more than an intellectual
workout. The point of knowing is ultimately doing. New-found
knowledge presupposes a new way of acting. Change is the
essence of life and coping with change is the essence of dealing
with life. Coping with change means being sensitive to just what
is changing and what *needs* to be changed. Using the devices
given here can help you devise guidelines for divining both. The
options are there; it's up to you to choose—and to choose wisely
for yourself and for the ones you love.

If, like most of us, you find it difficult to sort out just what
to do and what to change, you must realize that there are
resources you can tap into. You may want to seek the help of a
psychotherapist. Therapists can help you by exploring your
feelings and guiding you through the sometimes difficult but
always rewarding journey of your inner self. Your end-point
should be a harmony of being, with the ratings scored in these
exercises reflective of you as you wish yourself to be. While
therapy may take time, energy, and money, it can be the most
profitably spent period of your life. One woman said, "Therapy
gave me the ability not to trip over my own feet." Another put
it this way, "Before therapy (BT), my life use to go on without
me. Now that's all changed. I'm right up there with it—in it."

While your ratings on the scales here have alerted you to
your underlying feelings and behaviors, they should also have
sensitized you to the risks inherent in an affair. Most people get
into an affair because it makes them feel good. If it goes on for
any length of time, however, just maintaining it imposes a
burden, and there are other problems as well—deception, guilt,
expenses, leading a double life, and so on. At this point, you

may be tempted from time to time—especially in times of stress—to wonder if the whole thing is worth it.

Make no mistake, *you* are taking risks for the affair (never mind your partner for the moment), and *you* will have to face the consequences if the affair is discovered. You have every right to question seriously what the situation means to you, what losses you are willing to sustain for it, and which ones you won't.

One last exercise is included below for those who are involved in an affair now. As before, head a paper "Risks," and note down all the possible risks you feel you are running because of the affair. After that, begin probing to examine how the risks stack up against what you know you are receiving from the affair. Some of the questions you will surely want to include (among others) follow.

• Do I really feel anything's at risk? (No problem, my spouse and I understand each other? I'm smart; I won't get caught? We've had two glorious years of an affair and no one knows; why should anyone? I've had several affairs already and nothing's happened. My marriage is on the rocks; its loss is not a major concern?)

• Am I willing to see my present situation—spouse, family, social standing—change radically if the affair is discovered? (Looking forward to a change? Eager to begin anew? Unthinkable! Play is play and no more? What *actually* would happen if the thing came to light?) Be specific in listing the consequences of your affair being revealed.

• Is the affair really doing for me what I want it to? (At first, great. Now it's just another problem to be solved like the rest. I couldn't live without it.)

• Would I leave the marriage now if it weren't for the children? Do I need the marriage and the affair both?

• Can I handle all the roles of a clandestine affair without a hitch? (Without undue strain? Without guilt or regret? Without forgetting?) Are we careful or foolish in the affair? (Is the daring what makes it so exciting? Would making it more discreet make it more mundane?) Could I explain it to my children? Would I even try? (Something apart from everyday life? Beyond the problems I face all the time?)

• As a single person in an affair with a married partner am I just marking time? Am I going anywhere? (I don't want marriage and children; this is fine. This is the person I want; I'll take what goes with the territory. There's no chance for us. If I want something of my own, I'll have to find it elsewhere.)

The point of this exercise is to get you to begin thinking rationally about the very real risks you are running and the emotional satisfaction you are gaining. Viewing them side by side, you may come to some startling conclusions. The marriage may now appear no less desirable than the affair, and the risks of the affair may seem way out of line with the satisfactions it's providing you.

Conversely, you may conclude your marriage is largely over and the risk of discovery and subsequent breakup is non-threatening. This may be clear to you after you've done the scales. What has the self-awareness scale told you? Are you ready to stay in the marriage, leave the affair, or do the reverse?

Finally, if you are a single person in a triangle, you will want to look very closely at your goals and needs. An affair with a married partner can seem very satisfying at the moment. Perhaps you have been thinking that all the really smashing men/ women seem to have been snapped up, and this, at least, gets you out of that depressing dating game. But you could be stuck in a no win situation that will leave you alone and furious a few years later.

Using the free-associating and probing techniques, you can begin now sorting out your options and clearing the decks for a course of action. Some alternatives you can rule out immediately: "There's no question but that I have to stay in the marriage. The children and my deep beliefs make that essential." Or, "Come what may, I must get out of this marriage. I'll think about the rest later."

Once you've ruled out certain options as being, for whatever reason, impossible in your case, you can analyze what's left with a view to maximizing the benefits and minimizing the risks for all concerned—yourself not the least. This emphasis on self may seem a bit off-putting at first. Many of us are brought up with the ideals of service and responsibility as primary virtues, with the needs of self much lower on the list of priorities. Such ideals are most worthy and deserving of respect, and we don't mean to encourage here a mindless "Me-generation" approach to life. We've seen how sour and shallow such an approach can be.

No, when we speak of examining your marital and sexual relations in terms of your own needs, we are suggesting an exercise more along the lines of Socrates' "Know thyself" than Ivan Boesky's attitude that says, "Enrich thyself." Only when you begin to see yourself and your motivations clearly can you choose from the almost limitless possibilities the course of action that best fulfills your ideals and sense of rightness. It is the firm conviction of the authors that the development of such a sense of self, the development of what we have called the cohesive self, is the best service you can render to yourself and to others.

If the case studies here have shown anything, it is, we hope, the real potential for pain that we risk every time we act without thought or against our own deepest natures. Self-knowledge is not a panacea; it won't end all your frustrations or solve all your problems. Life will still be tricky, demanding the stolidness of an ox and the agility of a mountain goat. Nevertheless, if you learned here to regard yourself and your actions with a quizzical eye, we feel you will have gained an insightful method for coping with your problems. What's more, we believe you will come to think so, too.

REFERENCES

Andrews, Lewis M. *To Thine Own Self Be True*. New York: Anchor Press, 1987.

Avery, Carl S. "Flirting with Aids," *SELF* Magazine. July, 1988, pp. 80.

Bergmann, Martin S. *The Anatomy of Loving*. New York: Columbia Univeristy Press, 1987.

Cohen, Betsy. *The Snow White Syndrome*. New York: MacMillan Press, 1986.

Fatal Attraction. Screenplay by James Deardean. A Jaffe-Lansing Production, Paramount Pictures, 1987.

Forrest, J. C. and Fordyce, R. R. "U.S. Women's Contraceptive Attitudes and Practices: How Have They Changed in the 1980s?" *Family Planning Perspectives*. Vol. 20, No. 3, May–June, 1988, pp. 112–118.

Freud, S. "Civilized Sexual Morality and Modern Nervous Illness," *The Complete Psychological Works of Sigmund Freud,* Canada: Hogarth Press, 1959, vol. 9.

Gabriel, Trip "The Ambivalent American Bachelor" *New York Times Sunday Magazine*. November 15, 1987. Sec. 6, Part 1.

Gallup Poll of November 29, 1987.

Goldberg, C. "Replacing Moral Masochism with a Shame Paradigm in Psychoanalysis." Paper presented at the American Psychological Association Annual Convention, New York City, 1987.

Gould, R. E.: The Reassuring News about AIDS: A Doctor Tells Why You May Not Be At Risk." *Cosmopolitan*. January, 1988.

Hall, Trish "Infidelity and Women" *New York Times*. June 1, 1987, pp. B-8.

Hite Shere. *Women and Love*. New York: Alfred A. Knopf, 1987.

Horowitz, Simi "Sex Is Alive and Well" *Harper's Bazaar,* November, 1988.

Humphrey, F. G. "Treatment of Extramarital Affairs: A Summary"

Presented at the 95th Annual Convention of the American Psychological Association, New York City, August 28, 1987.

Kinsey, A. C., Pomeroy, B. and Martin E. *Sexual Behavior in the Human Male*. Philadelphia: W. B. Saunders Co., 1948.

Kinsey, A. C., Pomeroy, B. and Martin, E. *Sexual Behavior in the Human Female*. Philadelphia: W. B. Saunders Co., 1953.

Kohut, Heinz. *How Does Analysis Cure?* Chicago: The University of Chicago Press, 1984.

Lawson, Annette. *Adultery*. New York: Basic Books, Inc., 1988.

Masters, W. H., Johnson, V. E. and Kolodny, R. C. *Crisis: Heterosexual Behaviors in the Age of AIDS*. New York: Grove Press, 1988.

Mcgrath, Ellen. "Fatal Attraction": Movies as Cultural Beacons Warning The Women and Men of Today. *The Psychotherapy Bulletin*. Vol. 23, No. 4. Winter 1988–89, pp. 25–27.

Murstein, Bernard I. *Love, Sex and Marriage*. New York: Springer Publishing Co., 1974.

Plutchik, Robert and Kellerman, Henry (Eds.) *Emotion: Theory, Research, and Experience*. Vol. 1. New York: Academic Press, 1980.

Reage, Pauline. *The Story of O: Part Two, Return To The Chateau*. New York: Grove Press, 1980.

Starr, Bernard D. and Weiner, Marcella Bakur. *The Starr-Weiner Report on Sex and Sexuality in the Mature Years*. New York: McGraw-Hill Book Co., 1982.

Wallerstein, Judith and Blakeslee, Sandra. *Second Chances*. New York: Ticknor and Fields, 1989.

White, Marjorie T. and Weiner, Marcella B. *The Theory and Practice of Self Psychology*. New York: Brunner/Mazel, 1986.

Zubin, Joseph and Money, John (Eds.) *Contemporary Sexual Behavior*. Baltimore: The Johns Hopkins University Press, 1974.

APPENDIX

INSTRUCTIONS

This is a survey conducted by two professors researching the topic of changes in sexual behavior. Information is being collected regarding your feelings about AIDS (Acquired Immune Deficiency Syndrome) and sexually transmitted diseases (STDs) such as Genital Herpes. All responses are *anonymous*. THANK YOU FOR YOUR HELP.

Please check the appropriate responses below.

1. **How would you characterize your concern about AIDS?**
   $\Box_1$ Extremely worried $\Box_2$ Very worried
   $\Box_3$ Moderately worried $\Box_4$ Slightly worried
   $\Box_5$ Not worried   1

2. **How would you characterize your concern about other sexually transmitted diseases?**
   $\Box_1$ Extremely worried $\Box_2$ Very worried
   $\Box_3$ Moderately worried $\Box_4$ Slightly worried
   $\Box_5$ Not worried   2

3. **How would you characterize your concern about sexually transmitted diseases in the PAST (before learning about AIDS)?**
   $\Box_1$ Extremely worried $\Box_2$ Very worried
   $\Box_3$ Moderately worried $\Box_4$ Slightly worried
   $\Box_5$ Not worried   3

4. **Approximately how many articles or books have you read in the past month related to the topic of sexually transmitted disease (STDs)?**
   $\Box_1$ 0 $\Box_2$ 1–3 $\Box_3$ 4–7 $\Box_4$ 8–12 $\Box_5$ over 12   4

5. **Approximately how many lectures or radio/television programs have you heard in the past month related to the topic of sexually transmitted disease (STDs)?**
☐₁ 0   ☐₂ 1–3   ☐₃ 4–7   ☐₄ 8–12   ☐₅ over 12   5

Now, a few questions about your background. For each question, please check the appropriate box.

1. **Sex**   ☐₁ **Male**   ☐₂ **Female**   6

2. **Age**   ☐₁ Under 25   ☐₂ 25–30   ☐₃ 30–34
           ☐₄ 35–39   ☐₅ 40–44   ☐₆ 45–49
           ☐₇ 50–54   ☐₈ 55–59   ☐₉ 60 and over   7

3. **Marital Status**
   ☐₁ Married   ☐₂ Separated   ☐₃ Divorced
   ☐₄ Single (never married)   ☐₅ Widowed   8

4. **Place of Residence**   ☐₁ Urban   ☐₂ Suburb   ☐₃ Rural   9

5. **Place of Employment**
   ☐₁ Urban   ☐₂ Suburban   ☐₃ Not Applicable   10

6. **Strength of Religious Beliefs**
   ☐₁ None   ☐₂ Weak   ☐₃ Moderate   ☐₄ Strong   11

7. **Racial/Ethnic Background**
   ☐₁ White   ☐₂ Black   ☐₃ Oriental   ☐₄ Hispanic   12

8. **Education**
   ☐₁ 0–8th grade   ☐₂ Some high school
   ☐₃ High school graduate   ☐₄ Some college
   ☐₅ Two year degree (AA)   ☐₆ College grad.
   ☐₇ Some graduate work   ☐₈ Masters/Doctorate   13

9. **Employment Status**
   ☐₁ None   ☐₂ Part-time   ☐₃ Full-time   14

10. **Size of Employment Setting**
    ☐₁ Fewer than 25 employees   ☐₂ 26–200 employees
    ☐₃ 200 or more employees   15

11. **Are you employed in any aspect of Health Care Provision?**
    ☐₁ Yes   ☐₂ No   16

Now, a few questions about your behaviors.

1. **Are you currently involved in a sexual relationship with one or more partners?** *If Yes,* **how many?**
   $\square_1$ None $\square_2$ One $\square_3$ Two $\square_4$ Three
   $\square_5$ Four $\square_6$ Five or more partners   17

2. *If in a relationship,* **how long has the most recent of your relationships lasted?**
   $\square_1$ under 4 mos. $\square_2$ 4 to 12 mos. $\square_3$ 1–2 yrs
   $\square_4$ 2–5 yrs $\square_5$ 5–10 yrs $\square_6$ over 10 yrs   18

3. **In the past, how long did your relationships usually last?**
   $\square_1$ under 4 mos. $\square_2$ 4 to 12 mos. $\square_3$ 1–2 yrs
   $\square_4$ 2–5 yrs $\square_5$ 5–10 yrs $\square_6$ over 10 yrs   19

4. **Is this different from your current practice?**
   $\square_1$ No difference $\square_2$ Relationships last longer
   $\square_3$ Relationships are shorter   20

5. **Do you worry about AIDS with regard to any of your current relationships?**
   $\square_1$ Not at all $\square_2$ Somewhat $\square_3$ A great deal   21

6. **Do you worry about other sexually transmitted diseases with regard to any of your current relationships?**
   $\square_1$ Not at all $\square_2$ Somewhat $\square_3$ A great deal   22

7. **Since you have become more aware of sexually transmitted diseases, have your behaviors changed in any of the following ways?**
   a) **Number of sexual partners:**
   $\square_1$ Less than before $\square_2$ Same $\square_3$ More than before   23
   b) **Number of times you go to social meeting places:**
   $\square_1$ Less than before $\square_2$ Same $\square_3$ More than before   24
   c) **Number of dates before you engage in sexual intercourse:**
   $\square_1$ Less than before $\square_2$ Same $\square_3$ More than before   25
   d) **Use of prophylactics (condoms):**
   $\square_1$ Less than before $\square_2$ Same $\square_3$ More than before   26
   e) **Innovative forms of sexual practice:**
   $\square_1$ Less than before $\square_2$ Same $\square_3$ More than before   27

8. **During the past two years, have you avoided a relationship because of fear of sexually transmitted disease?**
   $\square_1$ Yes $\square_2$ No   28

9. **Do you ask prospective partners about any of the following:**
a) **whether they have sexually transmitted disease**
☐₁ Always   ☐₂ Sometimes   ☐₃ Rarely   ☐₄ Never   29
b) **about their sexual practices**
☐₁ Always   ☐₂ Sometimes   ☐₃ Rarely   ☐₄ Never   30
c) **how many relationships (partners) they have**
☐₁ Always   ☐₂ Sometimes   ☐₃ Rarely   ☐₄ Never   31

10. **Do partners ask you about diseases you have or may have been exposed to?**
☐₁ Always   ☐₂ Sometimes   ☐₃ Rarely   ☐₄ Never   32

11. **Have you *ever* been involved in an extra-marital relationship? *If Yes*, how many have you ever had?**
☐₁ None   ☐₂ One   ☐₃ Two   ☐₄ Three
☐₅ Four   ☐₆ Five or more affairs   33

12. **Are you *currently* involved in one or more extra-marital relationships? *If Yes*, how many?**
☐₁ None   ☐₂ One   ☐₃ Two   ☐₄ Three
☐₅ Four   ☐₆ Five or more affairs   34

13. ***If in an extra-marital relationship*, how long has the most recent of your relationships lasted?**
☐₁ under 4 mos.   ☐₂ 4 to 12 mos.   ☐₃ 1–2 yrs
☐₄ 2–5 yrs   ☐₅ 5–10 yrs   ☐₆ over 10 yrs   35

14. ***If you had past extra-marital relationships*, how long did these relationships usually last?**
☐₁ under 4 mos.   ☐₂ 4 to 12 mos.   ☐₃ 1–2 yrs
☐₄ 2–5 yrs   ☐₅ 5–10 yrs   ☐₆ over 10 yrs   36

15. **Has concern about sexually transmitted disease changed your practice with regard to extra-marital relationships?**
☐₁ Same amount as before   ☐₂ Fewer relationships
☐₃ More relationships   ☐₄ Never had any   37

16. **Of the following, my two greatest concerns about having sexual relations are: (PLEASE CHECK ONLY TWO)**
☐ Not performing well   38
☐ Not satisfying my partner   39
☐ Contacting AIDS   40
☐ Contacting herpes or other STD's   41
☐ Being rejected afterward   42

We have a few last questions about your attitudes toward sexually transmitted disease. PLEASE CIRCLE 1..E RESPONSE WHICH BEST DESCRIBES YOUR ATTITUDE ABOUT EACH STATEMENT.

1. **Since learning about AIDS, I have been more cautious about my sexual practices.**

Strongly Disagree	Disagree	Neither Agree nor Disagree	Agree	Strongly Agree	
1	2	3	4	5	43

2. **Since learning about other sexually transmitted disease, I have been more cautious about my sexual practices.**

Strongly Disagree	Disagree	Neither Agree nor Disagree	Agree	Strongly Agree	
1	2	3	4	5	44

3. **I am not very much worried about contracting AIDS.**

Strongly Disagree	Disagree	Neither Agree nor Disagree	Agree	Strongly Agree	
1	2	3	4	5	45

4. **AIDS is a real threat to me and my family.**

Strongly Disagree	Disagree	Neither Agree nor Disagree	Agree	Strongly Agree	
1	2	3	4	5	46

5. **AIDS is growing in epidemic proportions.**

Strongly Disagree	Disagree	Neither Agree nor Disagree	Agree	Strongly Agree	
1	2	3	4	5	47

6. **The media has blown the problem of AIDS out of proportion.**

Strongly Disagree	Disagree	Neither Agree nor Disagree	Agree	Strongly Agree	
1	2	3	4	5	48

THANK YOU FOR YOUR TIME

Additional Comments:

The following additional questions relate to recent trends in
extra-marital affairs. If applicable to you we encourage you to
respond. Thank you.

HOW OLD WERE YOU WHEN YOU HAD YOUR FIRST EXTRA-
MARITAL AFFAIR? _____

HOW LONG HAD YOU BEEN MARRIED? _____

HOW OLD WAS YOUR LOVER? _____

WHAT AGE DO YOU THINK IS MOST SUITABLE FOR AN AF-
FAIR? _____

WHY DID YOU HAVE AN AFFAIR?

WHAT DID YOU GET OUT OF THE AFFAIR?

WHAT WAS THE GREATEST RISK YOU EVER TOOK DURING
THE AFFAIR? DESCRIBE.

HOW DID SEX IN YOUR AFFAIR COMPARE WITH SEX IN YOUR
MARRIAGE?

HOW DID THE AFFAIR END?

WHAT WOULD BE AN IDEAL AFFAIR?

DO YOU HAVE ANY REGRETS ABOUT YOUR AFFAIR? IF SO, WHAT?

DID YOUR AFFAIR HELP OR HURT YOUR MARRIAGE? EXPLAIN.

WHAT IS YOUR PHILOSOPHY ABOUT EXTRAMARITAL AFFAIRS?